T0304862

Becoming Us

A story of transgender love, joy and family

JAKE & HANNAH GRAF

CORONET

First published in Great Britain in 2023 by Coronet
An imprint of Hodder & Stoughton
An Hachette UK company

1

All photographs © authors' collection, except p. 5
(top left) © Lezli+Rose; p. 6 (bottom) © Paul Grace

A CIP catalogue record for this title is available from the British Library

Hardback ISBN 9781399719186
ebook ISBN 9781399719209

Typeset in Celeste by Hewer Text UK Ltd, Edinburgh
Printed and bound in Great Britain by Clays Ltd, Elcograf S.p.A.

Hodder & Stoughton policy is to use papers that are natural, renewable
and recyclable products and made from wood grown in sustainable
forests. The logging and manufacturing processes are expected to
conform to the environmental regulations of the country of origin.

Hodder & Stoughton Ltd
Carmelite House
50 Victoria Embankment
London EC4Y 0DZ

www.hodder.co.uk

Jake: To my wonderful and most patient of mothers, Susie Brown, without whom I quite simply wouldn't be here, in more ways than one.

Hannah: To my brother Jeff, who never blinked an eye, and to my mum and dad, whose love never wavered.

Contents

Becoming Us

PART ONE

The Road Less Travelled

CHAPTER ONE

A beautiful kind of chaos

Hannah & Jake

Hannah

There's a moment in the afternoon, when Millie is at nursery and Teddie is napping in her cot, that the house seems to breathe a sigh of relief. I make a cup of tea, move the pile of my husband's film scripts from the armchair and sit with my eyes closed, allowing myself to feel, even just for a second, a sense of peace. Today rain lashes the skylight above me. In the garden, one of Jake's precious sunflowers has been felled by the wind. I haven't the heart to tell him yet.

Every single surface in our living room is covered in the miscellany of a busy life: unopened bills, invites to parties, baby toys, Millie's new football kit, a Christmas present we still haven't had a chance to give our nephew, laptops, books, kids' drawings. People think that soldiers live like they did in military training – everything in its place, with clothes folded into A4 rectangles – but since my time in that microcosm of order and routine came to an end, when I became Hannah and left my role as a British Army Officer, daily existence has spilled into a beautiful kind of chaos.

Jake

My wife says she doesn't believe in 'The Universe'. Obviously she does in an empirical sense – Hannah is super scientific and studied maths, further maths and most likely *even further* maths at university and is one of the brightest people I know. But when it comes to those things that defy explanation, the coincidences, the magic almost, of life, she's got little patience for any of it. I'm not exactly spiritual, but I do think things happen for a reason and that some greater power than ourselves can put us on a path – take us somewhere we were meant to be. If I consider all the twists and turns, the huge life decisions, the specific ways the stars aligned so that Hannah and I met when we did and built this family together – it's as far-fetched as a fairy tale. But as I dash around the house picking up my wife's clothes, putting away our daughters' safari park of cuddly animals and generally trying to make some sense of the 'beautiful chaos' created by my wife and offspring, I'm reminded, this is real. And even on a dark autumn day, when my to-do list spills over several A4 sheets, I have to fetch Millie from nursery in half an hour, there's a Covid case on the set of my new short film, we have company for dinner – and Hannah is just *sitting there* with a cup of tea and insisting on 'relaxing' while the baby naps... this is the life I longed for. And I tell myself, *Jake, this, really,* is *happiness.*

Hannah

The real mayhem will begin as soon as Millie, our eldest, is back from nursery. Jake is stressing because the house is a mess and I'm not tidying it fast enough – I like to listen to a podcast on my headphones, taking my time and putting everything methodically back in its place, when I'm on clean-up duty. It drives Jake mad because he runs around in a rush shoving anything anywhere – case in point, a side table is currently buckling under the weight of garden secateurs, old remotes, plant bulbs, hard drives, paperwork. He calls it his 'indoor gardening corner'. I call it a 'disaster'.

Our friend, Linda Riley, is on her way with her Pomeranian, Lucky, a firm favourite of Millie's. Linda and Jake are particularly close and she has been a great friend through many tough times. As a mother of twins and major influence in the LGBTQIA+ community, she has been there with help and advice throughout both pregnancies, preparing us for what to expect as an 'alternative family' but also for the sleepless nights, teething and other parental joys. She is what you'd call a 'power lesbian' and has founded events like the much-needed Lesbian Visibility Week, which now runs every April. She campaigns tirelessly for equality across the board but, in particular, has been an unwavering force of support for our much maligned trans community, sustaining vicious personal attacks online because of it. Despite that tenaciousness, she's so easy going, content with a burger and chips from around the corner. She doesn't need us to pretend to be anything we're not, nor to make the place look perfect for her arrival – I remind Jake of this and send him off to get Millie.

Most nights, especially in the warmer months, Jake will fire up the barbecue and cook me my favourite lamb steak or chicken wings with chargrilled lettuce (the deal is, he does all the cooking, washing, general upkeep of the house, I do all the baby's night feeds while he sleeps through, so frankly I don't worry too much about the leisurely cups of tea once or twice a day!). Once the children settle, we'll have a few glasses of Linda's favourite pink champagne and put the world to rights, usually peppered with a little gossip and some laughs.

I'm rubbish at maintaining relationships, whereas Jake excels at it. He's constantly at the wall calendar saying: '*We need to go and see this person. We need to go and see that person.*' He's really good at making the effort to show people that they matter to us and, as such, has friendships that have lasted over 40 years. It's just one of the many, *many* ways my husband and I are so different but somehow brilliantly fill each other's gaps. He's impulsive and creative. I'm logical. Jake talks more but has an ability to make anyone open up and share their worries. I'm quieter, more reserved. He does the emotional labour. I do the bills and admin.

When Jake arrives back with Millie, she struggles out of her wellies and raincoat (she's at that age where she insists on doing everything herself) and runs straight over to where I'm giving Teddie her evening bottle. She gives us both an enormous bear hug. I feel a rush of love. Sometimes I still can't quite believe I'm a mother. There was a time, even just a decade ago, that I couldn't begin to conceive of such a future for myself. I was in a dark place: alone, lost and only able really to be myself in the confines of my small room in

Fallingbostel barracks, with the door locked on my own private shame. These memories still haunt me, but there's nothing like children to snap you out of it and keep you grounded in the present.

Millie wants me and Jake to sit next to her on the sofa. She holds our hands and looks between us with the most pure, wide-eyed adoration. I can tell Jake's itching to get on with the tidying, but how can he resist? 'We're a happy family!' she trills in her sweet little sing-song voice. Thinking of the vitriol, the hate and baseless, cruel prejudice that she thankfully has no idea exists yet, scares me. I hope we can give Millie the self-belief she'll need to deal with it.

Jake

As soon as I sit down and stop for a minute, the tiredness hits. As much as I'm loving being squashed into a sandwich of a hug with my wife and our toddler, who is alternately planting sloppy kisses on each of our cheeks as six-month-old Teddie smiles at us from her bouncy chair, there's just so much to do. I start to wriggle my way out of their arms, but then Hannah gently tickles the back of my neck with her fingernails and my whole body suddenly relaxes. Another few minutes of this can't hurt.

The first three decades of my life – when I was so miserable, an alcoholic and a junkie and a mess – were such wasted years. Now, I work like a demon and say 'yes' to everything, while being as prolific as possible to make up for that time – I produce a film every year. It's exhausting yet exhilarating, and feels like making up for lost time.

Hannah is great at helping me realise when I'm taking on too much. She gets it like no one else really does as we have been through such similarly traumatic emotional reckonings to get to where we are today. With her, I work really, really hard, but it feels good. It feels like we're building something, and giving our daughters a good life. Not being busy scares the hell out of me. When I finish a project I feel lost and have to have something lined up to dive straight back into.

I'm a nightmare on holiday. I really struggle to switch off and relax. 'Shouldn't we be doing something, Hannah?' I'll say. 'Is there nothing we should be doing? I'm sure there's something we should be getting on with—'

You hear about these young creatives who are working four jobs at once, writing and designing and painting while also launching their own fashion line... well, I don't want to be left behind. It feels like *now* is the time, and nothing makes me feel calmer than ticking things off our vast and neverending list. We can't rest on our laurels. Now is the time to make our mark.

Hannah is giving me the *look*. It's the one she gives me when I'm spiralling or getting anxious, worrying about a few minutes of down time with my family. Although we approach life very differently, feeling like a team with Hannah makes it all that much easier. Life is a lot right now and she helps me hold it all together.

Preparing a salad to accompany tonight's dinner helps calm me down too, usually with the soundtracks to *Encanto* or *Moana* playing in the background, Millie's favourites.

Hannah is putting Teddie to bed and we've at least 20 minutes before Linda arrives, which is good going for us.

Millie potters around, occasionally telling me about what one of her toys has said or done, with such earnest innocence. Every little bit of babbled nonsense makes me feel like the luckiest man on earth.

As I carefully place burrata on a bed of shredded basil and heirloom tomatoes, I reminisce on my time as part of the lesbian community. I knew Linda long before I really became me, even appearing on the cover of her magazine, *Diva.* As a writer, I feel very fortunate to have lived within that community, the trans community and even the gay male community, while now straddling the mainstream as a married man and father of two.

Each experience is a layer of myself, and each one has brought me closer to the real me. Through all the upheaval and evolution, my dreams and the people I hold dear have held me like an anchor in a storm: my mother, my friends and my lifelong desire to have children of my own.

I often pause and take stock of how fortunate I've been. I never dreamt that any of this would be my life, and I'm awestruck when I recall the hopelessness of even a decade ago.

Hannah

You're here reading our book, so the likelihood is that you know a bit already about our stories – the Grafs, Jake and Hannah. If you don't, then allow me to start by dropping a bombshell that will give you a good insight into who we are. This is something that, when we tell people, gets a mixed bag of reactions. Some have been known to pull disgusted faces and claim they will never look at us in the same way again. It's caused arguments between those who think it's totally normal and those who can't actually believe it. But we stand by it.

Reader, my husband, Jake, and I are... people who eat dinner in bed.

I know, I know – this is *very* controversial. Maybe it's my Army background, maybe it's Jake's – er... *bachelor* background – but it wasn't long after starting to date that our shared penchant for dinner au duvet came out.

Roasts, curries, Nandos – you name it, we've probably enjoyed it in bed.

Oh, and we're both transgender.

Jake

My mother tells me that as soon as I could speak, I would tell her that I was a boy, and that was something that I knew unwaveringly. Obviously, back in 1980s' London, there were no visible transgender role models at all; in fact the word 'transgender' didn't even exist, it was 'transsexual', at best, and those representations available were far from positive. Living under Margaret Thatcher's vile Section 28 certainly made life that much harder for millions of young queer youths like myself, as this law forbade any discussions or reference to LGBTQIA+ identities in schools. The damage it did echoed across our community for decades.

I didn't see myself in the media, in film or on television, and it made for a very lonely and isolating experience, and a childhood where I felt very much like there was something seriously wrong with me. Even as a young child, I was absolutely aware that I was a boy, yet I was doubted and dismissed because of a lack of knowledge and understanding of what transgender meant. Those feelings of self-doubt and uncertainty during my formative years are ones that stayed with me well into later life. They still haunt me to this day.

Being trans means that the gender you were assigned at birth does not correspond with the gender you know yourself to be. When transphobes tell me I couldn't possibly understand something so 'abstract' as gender, or that I'm lying when I say I knew from two or three years old I was male, it makes me so angry.

In my privileged, Conservative and sheltered childhood in Notting Hill Gate, west London, I had zero external queer or trans influences to 'turn' or 'trans' me. I was born transgender, yet understood very little of what that meant, nor why I felt so uncomfortable and unhappy every single minute of my day, other than knowing I was a boy in 'the wrong body'. Yet I am constantly judged, maligned and attacked by people who don't know me, nor any other trans people or young folk who have experienced the same feelings. They purport to know more about us than the trained medical professionals who help oversee our transitions.

There have been some incredible strides forward for trans rights in the last decade, yet so much remains a daily struggle. Some of the biggest issues facing people like Hannah and myself stem from a government that has repeatedly attacked us, weaponising our rights in order to garner votes, clearly unconcerned that they are bartering with our lives, but there are countless other threats out there. The media has long since realised that we are clickbait, that the more anti-trans rhetoric they peddle online, the more hits they'll see, and that has spurred them on to manufacture as much hateful propaganda as they possibly can.

Trans youth is being relentlessly and cruelly torn down, ridiculed, vilified and doubted – as if the life of a young trans person were not already hard enough. Trans women are similarly crucified, slandered, referred to as *predators* looking to 'remove' cisgender women's rights, rather than just trying to quietly hold onto their own.

The bathroom debate rages on, some of the same arguments that have been used to deny equal rights and access to people of colour, that it would violate 'white' rights, now recycled to bash the trans community. Just as then the rights of white folk were not being 'removed' or 'threatened' by people of colour, nor are the rights of cis women being removed because trans people are also using those spaces. It appears that we don't learn from the past, with the same toxic lies bandied around with the same tired bigotry and vitriol. We would happily sit down with any of our haters and detractors and try to find some common ground but, unsurprisingly, none seem keen to take us up on that invitation.

Right now, though, as much as I feel I need to educate the world on the realities of the trans experience, we have company. Hannah asks ahead of time that we don't spend ALL evening focusing on the immense emotional toll that the current level of hate is taking on us and instead try to enjoy a pleasant dinner with our friend. It's certainly easier said than done, but I now have my coping mechanisms. Whenever I find myself overwhelmed by the amount of hatred and misunderstanding directed towards us, I focus on my loving wife and our beautiful children, and am able to recentre and breathe again.

Hannah

Why is it that whenever you *really* need the kids to go to sleep they won't? Teddie is only just down and now I'm sitting on the floor of Millie's room reading her *one more book,* which definitely will be more like three. I start stroking her hair as she begins to drift, gently singing one of her favourite bedtime lullabies; then my phone screen lights up next to me, drawing my eye. An Instagram notification glares back at me. My stomach turns as I read the words, comprehending the abuse invading the quiet peace of my daughter's bedroom

You're a man... I hope your kid dies.

I try to keep my breathing steady. Millie's eyes are closing finally and I don't want her to sense there's anything wrong. I turn my phone over and quietly finish the lullaby, but my mind is elsewhere.

What have I done to deserve this? I served my country in the Army for 10 years, now I work in the City fighting financial crime. I'm a good friend, a wife, a mother, a daughter. Yet, for too many people, my very existence offends. Why? In 2013, I changed my name and began my transition to become a woman – the gender I've always been, despite having been born in a biologically 'male' body. But why should that matter to anyone else but me? My loved ones? Why does me being happy and living a good and true life, in a body that feels, for the first time in nearly 30 years, that it belongs to me, take *anything* from anyone else?

These strangers vilifying me and my family online are acting as if I have personally attacked them, threatening the very foundations of their life by simply existing in the world. And my crime? Talking proudly about my experience of being a trans person and using the women's loo, without fuss or fanfare.

The phone lights up on the floor beside me as yet more comments come in...

It took me a long time, after years of compartmentalising and shame, to realise that I deserve love. Happily, I found it with Jake and, out of that love and deep understanding, we built a beautiful family. But every day, there's one bitter person or an angry mob or entire government that tries to chip away at that happiness, hoping to destroy it, for reasons I will never understand. Yet they think it's their right. Horrifyingly, these texts, these Instagram comments, this kind of intrusion into my daily life is nothing new. I gently kiss my daughter's forehead, pull the covers up over her and tiptoe out of the room. She sleeps on, blissfully unaware. Jake and I will do all we can to protect her, protect both our children, from this kind of hate.

Jake

Hannah walks back into the kitchen, her face a mixture of sadness and exhaustion. I wipe my hands and walk over to her, as she switches off her phone before throwing it on the sofa. She doesn't need to tell me what happened. I know that look. I get the same kind of messages.

We stare into each other's eyes and, with an inner strength that I so love about her, I see Hannah visibly push away the hate. 'My love,' she says, 'did you put Linda's champagne in the fridge?'

The thing about transphobia is, it's entirely futile. These people can say what they like, they can spend their days trying to frighten and destroy us in the hope that we will go away, but we never will, just like gay or lesbian folk. We exist. We have the right to be here. And, if anything, their vitriol makes us even more vocal and passionate about advocating for the people in our trans community who don't have the same privileges as Hannah and myself. Those people who say we're like a broken record banging on about trans rights fail to realise that if we were just left in peace to live our lives, we would be only too happy to stop talking about it. But while the haters still seek to do us harm and make our lives unliveable, we have no choice other than to keep on fighting.

Hannah's and my relationship with the press has been chequered, although largely positive. We've never said we are the 'first trans parents', but unfortunately headline-grabbing articles about us have used that wildly inaccurate description and many of our own LGBTQIA+ community have been angry about that, and rightly so.

Trans people have existed for thousands of years and of course trans people around the world have had children in all sorts of ways, well before we did. We just happen to have a platform because of Hannah's high-profile role in the military and my own background as an actor in films such as *Colette* and *The Danish Girl*. We could have chosen to remain quiet and keep our heads down but, as we've seen throughout history, even that doesn't guarantee safety. It's only by working to change the status quo that trans people will be able to live in peace.

Hannah and I are so hurt and saddened about the injustices facing trans people, and particularly trans youth, in the UK right now that there's no way we could have sat back and not used our voices to educate and fight for our rights. But the amount of time that I spend trying to reason with bigots and bullies online is just so wearing. I cannot understand how some people have absolutely zero empathy for us and our lives, even when we do try to keep our heads down and avoid engaging. I can assure them that it's hard enough being born transgender without the daily hate that we endure as a consequence, and I grew up already overly familiar with unfounded hate.

My father was a Jew who lost his parents in the Holocaust, and had warned me from a young age never to share that information beyond the family. I then lived as a lesbian for over a decade, experiencing first hand the persecution that life often brings, and now I find myself in the eye of the storm of this raging war on trans people.

So much unnecessary vitriol and damage.

So utterly exhausting and wearing.

Were it not for the kids, there would be days when Hannah and I would choose not to leave our bed.

Yet amid all of this abuse, there's also support. When we first realised that people were interested in us as a trans couple, we made the decision to embrace the mainstream media in the hope that this would give us the most opportunity to change people's minds and affect real change.

We've been on morning TV in the UK and the US, we've done articles with the *Daily Mail*, *You* magazine, *Hello* magazine and more. Our nation's sweetheart and morning TV host Lorraine Kelly has been a huge champion of ours for years, despite the online abuse that she receives just for showing us kindness and support. But our biggest project so far has been the Channel 4 documentary *Our Baby: A Modern Miracle*, following our surrogacy journey and birth of our daughter, Millie, in 2020, against the backdrop of the Covid pandemic. We expected some online hate around its release, but after it aired we received quite literally thousands of positive and supportive messages from people, with none of the anticipated animosity.

I remember one message:

I'm 74 years old, never met anyone transgender, just heard your radio interview and I'm now ashamed of the way I thought about transgender people. I will rethink moving forward.

That's all we can really hope for – that by telling our story and sharing our lives we might help change the way we're viewed and inject some love and joy and hope into the narrative around being transgender today. The documentary is now hosted across on-demand platforms worldwide and we regularly receive lovely messages from viewers in Australia, Israel or Finland, saying that we've helped dispel the awful myths around trans people. I honestly can't think of a better reason to be doing all of this.

Hannah

Recently Jake put a picture of us with the kids on Instagram and someone cut out Teddie's face on Photoshop and enlarged it; she was pulling this sweet, funny expression, bless her. I mean she's a baby and was probably passing wind at the time, but some troll with an insane amount of time on their hands tweeted this picture with a really nasty caption about how Teddie didn't look happy to have us as her parents. *Pathetic.* To come after our children is just shocking and honestly, how miserable and sad must their life be to even have the inclination to do such a thing?

It's a constant balancing act – sharing photos and content about our family life in order to demonstrate how 'everyday' we are and provide some hope for other trans people, while protecting ours and our children's safety.

When it comes to the day-to-day stuff that I deal with as a trans woman, stuff that Jake manages to escape by fitting people's idea of what a man 'should' look like, I'm quite pragmatic about it. We all live in a world that's been binary from day one. The division of boys and girls starts even before school and it continues throughout our lives. If someone in their forties and working in customer service has been told from day one that boys are one way and girls another, I can completely understand why it's confusing when someone comes in who is more androgynous or has a deeper voice. So when, for instance, someone refuses to believe I'm Mrs Graf on the phone, of course I don't like it. It's hurtful and frustrating and reminds me that I'm different, but I'm old enough and experienced enough now to know that they are not necessarily trying to be rude and that they're not inherently a bad person. Were I just to snap at that person then I would be reinforcing a negative stereotype of trans people, which would then have a more damaging effect that could possibly cause harm to the next person. However, once corrected and once I've explained that I'm trans, if people persist in misgendering me, then it's hard not to take offence.

It's funny that in our relationship neither of us really fits traditional 'gender' roles. I love sport. I can enjoy any kind of competition, but particularly rugby, cricket and American football. Jake doesn't like watching sport at all. He's in charge of the garden and all the jobs like unblocking drains and fixing things, but also does most of the housework, washing and cooking. I drive, I sort all the boring house stuff and accounts and Jake, as I said, does more of the emotional labour and keeping up with friends. But isn't it a bit old-fashioned to see these things as 'gendered' anyway?

Like so many couples, our roles in our relationship are based on what we're better at and enjoy more, rather than, 'oh that's a man's job' and 'that's a woman's job'. If I were insecure about my gender it might bother me, but my womanhood, my femininity isn't anything to do with the clothes I wear, or my ability to bake an apple pie and arrange a bouquet of flowers. I mean, come on, it's 2023 after all!

Being a woman is a deep, innate truth. I can't really define it, just as any other woman reading this might struggle to, if asked.

I'm a woman.

Jake's a man.

We're both trans.

It's as simple as that.

The doorbell rings. I run into the bedroom to change into a slightly smarter top than the milk-stained hoodie I've been wearing all day and Jake opens the door to Linda. I hear him greeting her, a bark from Lucky and our friend's dry chuckle. We are fortunate. Despite the fact that certain individuals and even an entire government seem intent on making life as hard as possible for trans people, I am personally happier than I've ever been.

There was a time, though, long before Jake and I met and began dreaming about starting a family, when we felt trapped in our own private nightmares, places so bleak and lacking in hope, and there seemed no other option. We're eternally grateful that our family, friends and, later, our relationship and children pulled us out of that darkness and into the best and brightest kind of light. How? Well, this is our story.

CHAPTER TWO

Finding Jake

Jake

My fraternal grandparents were Ashkenazi Jews who fled their home of Poland in the 1930s, amid growing antisemitism, in the hopes of a better life in France. They found a flat in Saint-Maur, in the eleventh arondissement of Paris, with their daughter, Berthe, and started a new life. My grandfather enlisted in the French Army to be able to stay in the country, and held a clerical job after his service. After living somewhat happily for several years, they welcomed their second child, Maurice, my father, into the world in 1939. They were always mindful of the growing threat of fascism across Europe, but believed themselves to be relatively safe in their new country.

As it became clear that Hitler was gaining in influence and allies, my grandparents braced themselves and hoped that the persecution would be short-lived. Like other Jews across the world, they prayed for their safety and that of their children. As the Nazis marched across borders, the climate of fear and self-preservation replaced people's humanity. It became fairly commonplace for people to report any Jews they knew or suspected to be living nearby, even friends or neighbours, to the authorities.

One day, one of those neighbours reported the Jews next door to the authorities. My grandparents, Esther and Charles Graf, were taken away first, with assurances that they would be back later that day. My Aunt Berthe, who was just seven, watched them go. My father, still a baby, was hastily hidden inside a cupboard. Berthe waited by the door for several weeks for her mother and father to return. They never did – they were already on their way back to Poland, and, finally, Auschwitz.

My father and Berthe were moved to the southern French countryside and taken in by a French farming family, sleeping in their barn with several other Jewish child refugees and brought up ostensibly as Catholics to hide the fact they were Jewish. Berthe later had a breakdown and spent many years in a mental institution, an utterly terrifying place to find yourself as a damaged 11-year-old orphan. She never fully recovered. Years later, just before we married, Hannah and I sat by Berthe's hospital bedside in her last few months. She would regularly cower and cry, speaking in terrified mutterings of the Nazis, making us promise never to reveal her Jewish identity.

My father also fared badly. After the war, he returned to Paris to live with his uncle, who regularly beat him, never showing the softness and kindness so vital to an already trau-matised young boy who had lost his family before his life had even begun. His parents had been murdered and, when he wasn't getting knocked about by the man who was supposed to be taking care of him, he was bullied at school because the other children had found out he was Jewish. It was a tough start in life but it made him the man he was. And that man was my hero until my own inner turmoil pulled me further and further from him. By the time he died of cancer when I was 18, we were barely talking at all.

As soon as he was old enough, my father left France and came to England, finding his feet in London. Casting off his old name, Maurice, he took up his middle name, Luc, a re-invention of sorts. Life here was initially difficult – he was a foreigner with only basic English, a Jew frequently beaten up by the local Teddy Boys, with little to his name. What he did have though was drive, a steely will to make something of himself and a real understanding of business.

Taken under the wing of a man we knew as Uncle Simon, the owner of a company called Simon Wigs, my father soon learnt the ropes, from how to knot a wig and managing staff to growing a business. After several years, Simon handed over the reins. My father quickly renamed it 'Wig Creations', eventually opening a Paris office and going on to become one of the biggest names in theatrical wigs and makeup in the world. Clients included Barbara Windsor and Joan Collins, as well as work on some of the biggest international film productions at the time, from *La Reine Margot* to *Legends of the Fall* to *Little Buddha*.

By the time he met my mother through a mutual friend in 1974, my father had already established himself as a savvy businessman. As fortune would have it, he had recently come out of a relationship with a woman whose family had ordered their daughter to break up with him because he was a Jew. Luckily, that background was of no concern to my mother, who even offered to convert for him after they married. My father, a proud Jewish man, declined as he feared what might happen if his children were raised in the Jewish faith. Years later, he would warn us about mentioning our heritage at school, a generational trauma that haunts many Jews and certainly made my sister and me aware of bigotry early on.

I had an affluent upbringing. We lived in a big five-storey townhouse in Notting Hill Gate. It was a tree-lined street near Hyde Park, quiet, friendly and just off the bustling track of Portobello Road. We knew many of our neighbours and very much enjoyed the community feel. From the outside it was a perfect childhood – my little sister Chloe and I had a rotation of lovely nannies who lived in the top room of the house and kept us entertained, and an ever-present mother whom we both adored.

I spent huge amounts of my childhood imagining other realities. I'd watch *Star Wars* and then desperately want to be Luke Skywalker or Han Solo, and spend hours lying on my single bed, staring up at the ceiling dreaming I was them. When I was seven or eight, I had this little pink diary that had been a present one Christmas. I filled it with stories in which I was a boy, solving crimes, saving old ladies or simply whiling away the hours playing with my (equally imaginary!) dog.

I didn't *want* for anything as a child. I was sent to the Lycée – a prestigious French school in South Kensington, where the likes of Madonna sent their kids, and we enjoyed wonderful holidays in villas in Mallorca and Malta. I loved being around the pool in my little swim shorts and bare chest. I looked just like the other boys and, on the beach, I'd often befriend them and we'd play together until my parents or Chloe would shout out my name. The bubble would burst when it emerged that not only was I a 'girl' but that I had lied to them. I lost these new friends as quickly as I'd made them.

No, I didn't want for anything as a child – except perhaps the most important thing of all – to be better understood by the people I was closest to. Because no amount of privilege could ever make up for the lack of love I had for myself. I was a little boy condemned to a biologically female body, and called by a girl's name.

*   *   *

My father was my idol from a very young age. Even though he could be quite a hard man, with me he was different. I was his little tomboy. We were very, very close and I think he related to me in ways that he might not have had I been a 'normal girl'. He would take me out to play tennis, or on bike rides on Saturday mornings or just out and about in the car. My younger sister was often left out and naturally became closer to my mother, not unusual but a source of some jealousy for me. Despite that, I idolised my father, wanting desperately to make him proud and hoping that one day he would see me as the boy I knew myself to be.

Even before I had the words to articulate it, I knew I wasn't just a 'tomboy' like my parents thought – I was a boy. I was so young and had no idea then quite how much was 'wrong' with who I was, how little understanding I would find, nor how badly it would affect the rest of my life. From the age of two or three, I'd tell anyone who would listen that I was a boy, and I was small enough for it to still be a cute affectation. Something adults would roll their eyes and laugh about. Nothing serious.

My dad spoke French at home and Mum was fluent too, having learnt it at school then worked for IBM in Paris for several years. As I learnt the language alongside English my world became gendered: 'La voiture' – female. 'Le jardin' – male. There was no escaping it and the feminisation of words associated with me became a kind of prison.

I loathed and dreaded being made to wear a dress and it was an endless source of arguments from a very, very young age. Strangely, in some weird throwback to that trauma, I still really struggle to put Millie, our eldest, in dresses because of the awful connotations for me, although I love her in pinks and pigtails. I can't easily shake off the years of misery that those simple garments meant to me. I have, however, promised Hannah that if Millie starts asking for dresses and skirts then I won't hesitate. I even bought her a very pretty tie dye dress on holiday in Spain last year, real progress for me. She of course looked adorable in it!

One of the experiences that most stuck with me, mostly due to the vast amount of photographic evidence dotted around the house as I grew up, was at Uncle Jean Michel's wedding. I had been bestowed the 'honour' of being a bridesmaid and I vividly remember the palpable dread I felt from the first fitting to the wedding day. The thought of appearing in public dressed in the white, ruffled dress, little white shoes and flowery headband kept me awake for weeks ahead, filled with misery and resentment.

That Saturday morning, I had been happily playing in the room I shared with Chloe, all of my He-Man figurines out on the floor or in the turrets of Castle Grayskull, waging war against the evil Skeletor. Those moments of escapism, the only safe place where I could be the boy I wanted to be, were what kept me going throughout my childhood. I heard my mother shouting my female name from the bottom of the stairs, bringing me crashing back to reality. Even at an early age, we would all brace ourselves for such occasions, my mother taking the lead but my father equally determined that I should wear a dress and look pretty for the extended family. I cried and pleaded and sulked all the way to the wedding venue.

I mostly hid in a corner, as much as I was able, but I will never forget my mother having to bribe me with Mars bars, through gritted teeth, to smile for the photos after the ceremony. I was in floods of tears crying 'I don't want to,' to no avail.

It was miserable because I didn't want to be a difficult child or cause any problems, it just felt so wrong and humiliating to be dressed like that. All I ever craved was understanding and approval for who I was and being marked as a 'naughty' or badly behaved child from such a young age was incredibly upsetting and damaging for me. I felt utterly powerless without the words to explain and so ended up being punished simply for who I knew myself to be. From my parents' perspective, and now as a parent myself, I can see how trying it all must have been. They didn't understand why I couldn't just be their little girl, yet, even at four, I didn't want people to see me in a dress like that. I needed people to see me as the boy I was.

Eventually I gave in, my will broken, and walked down the aisle tossing rose petals and feeling everyone staring at me. I might as well have been naked, for how utterly ashamed I felt. Afterwards at the reception all the other children were twirled around the dance floor by the grownups and given plates of wedding cake, but I found a quiet corner, pulled off the flowery headband and sat on my own watching the groom and his best man laughing and fooling around and wishing, more than anything, that I might grow up to be like them.

Shame dug its roots deep into me. I felt disgusted by myself as a 'girl' throughout my childhood and right into my late teens. This manifested mainly as anger and I would lash out at people, have tantrums or fall into terrible moods that lasted for days. I was a difficult child and I could be very cruel especially to my little sister, hiding her toys and calling her names, tormenting her and generally being a monster of an older sibling.

I loved Chloe from the second she was born, but, as I grew older and more riddled with self-loathing, showing any kindness became almost impossible. Still, I tried to be a good sibling, and protect her when I could. I remember one day at school, I must have been eight or so, and Chloe five. An older girl, Sabia, hit her in the school playground. She came to me crying and I was furious. I just saw red and I went and jumped on this kid. I wrestled her to the ground and sat on her, shouting: 'Don't you ever hurt my sister again!' I hated violence and was always more cutting with my words, but seeing someone hit my little sister pushed me to a new place of rage. Afterwards, I don't think we spoke about it, but I knew how important she was to me. I just struggled so much to show that love and care when I was so crushed by my own misery. When I think back now to myself as that lost little person I feel sadness and a lot of empathy but at the time I just thought I was a bad kid, someone who caused my family an immense amount of stress and misery.

This way of living in constant conflict and self-doubt and

with a heightened level of tension as a child has affected me hugely in my adult life. I constantly worry if I've offended someone or done something wrong, because I grew up being told off simply for trying to convey who I was. That completely destroyed my self-esteem and self-belief. I'm always second-guessing myself and going over and over what I've said or done in my head, worrying that I've upset someone. Hannah reassures me most of the time, and I've worked hard to build up my love for and confidence in myself, but I'll struggle to ever shake the feeling that no matter what I do, I'm always wrong. Even now, as a trans person, I feel the constant need to justify who I am, to try to convince people that we're just as valid as anyone else, and the constant judgement and nega-tivity is incredibly wearing and detrimental.

Some of the more ridiculous anti-trans narratives I've heard are that liberal parents, or diverse picture books, or LGBTQIA+ characters on TV, or drag queens reading stories at local libraries, have the power to turn a child trans. Growing up in the 1980s there was absolutely no outside 'influence' on me and yet still I knew so inherently that I had been assigned the wrong gender.

There was a big, very famous gay pub on the corner of our road in Notting Hill Gate called the Champion. My mum and dad would say, 'Just walk straight past, don't look, don't stop.' This was the height of Section 28, the policy that prohibited the 'promotion of homosexuality in schools', which in prac-tice made talking about anything other than heterosexual relationships and families illegal. It caused fear and shame not only for LGBTQIA+ students but for teachers too, and stoked a lot of bigotry and hate for the queer community.

When the government is propagating that hate, it has a very real trickle-down effect on the rest of society. My father, despite running a business in an industry largely populated by gay men, would never have been taught about diversity and inclusion or even the existence of different identities. My mum was a Sussex girl from the tiny fishing town of Shoreham-by-Sea, born to my beloved grandmother, a working-class woman from Croydon, and my solicitor grandfather, who I never knew: he died suddenly when my mother was very young. Neither would have had any knowledge of the LGBTQIA+ community, nor imparted any to their daughter.

So neither of my parents, who were Conservative voters for life, had any understanding of different identities, which undeniably made my youth that much harder. I think my father's experiences as a child had made him even more wary and closed off to anyone different. In my teens, as I became more opinionated, we would have blazing rows about tolerance and acceptance, creating further division between us. I used to wonder if experience of trans or queer people in my mother's life and deeper awareness would have made her feel and behave differently back then. Given how quickly and unquestioningly she accepted first my lesbian identity, and later my transition, my queer friends and trans wife, I am more aware than ever of the importance of teaching acceptance and empathy from an early age. When faced with those differences first hand, my mother never faltered. It's also important to remember that back then, in 1980s' London, no one was talking about trans identities. I didn't know the word transgender until much, much, much later in life. Back then the word 'transsexual' would have been used, but even that was not a word that would have been in my parents' vocabulary.

As I grew from being a cute little quirky kid who could get away with being perceived as 'tomboyish', to a child of seven or eight, my desire to be a boy crystalised to the point that I would put a pair of socks in my pants to feel more 'real'. Alongside this, my behaviour became a lot more problematic for the people around me. Life was about to get a lot harder.

School was the main problem. I hated going to the girls' bathroom and I hated my body. I was always trying to hide it. All the little boys could pee standing up, and I couldn't. It didn't feel fair. The Lycée was vast, one of the largest schools in London. When I first started there, I welcomed the ability to get lost in the crowd, an anonymous, nameless little face desperate to blend in. I was largely able to 'pass' as the boy I knew myself to be. My hair was very curly and I would beg my mother to let me keep it short, which she did – much to my relief. There was no uniform so I wore jeans or the green, yellow or red corduroy trousers that were popular at the time. I played with the boys and was so chuffed when they believed I was just like them. It was only when we were out and about as a family and would run into someone from school and their parents that the identity I'd built would crumble around me. 'Your son must come over for tea one evening to play with Nicholas,' my friend's mother said outside the school at pick-up one day. 'You mean my daughter!', Mum replied firmly as I pulled my hand from hers and hid, mortified.

Then as I moved up the years, teachers began to take the register. I'd be sitting on the carpet – my skin prickling with sweat, knowing my name was coming and dreading it. The sound of it made my skin crawl – it was not who I wanted to be and it outed me as a girl over and over again. Another addition to the daily anxiety and humiliation I felt as a young trans person. Each day the disconnect between 'me' and this idea of the girl I was supposed to be grew until it was a chasm.

Before puberty hit, for the most part I'd managed to still be considered one of the boys. I'd play football, marbles or palm tennis in the playground, or ride around on an imaginary motorbike with the wind whistling in my hair, while all the girls played the 1980s' craze 'Elastique', jumping in and out of a big length of elastic pulled taut between two people's ankles – which my sister threw herself into with wild enthusiasm. Instead, my little crew of boys and I would be spies and secret agents, hiding out in corners of the playground pretending we were keeping watch. Oh, and for a while I was in a rock band with my friend, Lorenzo, armed with an A4 folder of songs we'd go around with, dreaming of one day being famous.

Most days I could get lost in the moment, and forget that the world saw me as a girl until, unavoidably, I would need to use the loo. At the Lycée, home to some four-and-a-half thousand pupils annually, they had these massive toilets in the playground, which were open, so you could see in at all times. There were cubicles on one side, the sinks on the other. Every time I needed to go to the loo, I'd have to go into the girls' because I was worried about getting in trouble if I went to the boys'. Everyone could see me in there and it was just horrible. Occasionally there'd be a nice teacher like Mr Florent who, when I was around eight or nine, for whatever reason either understood who I was, or just realised that I was getting a hard time, and let me use the teachers' bathroom. But even that was riddled with anxiety because what if another teacher saw me coming out and told me off, or what if the kids saw me coming out and asked why? Once inside, I would stand there for ages, worrying about how to leave again, unseen.

I had so many anxieties from such an early age, having to worry about things few other children needed to give a second thought to. I'd sit in class obsessing over how I would manoeuvre my next trip to the loo. And the worry would just consume me. I'd try to wait until I was in class to ask to use the bathrooms because I knew then all the other kids would be in class too and I could go when there'd be no one else in there. I spent a lot of time trying to do things when other kids weren't around. Eventually, as I know many trans kids and young folk still do to this day, I stopped eating or drinking during the school day. It made life much easier and drastically cut down on bathroom breaks. Hunger and headaches seemed like a fair trade-off for that peace of mind.

I was good at putting on a tough exterior. I actually had lots of friends as a kid, but none who knew what was going on inside my head. And although I never admitted to them that I was a boy because I had neither the language nor the confidence to express it – it was clear I wasn't a girl. We were young enough for my friends to just accept it though. And over the years I learnt to squash down my true feelings. I learnt that society was by no means ready to accept me for who I was, as my identity caused issues wherever I went.

I had crushes on girls from my first year at school, but there was one in particular who I was crazy about for most of my childhood. *Emily*. She had green eyes and long brown hair and was just stunning. I was obsessed from the first time I saw her and didn't hesitate in telling my mum, who I think saw it as an innocent crush on an older girl. I was attracted to everything about her and would spend hours and years watching her across the playground, mostly aware that she would never like me back. I remember from around that age, three or four years old, knowing two things: that I was a boy, and that I liked girls. Neither made my life particularly easy and I hid them both once I fully understood how wrong they were perceived to be.

Other than my father, most of the closest people in my life were women. The nannies whom I mostly adored (and mostly fancied!), my dear old mum and my much adored nana, Marjorie Bayley, one of my favourite people ever. Much as she would have had no knowledge of what trans meant or why her 'granddaughter' dressed mostly like a boy, she simply accepted it all and adored me back. She never needed me to be anything but myself and I loved spending time with her in her house by the sea in Shoreham.

After my grandfather's death so young, she had never remarried, and lived for her children and grandchildren. She had polio as a child, which resulted in mobility issues, so when we visited we never really did much beyond talking and playing cards in her little yellow kitchen, with its outdated floral curtains and magic biscuit tin that she would open whenever we descended upon her.

Nana represented kindness, ease and gentleness. For whatever reason, I could do no wrong in her eyes and being around her was an absolute relief and comfort. There were lots of hugs and I remember snuggling with her in her bed in the mornings, teaching her the French words that I was starting to learn at school, singing the little French songs that she had never heard. Her house was like a sanctuary where I could relax and just feel happy, rather than on guard all the time. Like most grandparents, she would leap in and take my side if my mum or dad told me off or raised their voice to me. It used to drive my mother mad. It makes me smile when my mum does the same thing to me when Millie is acting up and I'm trying to discipline her, and I see the obvious adoration already present between my own daughter and her nana.

My grandmother enveloped me in kindness and my time spent with her remains among my very fondest and most cherished childhood memories.

*   *   *

I always knew my mother loved me, but she also despaired of me, and I can understand why. Now I'm a parent myself, I appreciate how frustrating it can be just trying to get a toddler to put their shoes and their coat on and get out of the house. Now imagine that struggle every day for 15 years, especially on those 'special occasions' when the kids are meant to toe the line. My parents started to give up on dresses when I became a teenager and I think there were even occasions when I was allowed to wear smart trousers and a shirt, an entirely euphoric experience for my young self. To my parents, I was stubborn and quite impossible in every sense. But for me the fact that the people I was closest to in the world couldn't see or understand that I was suffering, and weren't able to support me to find a way through it, turned me into an absolute ball of rage.

So many things that should have been nice and normal parent/child experiences became fractious arguments for us. Shopping for clothes, for example, was an exhausting negotiation. We'd go to St Michael (what's now M&S) on High Street Kensington, maybe once every three months as I was growing so quickly. Mum would drag me up the escalator and straight into the girls' section but at the first opportunity I'd run into the boys' area where everything was blue or black or brown and there wasn't a frill to be seen. Then the bartering would begin: 'Let me have the boys' jumper and I'll wear a pair of trousers from the girls' section,' I'd say. And on and on it went until we reached some unhappy compromise, one of us probably ending up in tears.

This is why labelling clothes as for boys or for girls is so damaging. Why not just call them 'clothes' and arrange them by age or style? Let people decide whether these clothes suit them, rather than trying to force them into these outdated binaries of what girls and boys 'should' wear. It certainly would have made seven-year-old me feel a lot less anxious about shopping and given my mum a sense of permission to dress me in clothes that an official 'boy' label turned into a transgression. In all fairness to her, for the day-to-day, trousers, T-shirt and simple jumper were pretty much the staple, but the battles we fought to get there were, to my young mind, unnecessary, hurtful and utterly nonsensical.

When I talk to Hannah about all of this, she agrees that clothes shouldn't be gendered but she also had a very different experience of childhood. Hannah never hated 'boys' clothes or felt frustrated that she was forced into traditional 'boyish' pursuits – she loved rock climbing and rugby – she joined the Army! Even today, post-transition, she's more comfortable in jeans and jumpers and flat shoes, although she does love a dress and heels on special occasions. I think there's an assumption that all trans experiences are the same. They're not. And being a trans man has nothing to do with what you wear, just as a trans woman shouldn't have to prove herself by wearing dresses and makeup. That's not what makes a woman. Gender is something we feel deeply within us, and then we choose how to present ourselves to the world in a way that feels good and right. I felt strongly and clearly I was a boy in a girl's body from the age of two. It took Hannah into her late teens to really acknowledge that she was a woman. Both these journeys are equally valid.

What makes me most sad, looking back, was that I came to dread any kind of special occasion as it meant I'd be expected to perform as a girl. I remember counting down the days to my 10th birthday with a feeling of dread, knowing that I would have to open all these cards addressed to my given name, wear a dress and pretend to like the girly things family friends who didn't know me well would buy me. Thankfully, at that point in the 1980s we had *Ghostbusters*, which was seen as an acceptable thing for me to be into as it wasn't entirely 'for boys'. So I was *obsessed* and most of the presents from people who knew me involved some kind of *Ghostbusters* merch. I remember playing the vinyl single on repeat every day for months, pretending I was about to go out with my ghost trap and save the stunning female lead, Sigourney Weaver.

Christmas was complicated. Like all kids I was so excited by the build-up, but I also knew I'd have to wear a dress on

Christmas Day and that truly marred the excitement for me. I'd open each little door in my advent calendar, the count-down twisting my stomach up in knots. When the big day arrived, we'd do stockings in the morning in pyjamas (my favourite bit of the day) and then have to change into smart clothes. When I was nine I managed to negotiate wearing a kilt so that I could feel slightly more masculine but, regard-less, it never failed to take the sheen off what would other-wise have been a magical day.

My dad would get angry and say, 'you're a girl, that's what girls wear'. And I get it, parents want their children to look nice. In the 1980s, gender 'divergence' wasn't understood or celebrated as it sometimes is now and my dad was fairly short tempered, so, while I could negotiate with my mum and these arguments would drag on for hours, with my father – there was no such thing. His childhood and youth had not prepared him for the empathy needed when bring-ing up a child riddled with emotional issues and challenges. Never having had a mother to look after him, or a father to be a role model, there was a lot of residual anger in him too and his patience by then was limited. I wasn't scared of him, but I wanted to please and impress him in a way I didn't with my mum. I wanted him to see me as his good boy, but once I realised that wasn't ever going to happen, particularly as my teens approached, I withdrew from him completely. With the benefit of hindsight, I realise that must have been awful for my father – like losing someone all over again. And feeling rejected by your children is horrible   I've only ever experienced it with Millie when she's going through a 'Mummy' phase and only wants Hannah and that breaks my heart a little bit. My father and I simply made for an explosive combination, and would eventually come to clash far too frequently.

From the age of around five I was a ball of nerves, self-doubt, self-loathing, lack of confidence, neurosis, anxiety. In a way it was surprising that my parents never sent me to a child psychiatrist but maybe I had a lucky escape. At that time the practice of conversion therapy was rife and children who expressed any kind of gender divergence were often subjected to verbal abuse, EST, behavioural modification therapy, all sorts of horrors. This is why the work the charity Mermaids does to support children like me is so vital. Had there been a charity that would help not only me but my parents and sister to understand who I was, life would have been immeasurably different, bearable even. Whether Thatcher would have allowed it to survive is another matter, but, having met hundreds of healthy, happy trans kids who have been saved by Mermaids, it really would have been the stuff of dreams.

Little things would have made such a difference – just calling me 'he/him', or letting me choose a name that I would have been more comfortable with, could have freed me up to just enjoy being a kid. It's what's known as a social transition, and it's all that most young trans kids ask for. To be allowed to present and be recognised in their correct gender. Nothing to do with hormones or surgeries, but enough to make our childhoods liveable and happy. It's hard to describe the sadness and disgust I feel when I read some of the slanderous rubbish that the press spreads about Mermaids.

A small charity originally started by the lost and scared

mothers of trans and gender nonconforming children, it does not help with medical transition, hormones or surgeries and is certainly not 'transing' kids, whatever that means. We've spent many weekends at retreats with both the trans youth that Mermaids has helped and their relieved parents, parents who have witnessed their often self-harming or suicidal kids not only recover but start to thrive.

It's criminal to attack such a vital organisation. I challenge any of the bigots and detractors to sit down with these young-sters and their parents, hear their stories and still try to tear down their only port of call. As a trans child who had an angry, unhappy youth due to a complete lack of help and support, it enrages me when those people say, *'Just let them enjoy their childhood. Don't worry them with gender issues and ideology they don't understand.'* It is nigh on impossible to enjoy a childhood as a trans young person unless your voice is heard and your correct gender is acknowledged. To believe otherwise shows a real lack of care and understanding for what we go through. Unless you are trans or have a trans child, you are in no position to comment on our childhoods nor on what we do or don't understand. The false concern is almost laughable.

A few years ago my mum dug out all of the old birthday cards and Christmas cards and Father's and Mother's Day cards that I'd written to my parents over the years. They were all signed by 'Mike' or 'Frank' or 'Charles', depending on which TV show I was currently obsessed with. I gave myself those names, asked my parents and sister to use them and was promptly and dismissively ignored. But simply writing them made me feel slightly closer to the boy I knew myself to be. It almost felt like the ink sealing my intention. Proof of who I was. If my mum had ever felt that me being trans were some kind of fabrication, here was the proof, in her hands, that this was nothing new. My gender had always been male.

There is also another nonsensical 'theory' from the bigots and transphobes, many of whom are intelligent people most likely aware of how ridiculous it sounds, that 'healthy gay and lesbian kids' are being pushed into transition by parents who want a 'straight' child. Again, laughable but also, for the more impressionable, a truly terrifying notion. So please, let's think about it.

First, you can't 'make someone trans', just as you cannot make them gay. A child would fight you kicking and screaming if forced into the incorrect gender role (as I did!).

Second, the idea that life as a trans person is 'easier' than that of a lesbian or gay person is ludicrous, and I again challenge you to find anyone who genuinely believes that.

Third, there are many gay, lesbian and bisexual trans people, as our gender has nothing to do with our sexuality. Our gender is who we are, our sexuality is who we are attracted to. Sadly, the press pushes these dangerous lies, which then become legitimised, doing often irreversible damage to our community.

I got through my childhood thanks to my rampant imagination and my loyal band of misfit friends. They comprised Pavlo, older (by a whole six months), cooler and born with club feet, so he spent a lot of his teens on crutches; Alex, a fellow troublemaker whom I homed in on; Calandra, who aged 13 was out most nights and had seen more than most 18-year-olds; Simon, who was into death metal and had hair down to his waist, and various others. We were this weird little group of oddballs who were all a bit bullied, but mostly left to our own devices.

I flew largely under the radar at school until May 1989 when we celebrated 200 years since the French Revolution by dressing as people of the time. Of course, I wanted to dress in the man's outfit, which involved a funny hat called a Bonnet Rouge, white stockings and culottes – hardly the manliest of looks, but nevertheless there was no way on earth I was wearing an eighteenth-century dress. To their credit my mum and dad spoke to the school to let me wear the boy's costume – it was fancy dress after all and, for whatever reason, they felt that in this instance listening to my protestations and letting me wear what I wanted would do no harm. The school allowed it and, although I looked a bit like a Smurf, I'd never felt prouder of my appearance. I remember adjusting the little red hat in the mirror and thinking that this, yes, *this* was a revolution. Sadly, my choice of costume came at a cost. It was the boldest demonstration of my gender I'd ever made and from then on the kids started calling me 'hermaphra-dyke'. It's a clever insult and something no 10-year-old could ever have come up with, so I can only imagine it came from a parent. Anyway, the name lasted my entire school career. That, combined with the occasional antisemitic aggression, calls of '*salle juif* ('dirty Jew') echoing down the halls, meant life at the Lycée was often a battleground. The more I was attacked, the spikier I became and I can't honestly claim that I was never a part of the very toxic environment that pervaded the school in the 1980 and 90s.

The thought that puberty was on the horizon was

mortifying – from the age of 10 I felt like there was a big ticking clock over my head ominously counting down the days until my body would start developing in the most horrifying of ways. My sister had some Judy Blume books lying around, and I'd secretly read them under the covers at night, shrouded in shame and cringing at any description of periods or growing breasts.

When that hormonal onslaught did eventually hit and things started changing and happening to my body, I overflowed with self-disgust and misery. I didn't want anyone near me. I didn't want to have a bath or shower – I didn't want to take my clothes off. I just wanted to be left alone. If no one was near me physically, then I could hide my physical self. It meant I pushed my family even further away and continued to widen the growing chasm between us. I'd look at Pavlo and Simon and all the other boys around me who were changing the *right* way and who were forming their stronger friendships and I honestly had no idea how I was going to survive.

CHAPTER THREE

A boy named Hannah

Hannah

When I look at images of myself as a little boy – cropped blond hair, a cheeky grin, some terrible combination of 90s' clothes, I feel nothing but love for the person I was, and for the person I have become. We all evolve throughout our lifetime. Some of us feel a strong sense of connection to our younger selves, others look back and see nothing of who they are now. Personally, I still enjoy the same passions as the kid in my parents' dusty old photo albums: sport, rock climbing, rock music, technology. I still have the same sense of humour (it probably should've matured but it hasn't), and I still adore my mum, my dad and my older brother, Jeff. But to all the world I was 'male', and now I'm female. Isn't that one of the most significant changes a person can go through in their life?

Well, yes. But I'm still 'me'. I changed my body and my name, and the gender marker in my passport, and I began taking hormones so that how I looked on the outside was closer to who I am on the inside. But transitioning doesn't magically turn you into a brand-new fully formed person. You are still an amalgamation of all your past experiences and the influence of the people you grew up with, for better or worse. I recognise how lucky I am that my past is a place I can remember with fondness. Many trans people want to destroy all evidence of their pre-transition selves. Their young lives were so traumatic or unhappy that to move on and find happiness they have had to rise from the ashes of these memories. But for me, childhood memories are my roots – solid and entwined with the people I love, and those roots have allowed me to grow into the woman I am today.

Family life in Wales was mainly very harmonious. My parents were both the first generation within their families to have gone to university and that's where they met. Dad was an avid rock climber and Mum had joined the Swansea Uni climbing club to be outdoors and also, I reckon, enjoy the company of the strapping men who ascended the rocks. One bright autumn day at the start of the second year of her psychology degree, she had gone with some friends on a climbing trip to Three Cliffs Bay, a beautiful spot by the Swansea coast. She was halfway up a limestone cliff when she got stuck. Now, my mum might not have been the best climber, but there is an inner strength to her. She grew up with her dad and brother, John, in a small Cornish town where everyone knew everybody else. Her dad was a foundryman and he spent long hours with an arc welder during the day, before working the doors at the local pubs in the night. They were poor and as John had learning difficulties, she took on a lot of his care and helped look after the house, making her own clothes and studying late at night when she had the time. A teacher at her secondary school saw her potential and really encouraged her academically.

Despite having little in the way of support, she got into university and that's when she was able to grow beyond a little town in Cornwall and start a better life. All this is to say – when she was dangling on the edge of that cliff, and my father climbed up to rescue her, she wasn't exactly a damsel in distress, yet it was the start of her fairy tale romance. They were married a year later.

My paternal grandad was a priest, so Dad had a very traditional upbringing in Leeds and Farnborough. They weren't wealthy by any means, but his childhood was rich in other ways – he was an excellent wicket keeper and played cricket every weekend. He also loved kayaking and other adventurous sports – something he really encouraged in me and my brother. His brain, like mine, has always worked in a very logical, pragmatic way and while he studied zoology at university, he's always been an engineer at heart. He was two years older than my mum and after he graduated and they were married, he got a job in Cardiff for a fledgling computer company called IBM. She would commute to visit him at weekends and holidays and, when she graduated, she also got a job there doing a very early form of computer programming. She did that happily until my older brother, Jeff, was born in 1985, when she quit to stay home and look after him. I was born two years later.

So far, so desperately 'normal', right? Beyond the hardships of many working-class families, nothing 'bad' or unexpected disrupted my parents' life. Their marriage had a rhythm and a structure that was happily predictable. So you can imagine that finding out their 23-year-old child was trans, was planning a medical transition and had changed their name to

Hannah was not something they were particularly equipped to deal with. But more of that later...

I was a very high-spirited child. Prone to sulking, apparently (still am!) but it was never anything a trip to the park wouldn't shake. There was something, though, a nagging feeling that I can only describe as like having a stone in your shoe – I always knew it was there but most of the time I could ignore it. When I was really little, it was no more than a tiny niggle – a vague sense that something about me was different to other boys – but it didn't make sense. It was only as I got older and tuned in more to what this feeling was that I was able to even start giving shape to it. And as this happened, my fear around what it might become was almost unbearable.

Before I started at primary school in the mid-1990s, Mum and I would go to the shops together once a week. On the bus into the centre of Cardiff, we would chat as Mum meticulously planned out our route around town on a little notepad from her handbag. The first stop was the department store BHS, where we'd have breakfast in the café and then wander around the clothes section as Mum flicked through the rails. She would tell me what she was looking for and I would help her pick out clothes and then sit on the little stool in the changing rooms while she tried them on. Sure, picking out the clothes was fun, but there was something else that captivated my younger self – the femininity that I, even at the age of around eight, felt an attraction to. The feeling I had, even now, is hard to explain because it was entirely instinctual. I had no way of intellectualising or contextualising it at all. I just knew that being in that changing room with my mum

48

was something I loved doing as much as I loved adrenaline sports and being outdoors. Because these other passions were seen as very boyish things to do, so much of my confusion around my gender came from the fact that I had this femininity inside me, but I still had all these things that fit in with the stereotype of being a boy. It was very hard to then go, 'Oh, I'm a girl.'

What I did understand acutely, however, was that this was not a feeling I should talk about. Even then, I knew on a subconscious level that whatever it was, others would think it was 'wrong'.

When I started school, Mum got a job as a teacher and so had high expectations of me and my brother in school. Nevertheless, I was naughty and quite disruptive in the classroom. Maybe it was a consequence of knowing I was different and dealing with that by acting out, or maybe I was just a bit cheeky and it had nothing to do with my gender. Either way, my behaviour was more mischievous than anything. I was boisterous and loved playing the fool and, for the most part, I got away with it.

I think a lot of my confidence came from having an older brother at the same school as me. Jeff always had my back, and does to this day. You will not meet a nicer man. He's not got a bad bone in his body. He's super intelligent – he got something like 13 A*s at GCSE and five As at A level, one of which he taught himself, and went off to Cambridge University where he got a doctorate. We like the same comedy, the same music, and I have very fond memories of playing computer games with him, going on holidays and spending hours in the swimming pool or on the beach, messing around. He was always patient with me, as I know I was extremely annoying and demanding of his time. But then one day, something happened that threatened our bond like never before.

This is hard for me to write about as it makes me feel very vulnerable and I still feel a really awful sense of shame about it despite being comfortable with who I am now.

I must have been about 10. It was a Saturday morning and Mum and Dad were taking my brother to Scouts then going off to do some shopping. I'd been left at home under strict instructions not to use the oven or make a mess. As soon as I heard the front door close I turned off the TV and tiptoed out of my bedroom, which was painted bright red and covered in Man United wallpaper with little pictures of Eric Cantona and Ryan Giggs (because that felt like the sort of thing a boy my age should have on his wall). I peeked over the bannister to check they'd all definitely left, then pushed open the door of my parents' room and walked towards my mum's wardrobe.

Maybe one of the reasons I'm reluctant to write about this is that it's a bit of a trans woman cliché – particularly when we see these stories acted out on screen. There's always that dramatic moment when the trans person 'discovers' the joy of dresses. They caress the fabric and look visibly excited; they slip into a dress then frolic around looking at themselves in the mirror like they're about to sing, '*I feel pretty, oh so pretty!*' I get annoyed with this because it equates clothes with gender in a really basic way. Plenty of trans women don't want to wear skirts or dresses, just as plenty of cis women don't. And yet somehow, that's the main reference we have for what makes a woman. I get that it's an easy way to dramatise a very complicated feeling when you're telling a story on screen, but it's very limiting because realising you're trans is about so much more than wanting to wear women's clothes – which is what it is so often reduced to.

So for me, excitement isn't the first emotion I'd use to describe the feeling of wearing my mum's clothes: it was more comfort – maybe. It wasn't 'nice' because there was so much self-hatred and shame attached to it. In spite of this, though, it felt *right*. And the fact that I was doing it in secret (and had been since the age of about seven) did add an exhilarating element to it, even if it wasn't particularly positive or enjoyable exhilaration.

It wasn't the clothes themselves that appealed to me. I wasn't looking for sequins or sparkles or anything particularly fancy or feminine. I'd pull out a skirt, a T-shirt, maybe a pair of leggings. It was about what these items of clothing signified and my fantasy, if you can call it that, was that wearing these clothes would be a total non-event. I liked to pretend that me wearing a giant skirt and baggy pink T-shirt (I was 10 remember, and small for my age) was the most normal thing in the world. The intoxicating part of it was just being myself in these clothes. So once I had hurriedly pulled off my T-shirt and shorts and put on something of my mum's – I would carry on doing whatever I'd been doing before. So, I'd go back to the sofa and watch TV. I wanted to feel what it was like to *live* like this. It wasn't about the dressing up. I certainly hadn't made the cognitive leap to understand this meant I didn't just want to wear girls' clothes, I wanted to be *the girl* wearing the clothes.

On this particular Saturday morning, I was in Mum and Dad's room – I had donned a dress and was putting on a pair of tights – when all of a sudden I heard the front door open. I froze, not knowing what to do, as Jeff bounded up the stairs and appeared at the door. He'd forgotten something, and they'd driven back so he could run in to get it. We stared at each other, a tsunami of shame rearing up and crashing over me. I'll never forget the look of complete confusion on his face. I ran and hid behind the bed.

Crouching down with my head between my legs, adrenaline coursed through me and I was shaking. I just wanted it to be over. Jeff ran to his room and then, without saying a word, headed back down the stairs and was gone with the slam of the door. I was terrified that he might tell Mum and Dad what he'd seen. I sat there on the floor for a while, then I slowly pulled off the tights and lifted the dress over my head. Words cannot describe my mortification. I hung the dress carefully back in the exact same place in the wardrobe. I had also memorised, as if they were landmines, the precise location of every makeup brush and perfume bottle I might have moved on her dressing table. If everything was in its place, I believed Mum would never know. This was the first time my cover had ever been blown.

I went through periods where there was so much guilt that I just stopped wearing Mum's clothes and makeup. After my brother walked in on me I promised myself I'd stop. I must have lasted about 18 months until the desire to scratch that itch became impossible to ignore.

Before coming to terms with their identity, it's not uncommon for trans women to indulge their true gender identity by purchasing clothes, makeup or other such signifiers that validate their sense of self, and then after splurging on stuff or wearing it secretly the shame builds up, resulting in a purge and they will chuck everything out, vowing to never do it again. I would definitely do this as I got older, but even at 10 I would suddenly think, *I'm so dirty, I'm so wrong. I'm so so messed up. I've got to stop doing this.*

*   *   *

I threw myself into 'normal' life. Every summer we would drive down to Cornwall and spend a week with my grandad (my mum's dad) in his freezing old house. I loved these trips, and dear Grampy, who sadly died in 2012, so much. He was a real character – constantly making rude jokes, and with a big booming laugh. Ironically, he embodied the most traditional masculinity you can possibly think of, but at that young age I just thought he was a lot of fun. He gave me catapults and took me fishing and told me these amazing stories about all the pranks he'd played on his mates in the pub. We'd go on long walks in Liskeard together and he'd get his walking stick out, turn it upside down like a golf club and hit cow pats at me. In a very unexpected way we were kindred spirits. We just clicked.

My mum's brother, John, always lived with Grampy and while they were both Cornish through and through, we were their only family, and so, when I was in my early teens, they moved to Cardiff to be closer to us. I have such fond memories of sitting around a roaring fire, staying up past my bedtime to play the card game Euchre with them both. Grampy was of the world where you had to be able to take the piss out of each other and yourself and I loved that – it certainly set me up well for my time in the Army! As a child of the Second World War, he was beyond proud when I joined the Army and, given his working-class background, even more so when I made Officer. He had photos of me in uniform all around his house.

Grampy passed away before I transitioned and I never came out to him. Perhaps it was for the best that we never had to confront that together – we loved each other so much, but I just don't think he would have been able to comprehend it and I think it would really have affected our relationship.

I do still wonder though what he would have thought. I can't imagine that it would have been good, but he was also a very kind man at heart and so perhaps he might have surprised me. Either way, I'll never know. Transitioning is a journey for everyone involved in that person's life and, when you are the one embarking on it, it's almost like going into a military conflict – you know you're going to suffer losses.

We were such a 'normal' family, there was no reason little seven-to-ten-year-old me could think of to explain why I was feeling the way I secretly did. I just thought there was something wrong with me, and that I was a freak and that was it. So what I started to do then, and what I managed to do very successfully right through my teens and into my early twenties, was to compartmentalise.

It was like having a little box, and I would place all those feelings, thoughts and questions inside and that's where they would stay, safe and undiscovered. But in those quiet moments, when no one else was around, I'd open the box up, play around with what was in there, see how I felt about it. Then real life would intervene and the box was shut again and that was that.

I spent the whole of that fateful Saturday feeling disgusted by myself and so panicky that my world was about to come crashing down around me. I avoided my brother for most of the day but later that evening, when my parents were in the kitchen, Jeff quietly sat next to me on the sofa. I couldn't look him in the eye as shame washed over me once more. He asked me if I wanted to talk about earlier and the word 'No' burst out of my mouth before he even finished his sentence. He simply nodded, stood up and walked away. To his credit, he didn't mention it to me or anyone else for nearly eight years.

What was really beneath the shame? What was really beneath that fear of getting found out? It's simple really – societal misogyny.

Young boys grow up being taught to reject anything feminine. Every TV programme, every book you read, every conversation at school is riddled with the idea of what a man should be, and any boy who is at all 'different' will be laughed at, ridiculed and sometimes physically hurt by people who are supposed to love them.

I am fortunate and yet I still felt guilt at my feelings. My mum and dad are actually very open-minded people, that's certainly how they brought Jeff and me up and they never had a bad word to say about anyone, but no one is immune to a lifetime of consuming societal discrimination. So there would be moments when my mum would whisk me past the local drag club in town, instinctively and without much thought, but to me it really reinforced what I already knew – to be queer was not good.

*   *   *

Many cultural influences rammed the message home that being feminine as a boy was at worst deviant, at best disgusting. When I was 11 some friends and I rented the movie *Ace Ventura: Pet Detective*. I sat in my living room, my friends either side of me, and laughed along as Jim Carrey's character searches for a lost dolphin in typical slapstick fashion. We watched as he kissed police lieutenant Lois Einhorn, played by the stunning Sean Young, a pivotal prelude to the film's big twist – Lois Einhorn is 'a man!'

My immediate reaction was one of excitement; the idea of a transgender woman as this beautiful, sexy police officer was quite intoxicating. But that moment of exhilaration was short-lived. When Ace Ventura finds out that she's trans, he vomits and burns his clothes, weeping as he washes his mouth out, finally scrubbing himself clean in the shower. At the very end of the film Einhorn, Sean Young's character, is stripped naked with her genitals on show, causing the police officers to simultaneously start throwing up around her. It was so distressing to find myself relating to that trans woman but also to witness the hell it was to be her. The self-hatred that scenes like that inspire in young trans people is utterly toxic and destructive. Thankfully, we now have more positive depictions of trans men and women in the media, but that film is still wheeled out regularly on British TV, classed as a 'family film', doing the same damage to this generation of young trans people's self-esteem and worth. It's quite telling that a lot of the outdated representations of people of colour, women and gay people have slowly been removed from our television screens, yet those portrayals of trans people still remain.

Suffice to say that growing up I was close to my family and I loved them all dearly, but knowing I was keeping this awful secret from them was eating me up inside. By the age of 12, I was the Marie Kondo of emotional compartmentalising.

CHAPTER FOUR

Seeking oblivion

Jake

I often have to remind myself to stand upright. I spent the entirety of my teenage years hunched over, trying to hide my chest and generally shrink into the background, and it still now affects my posture. If I catch myself sinking inwards today I'll take a deep breath and roll my shoulders back. I'll lift my head and my heart – proud of the man I am. But rewind a few decades and you'll have found me drowning under baggy T-shirts that I'd layer over each other to hide any hint of breasts. I did briefly try binding my chest with Boots bandages but in those days there were no YouTube tutorials to help you do it safely or specially made binders that protect your neck and back. It was so uncomfortable I couldn't bear it. Luckily I had developed a passion for grunge and heavy metal music and could dress accordingly in ripped jeans and oversized tops.

My two best friends, Alex and Pavlo, were both boys raised by strong mothers. They probably had a better under-standing of 'girls' stuff' than I did, as I'd recoil from any conversation about bodies or sex, finding such subjects skin-crawlingly awkward. But the boys didn't include me in their whispered *boy* chats either so I was somewhat ostracised, neither fish nor fowl and with no sense of belonging whatsoever.

* * *

By age 14, my reputation as a 'hermaphradyke' was etched deeply into school folklore. It was thought of as hilarious to push me towards guys at school discos. The boys would laugh and push me away, which, of course, meant more humiliation and more self-loathing. I wouldn't say I was particularly singled out for bullying – everyone was fair game. It was assumed I was a 'dyke' and was bent out of shape because of that. I was regularly called k.d. lang (the only famous lesbian anyone could reference). Having to get changed for swimming or sports in locker rooms with naked girls all staring at me like I was a freak, and me trying to look anywhere but at them, was a horrific ordeal. Being forced to wear the regulation one-piece swimsuit for lessons felt like the worst kind of punishment and left me nowhere to hide my shame.

I'd try everything to get out of PE – but my school was strict and any complaints about how I *felt* wearing the swim uniform would have been dismissed outright. I dreaded those lessons and the only way to survive was to disconnect from myself, to stop thinking and definitely stop feeling anything. If I could numb myself to it all, I could just about get through it, but it took all of my willpower. Even casting my mind back to it today makes me feel sick and anxious. Those terms when we had swimming every Monday left me riddled with misery and self-loathing, despite my best efforts to disassociate.

My attempts to remove myself from traumatic situations became the bedrock of my teenage years. I sometimes struggle to remember the details of my life back then, mostly due to working so hard to mentally escape it all. But I remember the anger, the resentment, the humiliation at being forced into a gender that just felt so wrong. And that anger became rage, and I became an utter nightmare. It was a surprise to no one that I was eventually expelled from the Lycée for a litany of bad behaviour, including playing truant, smoking weed and mouthing off in the classroom. By the time my parents were called into the head teacher's office to be informed of the decision, a week before I took my GCSEs, aged 16, I think we all realised that it was for the best.

*   *   *

After a summer of avoiding my parents, drinking and listening to Metallica on repeat in my bedroom, which was plastered in images of 90s' supermodels and a life-sized poster of Dannii Minogue, I enrolled in a sixth form college in west London called Collingham.

Housed in a red brick, Georgian townhouse and costing thousands a term to attend, this was a place for misfits, black sheep and the troubled offspring of affluent parents who had more often than not been kicked out of their elite private or boarding schools for bad behaviour. I loved it. I went from being in a class of 32 to a class of 8. It was calm and quiet. Without the baggage of the Lycée, I made new friends who were unaware of my past and didn't immediately see me as a figure of ridicule. Many of these kids were slightly older, more worldly, more open-minded. There I even felt confident enough to come out as gay. I reasoned that as the world perceived me as a woman and I was attracted to women, and having never seen nor met a trans man, the lesbian identity was the one closest to mine. I first told Pavlo, who was still at the Lycée, then his girlfriend, Georgia, another boarding school exile who was kind and wise and seemed much more accepting than anyone I had met so far. They took it in stride, barely blinking.

I guess by then it was news to no one that I was queer.

And as my friendships grew, so my defences started to come down, and as we became closer, some of these new friends introduced me to drugs, beyond the weed that I smoked daily by then. The thought of being out of control really scared me, and still does. I had devoted my young life to artfully stage managing myself. Hiding my true identity and keeping a lid on my feelings. So I didn't exactly throw myself into Class As headfirst. I hung back, watched and learnt. We would go to Camden Market on a Saturday, resplendent in Doc Martens, bomber jackets and rock T-shirts and buy the little bags of legal highs. At that point it was whatever we could get our hands on to feel a buzz. For a while we all smoked banana peel, as some bright spark had read that it had hallucinogenic properties. It smelt like banana flambée, and was far less pleasant. Soon after that we moved onto dried lobelias, my father's garden quickly cleared of the pretty blue and white basket fillers. Then we tried nutmeg. *Terrible* idea. Even then, I approached getting high with some trepidation

I wasn't one of the kids that was all like: *Yeah, let's just go for it.* I was always very cautious about doing these things. But then as soon as I'd done it once I figured: *Ah, that was nothing.* So I'd do it a bit more and a bit more and it was a slow build from weed to ecstasy to cocaine.

Despite my leaving the Lycée, Collingham was only minutes away and I retained all of my friendships. For several years, my best friend was a guy called Ollie. He was another ex-boarder and troublemaker who had ended up in South Kensington, London's Little Paris. Tall, lanky, with long blond hair and a souped-up 2CV that we tore around in, music blaring; Ollie and I were absolutely awful influences on each other.

Every weekend I'd buy weed and smoke it in my bedroom then head off to a house party or nightclub. We used to go to Turnmills in Farringdon with Pavlo and the rest of the gang, and feel really grown up as we were all underage and out of our depth. Everyone was there for the music, which was mindless, banging techno rubbish that I hated, and I had never enjoyed dancing, far too self-conscious in my own skin. But there was a pinball machine, and I'd spend most of my night playing that, or sitting in a heap with friends on a dance-floor break, high and, for once, happy.

One night, someone scored some E, and excitedly handed around the little white tablets that I would come to know well. It was my escape from myself, from the invisible weight of unhappiness that I carried with me every day. It showed me what freedom from self-loathing felt like, and slowly allowed me to start releasing some of the anger and misery of the previous 17 or so years. While E was never really my main problem, it's hard not to form dependencies on a feeling quite so heady and utterly freeing. Back then, in the innocence of first discovery, it was all love and light, and I started living for the weekend when I could get off my head and talk happy rubbish all night.

So while the weekends had become wild escapism, Monday

to Friday was college, and, after the decade of difficulty and distress at the Lycée, Collingham was a breath of fresh air. Here, we were nurtured and the contrast could not have been more stark. We were listened to, had several truly phenomenal teachers who treated us like adults and started reading books in which queer characters and culture weren't taboo. Margaret Atwood's *The Handmaid's Tale* was a particular favourite, the heroine's best friend, Moira, a lesbian. We were now at the age where homophobia and any kind of discrimination were very much 'uncool' and I breathed a sigh of relief that my identity was slowly becoming almost fashionable.

Although the weekends could be fairly hedonistic, I was largely present at school. Home was a different matter and I spent as much time out of the house as possible, or locked in my room, away from my family, to spare us all the tension and by now icy relations. I was driving my parents to a new kind of anger and frustration. By then, I was so detached after years of shutting myself down from family life that it was almost impossible to re-engage. Lengthy therapy in my thirties eventually helped me to feel again and move past all the bitterness, but at the time and with all the substances in my system, I was very much switched off. I know that for my parents, it must have been heartbreaking. They had given me everything, but still I was a complete mess. '*Why?*', they would shout at me. '*Why, why, why?*'

Looking back now, I can't imagine what my mum and dad were going through. I avoided them at all costs, because I quite simply hated myself, loathed who I had become and knew the pain that I was causing, but with no means to stop it. I became adept at listening for the noises that meant they

64

had left or gone to bed and only then would I venture out of my room. I had no way of connecting on any kind of level. Of course it broke my heart too, but by then I knew myself to be the most devastating disappointment in their lives and that both enraged me and made me want to weep. I will move mountains to ensure that such chasms never form between us and our kids. The thought terrifies me.

*   *   *

My friends were getting girlfriends or boyfriends and it was obviously all very straight. I remember when occasionally I'd hear about two girls who'd kissed at a party and become obsessed with them, unable to stop thinking: *My God, are they gay? Are they gay?*

As anyone who grew up LGBTQ in the 1990s will relate, I was grasping for whatever scraps of queerness I could find. For several years, that was an obsession with the Spice Girls, and more specifically Sporty Spice, Mel C. My Dannii Minogue pics were quickly replaced with life-size posters of Melanie, bedecked head-to-toe in Adidas and, despite the devastating news that she was in fact straight, it made the 16-year-old me feel a little less alone.

And I was lonely.

Even though I had lots of friends, they were all hooking up and dating and there was no one for me to do that with. So, I threw myself into getting high instead. I wanted to be out party-ing all the time. The only family member that I would let in was my nana and I would call her every single day, and often visit her for the weekend, finding such calm and comfort in her little seaside cottage that drink and drugs were simply uncalled for.

I think my close friends realised that I was frustrated at always being on the fringes, unable to participate in the thrill of sex and relationships first hand. One Saturday night during our final year at Collingham, Ollie pulled up outside the door to my house in his red 2CV and tooted the horn. My parents were very fond of him. He was so sweet and laid back, unlike me, and, even though I'm sure they guessed at some of what we were up to, they liked me having a friend and largely left us to it. My mum waved to him cheerily from the doorstep as I ran over to the passenger side, slamming the door behind me.

'What's the plan?' I asked as I flicked through the CD wallet he kept in the glove box and slipped a Café de Paris compilation into the CD player.

As the Balearic beats blared out on the customised sound system, Ollie looked at me and said, 'We're going to Soho, mate. Check out a gay bar?' At the time, Bar Freedom was *the* place to go out gay, and as it was a mixed clientele it seemed less daunting than some of the lesbian haunts. Driving down Old Compton Street with the windows open, we thought we were so cool. I was tipsy, nervous and excited. Having liked girls since I was 3, and now aged 17, it felt rather momentous to be venturing forth. Although my self-esteem and confidence were at rock bottom, at least I would be around like-minded people.

We parked the car on Soho Square and walked to Wardour Street. I was wearing a black v-neck T-shirt with baggy jeans. My curly black hair was scraped back into a tight ponytail. It was cold and I pulled the collar of my leather jacket up and crossed my arms. Outside the bar a queue was starting to form; we joined it and promptly sparked up cigarettes. Standing in the cold, bristling with nerves, I began to notice more and more girls who looked like me, or who at least *didn't* look like the straight girls I hung out with. Ollie smiled inanely at the women around him, none of them paying him much mind. I began to lose my nerve, just as we made it inside. We handed over cash at the door and I held out the back of my hand to be stamped. A mark of belonging.

I was instantly swept up in the mood, even though I felt way out of my depth. Beautiful people were knocking back cocktails, a DJ played funky house and downstairs a giant disco ball cast a constellation of stars onto the dance floor. We made our way to the sofas on a raised platform behind which was a giant aquarium of tropical fish. Within about 10 minutes a cute and very forward French girl started chatting to me. She was 24, which felt very cool to this only-just-17-year-old. She told me she worked as a nanny and insisted we swap numbers (this was a time when you'd give your landline as a primary point of contact). We kissed and for the first time in my life I felt the thrill of being desired.

The rest of the night passed in a blur. Ollie must have driven me home at some point as I still had a curfew, and I remember getting into bed, slightly drunk but mostly utterly incredulous that anyone had shown me any attention, had apparently found me attractive. The next morning at 8.30 I was woken up by my mother knocking on the door telling me, 'A girl is on the phone for you.' It was the French girl! I was mortified, and a little surprised that anyone would think it acceptable to call someone at 8.30 on a Sunday morning. This was a warning sign, but I certainly wasn't backing out now. She asked if I'd like to go to her place the following evening and I agreed, curious to see it through.

On Monday evening after college I went over to where she was living as an au pair. She had a room downstairs and she snuck me in and locked the door so we could become better acquainted. After two days, she told me she was my girlfriend. This did make me nervous as it was all happening so fast, but I thought maybe that's just how lesbians operate. After four days she told me her full life story, and showed me what must have been about 300 solo photos of herself. Warning bells were starting to ring but I was just so grateful that she was into me, I tried to ignore them.

She came over to my house one night and Ollie and Pavlo and my sister all made a big effort to welcome her into the fold, but my heart just wasn't in it. She was so overly familiar with all of them, and was talking about me like we'd known each other our whole lives. When she left, Ollie and Pavlo looked at me a bit shell shocked.

'Really, dude? I'm not sure that she's for you.'

Despite some feeble denial, I knew that they were right. I dumped her in the only way a 16-year-old in the 1990s knew how. I asked my mum to say I was out, and stopped taking her calls.

Apart from falling straight into the cliché of an intense lesbian relationship that ended badly, that night out at Freedom felt like the door to Narnia had been opened for me. As well as my first snog, I met a Greek woman called Kate who ended up being my gay fairy godmother. She was in her thirties and noticed I was new to the scene. Kate and her girl-friend took me under their wing, introduced me to other gay girls and showed me all that Soho had to offer. I was hooked.

It was Kate who introduced me to the Candy Bar for the first time. This small bar and basement nightclub on Carlisle Street was an *institution*. It was one of the few lesbian joints in London and it pulled in a crowd of hot young women every night of the week. By then I had met another girl at my weekend job at the enviably named Reject Shop in Bayswater and she and I became regulars. Steph was pretty and blonde and for whatever reason thought I was a catch. She was my first 'real' girlfriend.

A few days after I turned 18, I began working behind the bar, their youngest ever employee, becoming very friendly with one of the managers, Jo Gell. Jo was cool beyond belief, a few years older and quite iconic within the London queer scene. Suddenly, and for the first time in my life, I belonged. My difference was what made me part of the club, rather than excluding me, and it felt utterly euphoric. Most of the girls there were quite 'butch' presenting, and it wasn't long before my colleagues suggested I cut my hair rather than keep wearing it in a ponytail. I remember Jo taking me to her local Soho barber and giving him some brief direction before the guy just sheared it all off. A short back and sides. After a little getting used to it, I now felt more than ever like a member of some secret and sexy gang.

With my new queer haircut and much sought-after job at the Candy Bar I threw myself into the lesbian scene. I didn't think about anything beyond where I'd find the next party. I was drunk every night, and just about managed to keep it together to serve people at the bar. A few lines of cocaine would sober me up, give me the energy to power through and then when the shift ended there was always a lock-in that went on into the early morning.

The more attention I got from girls, the better I felt about myself. I'd felt so ugly for so many years, being desired was a truly intoxicating sensation. At last, I had found my people. It was the closest I'd come to happiness. The women at the bar evolved into my chosen family. Jo was one of my best friends but there was also Krista, the stunning Scottish model who always had my back, Liz, who worked on the door, an ex-copper who also made me her little protegé, Jacquie and Lucy and too many others to remember.

Many had lost their own families after coming out, and we became one big 'chosen family'. Surrounded by the older girls who looked after me, I would do the same for the younger newbies who would sidle into the bar, looking as lost and scared as I first had. It made me feel good to welcome them, show them around, invite them out with us as the bar closed for the night. Many are still my friends today, which gives me some comfort that I wasn't all bad. My old school friends would often come in for drinks at the start of the night – men weren't normally allowed in without a female chaperone, but they made an exception for Ollie, Pavlo and Alex, the Lycée boys I'd grown up with. I loved that my queer identity was joining up with other parts of my life – to a point.

Relations with my parents had reached a new low. They knew I worked in a bar in the West End. They didn't know it was a gay bar. I imagine they began to dread the sound of my key in the lock as they sat eating breakfast at the weekend and, while I still craved their love and affection, I was falling deeper and deeper into an abyss from which I wasn't even sure that I wanted to escape. Oblivion. Belonging. And an end to the years of self-loathing, at least superficially. Looking back it's all too clear what a disaster my life had become, but at the time it felt like happiness.

Then one dark February afternoon shortly after my eight-eenth birthday, as I left for a shift at the bar, my little bubble finally burst. My parents and my sister were in the living room, and my father called my name and I reluctantly joined them. My mum had clearly been crying and my sister looked scared, which quickly spread to me. My dad struggled as he said: 'I've been told I have cancer.'

The room started spinning. I steadied myself on the mantel-piece, where a picture of my mum and dad on their wedding day smiled down on me. It was mesothelioma and he'd been given a year to live. My mouth was dry, my eyes prickled but tears couldn't come. My true feelings were beneath so many layers of dysfunction that the right words were impossible to grasp. I should have hugged him, offered some semblance of comfort, but instead a sharp numbness took hold. I muttered something and left the room.

On the tube into work the inconceivable truth hit me. My father was going to die. And it happened sooner than any of us had thought. In those weeks before his death, just three months after the diagnosis, my father tried to talk to me, but I just had no capacity. We both clearly wanted to reach out to the other but neither knew how. He was as angry as I was at his diagnosis and we just weren't able to find each other. I was so emotionally bereft, still so hurt and enraged at the world. The walls around me were too high by that point and there was no getting in. I wanted so badly to be able to communicate with him, but was completely emotionally immature and broken by that point. I had withheld my feel-ings since I was six or seven years old and the worse life became, the less I was equipped to handle it.

He very quickly declined, my hero dying in front of my eyes. I couldn't bear it. I was utterly devastated, terrified, helpless. And the more scared I became, the more I searched for oblivion, for a means to numb the pain that just kept coming. I was spiralling out of control and just wanted the hurt to stop.

I remember being with Ollie and Pavlo after college one afternoon in May, sitting by the big tree outside the Lycée smoking. Ollie was the only one with a mobile phone and my mum called him from the hospital saying I was to pick up my sister and go there immediately. My father was rapidly declining and could die imminently. My sister was in the middle of her GCSEs, as I stumbled through my A levels. We'd both had exams that day. I waited for her outside the school and then Ollie drove us to Chelsea and Westminster Hospital.

Mum was waiting for us in the reception area. She looked devastated. 'Take your sister somewhere,' I remember her saying to me. 'I don't want her to see this.' We found a little garden and stood under a pink apple blossom tree. We picked flowers up from the floor and made stupid small talk as our father lay dying. After about an hour, we went back into the hospital and looked for my mum on the ward. My father had died and we weren't there.

There are parts of me that wish we had been in the room as he left us, but we were both so young, so damaged already. My hero was no longer recognisable and the pain had just become too much to bear. Either way, I feel a huge amount of regret and shame that I wasn't there, emotionally or physically, for my family when they needed me most. But I couldn't take care of myself, and I had zero capacity to take care of anyone else.

CHAPTER FIVE

A question of identity

Hannah

My bedroom walls were blue. By the time I turned 15, I had covered every single inch of them in posters ripped from music magazines. As a rock and pop punk fan, I had all my favourites up there, ranging from the Offspring to Slipknot. But one image, in among the pictures of bands adorned in ghoulish masks, was one that I eyed more than the others.

I'd tacked it up where I could see it from bed.

Stacy Jones – lead singer of American Hi-Fi. My first crush! He had mid-length wavy blond hair, and these big brown eyes – Kurt Cobain meets one of the Hanson brothers. Pretty, but boyish. And I loved his tight-fitting logo T-shirt and skater jeans vibe. It had taken me a while to start getting *those feelings* and it was reassuring when I finally did fancy a boy because it seemed like most of my friends had been deep in teenage lust with someone since they were 12.

I suppose you could say I was a late bloomer, but my attraction to men was complicated because of how I felt about myself. I definitely knew I wasn't into girls sexually. But I *liked* girls in a powerful way. I had better conversations with them. I enjoyed their company most. I wanted to be part of their world. This misguidedly led me to agree to 'go out' with some of my female friends at various points, sharing the clichéd kisses in the back row of a dark cinema. It felt all kinds of wrong and it quickly became clear that we were better off as friends.

Meanwhile, I developed a massive obsession with the lead singer of the band Placebo, Brian Molko. He was openly bisexual, which at that time felt very brave and exciting to a young person like me who was starting to make some sense of their queer identity, even if it would be a long time before I really understood it fully. I was incredibly drawn to the way he played with gender – beyond the drag queens whose acts I would see advertised outside the local gay club, it was the first time I'd encountered someone doing what I did in the privacy of my room in the open – without being completely ridiculed for it. He wore eyeliner and mascara, had longish, slicked-back hair, and even painted his nails. He dressed in a beautifully pared-down, androgynous way and I wished I was cool enough to pull off that same look without anyone thinking I was weird or wanted to be a girl. Because that *definitely* wasn't the case.

Or was it?

*   *   *

After Jeff caught me wearing Mum's clothes and I promised myself I'd stop that little habit, soon enough I was at it again. Whenever I experimented with makeup or secretly wore clothes from Mum's wardrobe that made me feel feminine, I allowed a little bit more of my true self in, like sunshine peeking through a gap in a heavy window drape.

Inch by inch I was opening it up, allowing my eyes to adjust to the brightness.

As I got older I realised that my mum's wardrobe wasn't quite what I was into style wise (sorry, Mum!), but needs must. The internet was in its early iteration, and online shopping wasn't yet a thing. There was no way I could risk anyone seeing me buy something 'for girls' in a shop and no way I could get away with hiding it in my own room. But as I've said, it was never really about the clothes themselves, more what they signified – a *femaleness* that I inexplicably was drawn to. So, I didn't discover much about this feeling online, or find out that I wasn't alone in it. Instead, TV and film were my only reference points.

I remember there was a BBC documentary that took five cis guys and five cis women and made them live in role as the other gender for a week. So the women had to pretend to be men and vice versa in different situations. It was meant to be insightful, but God, you'd never get away with making a show like that today. It was very sensationalist and riddled with gender stereotypes, but I couldn't tear my eyes away from it. With such a lack of representation out there, I grasped on to anything that contained even a glimmer of queerness, particularly in terms of gender. I remember watching the show sitting on the sofa in the living room, with my mum and dad either side of me and my brother on the floor in front of us. I was immediately gripped but had to desperately try not to let on. I pretended to find the whole thing silly and boring; if there was an Oscar for feigned indifference I'd have won it.

I doubt the show even registered with Mum and Dad, but my interest in it and what it reflected back at me stirred those common feelings of shame and disgust, so I avoided it when my family were around. I tried to watch the rest of the series on my own, without anyone noticing, hoping to clutch some modicum of gender queerness despite how sensationalised and cringeworthy it actually was.

As I have already mentioned, as a teacher my mum approached our education in quite a strict way, but was always reasonable and very kind. Jeff was the golden child – he studied hard and was never in trouble. I, on the other hand, would get the bus to school in the morning in my shiny shoes, immaculate uniform and tie, with neatly combed hair, and, as soon as the bus rounded the corner of my street, I tousled my hair, loosened my tie and switched my uncomfortable school shoes for a pair of trainers I'd hidden in my bag.

I was always getting into trouble. We had these school-issue diaries that teachers would write in using 'scary' red pen if you were badly behaved. I just ripped out the pages with the bad comments on. Easy! Eventually my mum cottoned on to the fact that my year diary only had about 20 pages left in it. She was not happy and neither she nor my died shied away from telling me so. I think deep down they could see the funny side of my naughtiness but they never let me know that and *always* sided with the teachers, much to my frustration.

Not long after, the school had written home after I had bowled confidently into English (my worst subject where I rather ironically questioned the point of it all – after all, it wasn't like I was ever going to write a book...) with my best friend, Emily, late as usual, as we'd been messing around in the playground. For some unknown reason, when the teacher asked what I'd been up to, I said, without missing a beat, 'Having sex around the back of the bike sheds, Miss.' The class burst out laughing. I loved the approval that kind of idiocy got from my peers. But honestly, what was I thinking? The look my parents gave me when they heard what I'd done pierced straight through the cocky armour I'd built around myself.

I wasn't ever as clever as I thought I was. Case in point – I had a tag. Come on, this was the 90s – you were a nobody if you didn't have a poorly rendered 'graffiti' name. Mine was 'VOR'. Don't ask me why. I scribbled it on everything. Desks, walls – all over the school basically. I even got into spray-painting. But being the pretty innocent 'tearaway' I was, I only ever used the spray paint in places you were allowed to graffiti, like an old car park and disused ferry port.

Once, in a French lesson, we were given a test and I just decided it was pointless and I didn't want to do it. So instead of answering the questions, I spent the lesson practising my tag all over the test paper. Of course, I had to hand it in at the end of class, and yep – you guessed it – I was busted. Turns out my teachers weren't as stupid as I thought they were and they recognised the tag. I had to spend three consecutive after-school detentions cleaning the walls and desks. So you get the idea: I was trouble, but I wasn't *troubled*. There's a big difference.

After the 'sex behind the bike sheds' incident, which factually couldn't have been further from the truth, my parents told me I needed a focus. They insisted I take on an extra-curricular activity to replace Scouts, which I'd loved but had stopped when my dad (who was a Scout leader) had to quit due to work. So, I signed up for Army Cadets. I don't think anyone could have predicted quite how much I would end up loving and excelling at it, because it involved delving deep into what is perceived as a very masculine world.

Before every session I'd have to get all dressed up in boots, a green jumper and a military beret. Something about putting on that uniform really appealed to me – it was an identity. It signalled my entrance into this Army environment and, as I've mentioned, I was very good at compartmentalising, so 'Army Cadets' became another part of myself that I could switch into and out of. The kid who didn't feel like a 'boy' but couldn't comprehend what it would mean to be a girl didn't exist here. I was an Army Cadet, and for that evening every week I wasn't anyone or anything else.

We did drill (marching) and some basics like fieldcraft lessons and first aid. There was even a little rifle range where you could fire a .22 rifle. I took to it very naturally. I suppose my time in the Scouts and my love of the outdoors prepared me well for Cadets, and despite all my silliness at school, I was getting a good education, so the cerebral element – map reading, logic, that kind of thing – I found suited me too. I loved that I could be so entirely in the moment with Cadets; it took me out of myself and that feeling was exhilarating.

Meanwhile at school, my female friendships were deepening and there was no more needing to go on pretend dates with girls, thank God. We'd just hang out in each other's rooms listening to music and laughing about stupid stuff that happened in the classroom – usually involving me being an idiot. I was quietly coming to terms with my queerness, and being gay felt like the best and really only option I had, but deep in my heart I knew it wasn't the truth.

One evening after school, I sat at the family computer, which we kept in the office, and on a whim I started an MSN chat with Emily, and I came out to her as gay. It was a terrifying moment, made somewhat easier by using an online chat, but she was totally fine about it – even quite pleased I think to have a gay best friend. I started telling more of the girls and fell into the GBF role, which was fine in some ways, as it gave me licence to be into 'girls' stuff', like clothes and makeup, and crushes on boys, but the more I was seen as the gay boy in the group the more wrong it felt.

Privately I'd been daring to consider the possibility that I was different. I hadn't heard the term 'transgender' yet. It was all hugely scary as there were zero positive role models for me, but I was starting to understand that there were other people out there who *felt* like me. I'd say it was a kernel of a realisation – something I was keen to give space to grow, explore and maybe even talk about with someone I trusted.

*   *   *

I went on a two-week Cadet camp in West Wales, when I was 14. It was the first time I'd ever been away from my family for so long.

I was nervous about being away from home and not having those stolen opportunities to explore my gender in private but I knew well how to switch that part of me off. And I excelled at camp – I won an orienteering competition, rifle shooting and was given the award for Best Cadet Overall. The only time the box with the queer part of me in was prised open a little was when this very sweet Welsh guy who I'd noticed giving me the eye in the canteen one afternoon told me he was gay and asked if I was too. It was discombobulating to be 'read' in that way by a stranger, and to have 'gay me' and 'Cadet me' in the same place. Up until that point we'd been like Superman and Clark Kent – never once seen together. But once I got over the initial jolt of recognition we started hanging out, and on the last night before the end-of-camp party he pulled me behind some bike sheds (oh the irony) and kissed me.

I wouldn't say I didn't enjoy it, he was a sweet guy and there was of course an excitement to it, but I realised then that being a boy kissing a boy just wasn't me. The whole thing was just too complicated for me to get my head around and I was terrified we'd get caught and worried about how people would react to us. Being gay in the Army then was illegal so there was a lot at stake.

'I'm sorry. I can't.'

I pushed him gently off me and ran into the NAAFI (a little shop and entertainment hall on a military base) where 'Wonderwall' was playing and kids were jumping up and down in that generic teen way of dancing (to be fair it's still how I dance now). I ignored him for the rest of the night and as he was from a different Cadet squad our paths never crossed again. I do hope he has settled down with a nice guy by now... but either way, it was fun to go home with a story to tell my girlfriends.

However, just before we all jumped on the minibuses to drive home, an instructor on this Cadet camp who was in the

Territorial Army took me aside and said, 'You could do this, you know. You could be a soldier . . . an Officer.' He asked me about my grades, which believe it or not were fairly good, and he told me about an Army sixth-form college called Welbeck. If I worked hard, if I trained physically and presumably if I didn't get caught kissing a boy or wearing my mum's clothes, I could go to this incredible-sounding boarding school, which was the first step to becoming an Army Officer.

So I applied. The application process started with a pretty simple form, but soon escalated to an interview with a retired Brigadier and ultimately a two-day assessment at a military base including IQ tests, leadership challenges and planning exercises. It was a bit of a whirlwind experience and made me only want it more. I was told that I would find out if I was successful some months later, but any potential offer was conditional on getting good GCSEs. I stopped tagging and kept my mouth shut and my head down at school. The idea of going to this boarding school in a stately home to be groomed for the British military seemed like a great way to have a purpose, and, more importantly, to have an identity bestowed upon me. At least that way, I wouldn't have to keep grappling with my own.

The only time I didn't think about my gender identity was when I was engrossed in some sort of outdoor pursuit such a rock climbing or kayaking or running around a muddy field in combat gear doing fieldcraft. By the time I was in my final year of school, about to take GCSEs, the internet had become a slightly better resource, and some late-night browsing (coupled with careful 'history' deleting) had led me to discover the term 'transgender' and the fact that other people, including 'boys' my age, felt like they were girls. It was a revelation and a relief but it also led to more questions than answers.

The more I read about being trans the more confused I felt. Was I trans *enough*? These other trans girls were super feminine. They'd been into dolls and dancing and all that sort of stuff from the age of two. I was into white knuckle sports. I was in the Cadets – heck, I was thinking about joining the Army. I couldn't possibly be a girl, could I? How limited and limiting my inherited ideas of what defines a gender had once been.

The first time I ever said anything to anyone about all this was towards the end of my last school year. I was early to English for once and Emily was too. She sat up at the front and I was at the back. Spontaneously, I walked up to her desk, perched on the side of it and whispered, 'Sooo... I've been thinking. I want to wear girls' clothes.' This was just an easier, safer way of explaining it. Plus, I was still quite far in my own mind from coming to terms with my gender, particularly when confronted with the fact that I wasn't exactly 'feminine' in the way society deems it. So there was no way I could have said, 'I'm a girl' even though I was starting to think it. Going with the clothes angle was about trying to make it a softer blow – Emily could think, oh, a gay guy wants to wear girls' clothes, rather than being blindsided by me saying, 'I'm not a gay guy, I'm a girl.' That felt too big, too radical for now.

Very sweetly Emily said, 'What kind of clothes?'

She was probably thinking I meant ballgowns or something. But the fashion then was for girls to wear baggy jeans and hoodies. As you might have guessed by now, I had no interest in being hyper femme. But I wanted to be like my female friends. I started to feel nervous as other students filed into the class, so I muttered, 'Just like a hoodie and stuff.'

'Come over to my house then, and try on some of my clothes,' Emily replied as if it was the most normal request in the world. I smiled, feeling unburdened in one way but also like I'd opened a Pandora's Box I almost instantly wanted to slam shut again. I went and sat back at my desk, my pulse racing.

I never did go to Emily's to try on her clothes, and we never spoke of it again. Because a month after this conversation, mine and Emily's lives went in very different directions.

CHAPTER SIX

Spiralling

Jake

I lined up six shot glasses on the bar, grabbed a bottle of tequila from the shelf behind me and poured. The DJ played Missy Elliott as girls in bandanas, tank tops and baggy jeans ground up against each other. It was hot and getting to that moment in the night when the mood shifted because everyone was too drunk or high. My head throbbed. I hadn't slept more than six hours in three days. I'd been rolling from lock-in to nightclub to after party. Everything was out of focus. I was still reeling from losing my father and completely unequipped to even begin to deal with that grief. I was too young to lose a parent, especially a parent who had been my hero growing up. Seeing my superman wither away had been unbearable and his subsequent loss even harder. The Candy Bar girls rallied round when I told them what had happened. I got a lot of attention and support but no one offered what I really needed, which was probably a detox and some intensive therapy.

I pushed the drinks towards the woman who had ordered them, spilling tequila all over my hands. Smiling at the customers had long since gone out of the window; my attitude to the world was rapidly deteriorating.

I turned and crashed into Jacquie, who was topping up a glass of rum from the Coke dispenser next to me.

'For God's sake, pull it together. We're slammed!' she said sharply, gesturing at the throng of women queuing for drinks. 'Are you gonna serve them, or what?'

The words felt stuck in my mouth. I couldn't talk.

The manager, who was standing at the door, clocked my erratic behaviour. She marched over and pushed her way behind the bar. With two steadying hands on my shoulders she looked me in the eyes: 'Go home. Come in early tomorrow and we'll talk. I'll call you a cab.'

As I sat in the back of that black taxi, rain lashed the windows and lights from the passing cars swam in a technicolour blur. I've no idea how I even managed to unlock the door and stumble upstairs to my bedroom, past my mum and my sister's rooms, their doors firmly shut.

I woke up around 3 p.m. the next day and as usual felt like death. Fragments of memories faded in and out. I knew I had to pull myself together and get into work in the next hour to beg forgiveness from my boss if I had any chance of keeping my job.

It was too late.

In the backroom of the Candy Bar, I sat on an office chair and wept as Clem, the manager, told me enough was enough and I was fired.

'It's just been a really shit time. Please. I'll be better, I promise.'

She shook her head. We both knew I'd been partying too hard and making mistakes behind the bar for some time. But this wasn't just any old job for me. The bar had become my home, my solace, my safe place. Its staff – my chosen family. Getting kicked out of there, honestly, felt like my world was ending again. I was 18 years old, a complete mess, wracked with grief, an alcoholic and, once again, outcast.

I walked down Old Compton Street that afternoon, not knowing where to go or what to do. I felt like I'd lost everything. There was another lesbian bar in Soho called Vesper Lounge, which was a bit more chilled than the Candy Bar. It had a few big pool tables in the middle of the space, which the butch girls in their stonewashed jeans and tucked-in shirts would commandeer for the whole night. My reputation preceded me though, and I wasn't able to get a job there. Instead, I started working as a waiter in a Soho restaurant, and promptly got fired from there too. I was a walking disaster.

Somehow, in spite of everything, I managed to get four good A-level grades at college. I applied to study film at Westminster University and I got in, but deferred a year to give myself some breathing space. The thought of even attempting further education then seemed pointless.

I'd cleaned up my act enough to at least look like I was making an effort and, despite my messy behaviour, I was eventually allowed back into the Candy Bar. I found a real kindness there from some of the women and various regulars who genuinely cared and fussed over me, which meant the world.

This was around this time that the word 'transgender' first properly entered my consciousness. Occasionally an older trans woman, Natasha, would come into the bar, and for reasons I didn't yet understand I felt this strong urge to talk to her and hear her story, although certainly didn't have the nerve to ask her! Those feelings I'd had of knowing I was male hadn't been forgotten by any means but life as a woman had, to some extent, become liveable. I was fitting in quite well as a butch lesbian, and despite my extensive troubles was a big part of the community. I certainly wasn't about to give that up. Besides, I had no idea of the possibilities for trans men, never having met one. There was a big part of me that doubted we existed, so it was hard to imagine that for myself.

I was 19 when the film *Boys Don't Cry* came out, in 1999. Everyone was talking about it and it was quite honestly the first time I had ever really heard of the existence of a transgender man. Hillary Swank played the lead and, as both a fan of hers and someone struggling with their own trans identity, I was desperate to watch it. On the day of the DVD release, I bought it and excitedly rushed home to watch in the privacy of my room. For those who don't know, the film is the true story of a young trans man, Brandon Teena, who lived in rural Nebraska. After transitioning and finding love with a local girl, her brothers discovered that he was trans, beat and raped him, then shot him dead. It was unimaginably horrific and left me shaken and depressed, convinced that I would never be able to live honestly and openly. Brandon's was the only trans male representation I'd ever seen, and to witness the graphic violence and death of a young man just like me was terrifying. He had lived in constant fear of being discovered, and finally had been murdered for his difference. I couldn't begin to contemplate living like that, and once again pushed down my male identity, more scared of the looming threat of violence than of continuing to live a lie. Lesbian life would do for now.

And so it went on – late nights at the bar, drugs, tequila, lock-ins. A tube home in the early morning as the rest of the world was heading off to work. I'd sleep till the afternoon, wake up, make some food, avoid my mother or make stilted conversation with her that would quickly descend into a row if we happened to be in the same room for more than five minutes, and then back on the tube from Notting Hill to Tottenham Court Road, where the night circus would begin again.

I thought I was enjoying myself, but I was too intoxicated most of the time to really know for sure. But I was *in it*. I was part of a scene and that made me feel like I mattered.

Then my beloved nana died.

It happened on my 21st birthday. Nana had been my world, the only source of uncomplicated love and comfort I'd had in my life. As her health began to decline, I would go and visit her as much as I could. The thought of losing her was never off my mind. I was overcome with the terror of her dying and being in a world without her. I knew it was inevitable and I couldn't bear it. I would lie awake and worry about it at night. I would cry about it in quiet, sober moments, never missing our daily phone call and doing my best to see her as much as possible, cooking her meals to try to get her strength back up, to little avail. She became seriously ill over Christmas, and moved to hospital on Boxing Day. By my birthday in early January, she was barely hanging on. I was almost unable to function.

That evening I went to the hospital in Paddington to be with her. My uncle was already there and, for reasons known only to him, he demanded that I leave. He was aware of how close we were, that I had been there for the many years that he had been absent, and perhaps felt some anger or shame over that. Either way, I was too young, too scared to stand up to him and decided to go back the next morning, once he was gone. It turns out he left her alone only moments after my departure. When I returned early the next morning, it was too late. Once again, I had missed the chance to be there for someone I loved as they left this Earth.

The feelings of guilt were overtaken only by the utter devastation that Nana was gone. Like the guilt I carry over my father, my feelings of shame that I didn't fight harder to stay still haunt me. I know that my grandmother would hate for me to still feel such sadness and instead want me to remember her only with love and happy memories, but that's easier said than done. I still think of her every day.

After another huge loss, grief was running thick and fast through my family. Everyone was trapped in their own private hell, too much heartbreak to bear. Relations at home had reached a new low. Once again, I leant on my friends and girlfriend for support, feeling that I was letting down my family. Steph came round a lot and was always nice and polite to my mum at a time when having a buffer was a relief, but everyone still thought we were just friends.

As Steph and I approached the nine-month mark, I decided to finally come out.

Standing in front of my mum in our slightly dated, wooden-clad kitchen, all bravado slipped away and I began crying and shaking. Despite our fractured relationship, I was suddenly terrified of rejection, of losing my mum too.

My voice wavered as I told her: 'Mum, Steph's not just a friend. I'm gay.'

I was prepared for an onslaught of judgement, for her to disown me, challenge or shame me. But my mother had only ever wanted to take care of me, and I'd only ever thrown all her efforts to love me back in her face. So I was braced, ready for a negative reaction.

'As long as you're happy, that's fine,' was all she said.

I was totally blindsided, completely unprepared for her kindness or acceptance. I broke down and she hugged me. We pulled apart and before she could say anything else I thanked her and left the room. Despite having lost her husband and her mother, and with her firstborn a hot mess, my mother's kindness that day stirred something in me.

It gave me a glimmer of hope that all was not lost.

*   *   *

The following year I deferred university again, remaining in what was my longest job to date, now promoted to selling Persian rugs at the Reject Shop in Whiteleys and making pretty decent commissions. I was still living at home and, despite maintaining my immersion in the queer nightlife, things felt somewhat calmer. Finally, two years after leaving school, I took up my place at Westminster University to study media and film. I couldn't move into halls as the campus was so close to my home, so even before I'd started I was missing out on feeling part of the student community and experience.

I remember my first day, lost in a sea of eager, happy students, most of whom had already formed connections and friendships, feeling completely out of my depth. I was so socially awkward, used to socialising only when drunk or intoxicated, and the thought of befriending these confident-looking strangers terrified me. Suddenly my visibly queer hair and attire made me stand out, and once again I felt like an outsider. I hated having to introduce myself using my given name and all those dysphoric feelings came flooding back. The place was so big and alien to me, I felt lost there.

I managed two or three months before I dropped out; something else to add to my list of life regrets as had I stayed, my whole life might have been different. The film programme there was pretty top notch and we were learning how to storyboard, to shoot, to cut film and digitally edit. We made three films in the first few weeks alone. It would have been great for my future career in film, but I just wasn't thinking about anything other than my grief, my social anxiety and getting back to a safe space. I didn't for a second imagine that I would ever make anything of myself, be anything of note or worth, and I certainly didn't think that one day I would be making films. The notion of ever having a career, family or kids seemed totally ludicrous to me, something that only happened to other people, so I genuinely didn't see how much I was robbing myself of.

Telling my mum I'd dropped out was one of the worst conversations of my life. I had recurring nightmares about it for years afterwards. I imagine that by then she had given up all hope that I would ever make something of myself. Seeing the disappointment in her eyes, yet again, was just too much.

'You don't understand,' I'd tell her, desperate to be able to tell her about the drinking, the addiction, the darkness that always seemed to follow me.

'All I've ever done is try to understand you,' she would reply, exasperated.

With hindsight, I know that if I'd told Mum what was going on she would have helped me, done anything she could to pull me out of it, but I was so filled with self-doubt and loathing that I convinced myself I would lose her. We couldn't be around each other any longer. Finally, and much later than most parents would have, she told me I needed to leave.

Steph and I had fizzled out, so there was little to keep me in London. A couple of good friends from the scene were moving to Brighton, and so I thought that could be the fresh start I needed.

But of course, Brighton being the lesbian enclave of the south, I soon fell right back into the very same, destructive patterns. There was a branch of the Candy Bar there, so there was nothing 'fresh' about what my life descended back into except maybe the brisk sea air it now came with.

An old school friend heard that I'd moved to the city and invited me to share a room with her. I was nervous about sharing a room with anyone by that point, but had nowhere else to go, and we had been close since we were kids. I arrived in Brighton with a backpack, a lot of trepidation and about a hundred quid.

As I met my friend at the station, happy to see a familiar face, she took me back to a squat. Now, despite my torrid past, I was really innocent in lots of ways. My London life had been seedy and troubled, but I was still going home to a big beautiful house in Notting Hill every day. I was doing drugs and I was a mess, but never in a way that I had steal or do anything dodgy, because I was working and lived at home. As I walked up to the door, my friend showed me the 'trick' for kicking the door open. A dank, rancid-smelling staircase led up to our room. A feeling of absolute terror ran through me, and all I wanted to do was tear back to London.

CHAPTER SEVEN

Express yourself

Hannah

'It's here!' my mum shouted. 'The letter's here!'

I bounded downstairs and grabbed the white envelope out of her hands. Standing on the doormat, I ripped it open and the black type swarmed in front of my eyes, '—*pleased to inform you that your application to Welbeck Army Sixth Form College has been—*'

The words suddenly came into sharp focus and I gasped, 'Yes!'

Mum had been standing over me as I read it. She gave me a huge hug and started crying. Hearing the commotion, Dad and Jeff appeared from the kitchen and when they saw my face they rushed over and embraced me, congratulating me and telling me how proud they were. We called Grampy to share the good news. And with that, one chapter of my life closed and another began.

I'd become almost compulsively good at keeping the various parts of my life separate, so I very easily and very selfishly jumped into this next chapter without really sparing a thought for Emily and my other girlfriends. They were all staying at the same school for sixth form; I was going to a boarding school 200 miles away. They knew I had applied but I'm not sure they ever really believed it would happen and I didn't have the emotional intelligence to think that they might feel betrayed when one of their closest friends just upped and left to start a new life, one which apparently didn't include them at all. Of course, they were upset, and rightly so, but I was blind to it, completely focused on the upcoming move.

My exciting new school was all-consuming and I soon forged new, lifelong friendships. Despite that, I will always be sorry for neglecting the relationships that had been so formative in terms of feeling safe enough to come out as gay and start discussing my gender.

There is a theory that transgender women sometimes choose stereotypically masculine careers as we try to prove to ourselves and the people around us that we are the 'men' society says we are. Now I wonder if going off to a military boarding school was, in part, driven by a subconscious need to distance myself from the very scary possibility that I was transgender: my friends back in Cardiff were a casualty of that. I did stay in touch with Emily and my other friends, but something was lost and we gradually drifted. Despite my belated efforts in later life, it was never really the same again, and I will always regret that loss.

As soon as I got back from that Army Cadet Camp, I asked my parents if I could apply to Welbeck and commit to a career as an Officer in the British Army. Dad was cool about it but Mum had her reservations, obviously, about her child joining the Army. As with everything I'd been passionate about, like adrenaline sports, she eventually found a way to put her fears aside and support me. I hope I can be the same with my daughters. Now I'm a mother, I realise how hard that must have been for her.

The whole point of Welbeck was to build a pipeline to produce technical Army Officers at the end. They didn't accept just anyone and the application process was a massive undertaking, but I was determined to succeed. It was legal to be gay in the Army by this point, but trans? I had no idea how that would work. Why did I want this life so badly when I knew it meant hiding a part of myself? Well, for one thing, I genuinely loved it. And for another, I felt it would actually make my life easier. The military is more than a career; it's a lifestyle, and so it somewhat moulds your identity to fit into that life. For me, embodying the life of a soldier gave me the perfect way to be 'something', while I worked out exactly what and who I was.

Welbeck was all about finding the leaders, the Officers, of the future. They were looking for a very particular kind of character and the deeper I got into the application process, the more certain I was that I wanted it. After passing a few written exams and physicals, I was invited to have an interview in Shrewsbury. It consisted of an hour-long meeting with a retired Brigadier and he asked me all sorts of things about myself. Towards the end, he posed: 'if you could do anything and get away with it, what would it be?' I thought about it for a minute and then I told him I'd get my maths teacher sacked, but only if he knew it was me.

It isn't the interview answer I would recommend to someone today, but I really, really, *really* disliked my maths teacher, and so did my parents as he was a bully, particularly to Jeff. I guess the Brigadier wasn't too perturbed by my questionable ethics. Perhaps he saw something in my attitude, a confidence that he ultimately felt was worth taking forward.

The next stage was two nights away at an Army base in south England with a load of other 15-year-olds all desperately wanting to go to Welbeck. We were put into different groups and had to wear olive boiler suits and a coloured bib with a number on so we could be identified. Assessors were watching our every move. Jogging through a field on a freezing November evening, long grass brushing against our legs, I looked down at my bib. Blue 14 – the anonymity, the relinquishing of self, weirdly felt like a weight was lifted from me. I stood on the spot, focusing on nothing but the metal frames and ropes in front of me. I was plotting my route across this fictional minefield – considering all the tools I had to work with, so that when the whistle was blown I had a plan to lead the team to the other side. I relished these moments of pragmatic certainty when so much in my head felt insecure and confused.

It was a fun and exhilarating experience and I was in my element.

We were being marked by adjudicators who hung back and just quietly watched how we all worked, how we interacted, listened, what ideas we brought to the table and how we motivated others to go with our idea. Even in that short two-day period, we bonded as a team, finding connection not just in our outgoing attitudes or love of the challenge but a common drive to succeed.

The final exercise was an obstacle course. In a field hidden from view sat 10 different physical challenges, including hurdles, walls and rope swings. We all waited in a holding pen around the corner as the instructor briefed us on the rules. We would be taken to the field as individuals and given two minutes to manoeuvre through the obstacles as fast as we could. I stood there waiting for my turn, my breath hanging in the cold air as I looked around the apprehensive faces, reflecting my own nerves back at me, not least of all because I was relatively unfit compared to the rest of the group. Eventually my turn came and I was led to the start of the course where, just a few metres in front of me, stood a brick wall with a window cut into it. Before I could give it any thought, the whistle blew. Adrenaline kicked in and my legs started pumping, driving me forward towards the wall, and without any conscious decision I leapt through the window headfirst, landing in a roll on the other side before jumping to my feet and charging on to the other obstacles.

In the end, I did OK. I got through all of the obstacles and a few extra in the two minutes, but what I hadn't appreciated at the time was how much of a test that first wall was. The assessors were really looking for people who, when confronted with a challenge, had the courage to dive at it headfirst. In that moment, I managed to do it and I remember being really pleased with myself that I had. Perhaps it hinted at an inner courage, the seed of something that in time, I would have to depend on.

The selection process was rigorous. The people who, like me, had eventually passed all the tests to get a place at Welbeck College had what was considered the potential to become an Army Officer. This meant everyone had something about them, not necessarily extroverted (although many were), but able to get on with new people and be part of something, not just shrink away. All of a sudden I was surrounded by people who were cool and fun and more like me than I'd ever really experienced before.

It's rare for any 15-year-old to know exactly what they want to be when they are older, but starting at Welbeck put me on a clear trajectory towards a future career. A huge part of the insecurity I felt about what lay ahead in life was pushed to the side as I focused my energy on one thing.

One crisp September morning, instead of going back to school with everybody else, I headed off up the M4 with a few duffel bags of my most precious possessions and an ironing board in the boot of the car. Dad drove and Mum did her best to hold herself together as she contemplated leaving her child at a boarding school.

The further north we got the further I felt from the life I was leaving behind – a secret life, riddled with shame, but also with my girlfriends and the growing understanding that I wasn't happy in my birth gender. Choosing a military career certainly seemed simpler. It meant I could avoid having to confront that part of me, I could throw myself through a metaphorical window into something new and leave that all behind.

As we drove down the grand, tree-lined avenue that led up to the imposing Welbeck Abbey, a magnificent seventeenth-century country estate in Sherwood Forest, my heart beat fast in my chest. I'd never seen anything like it. This sprawling mansion was surrounded by acres of gardens, there was a forest and a lake with actual swans in it. And this was going to be my home for the next two years. It couldn't have been further from my comprehensive school in Cardiff.

I'd been very, very nervous and quiet during the car journey but I knew I had to pull myself together and make a good first impression. We were asked to arrive wearing a suit, so my parents helped me get my bags from the boot – and the ironing board that we'd been told we *had* to bring with us – and before I knew it, they were giving me a big hug – all of us fighting back tears – and they drove off, leaving me there with my two bags, my arm wrapped around the ironing board standing next to me. As I waved Mum and Dad off, I tried not to let the full realisation that I had essentially left home get the better of me, before being whisked away by one of the senior students who were guiding us to our rooms. Apparently five minutes after they left, Dad had to pull into a layby so he could comfort Mum, who had burst into tears at having, as she put it, 'lost her little boy'.

I shared a room with two others, Tom Dunbar and Alex Rafferty, who we called Raff. Dunbar's best friend, Woody, was in another dorm but spent a lot of time in our room so we became a friendship foursome. Like any young queer person going to a new school, I wasn't going to announce my sexuality straight away – maybe it's different nowadays and that's great, but back then it was sensible to suss people out before saying, 'hey, I'm gay'.

There was no privacy or any way to explore my gender and femininity in this situation, so I kept that box firmly shut and perhaps over-compensated by throwing myself into the hypermasculine culture of teenage boys all living together.

Dorm wrestling became a regular occurrence and pranks were very common. It was never malicious and everyone gave as good as they got, learning quickly that the best way to deal with it was to be able to laugh at yourself and not take any of it too seriously. For the most part, the pranks were simply annoying. There was one called 'Upside Down Life': when someone was out, you'd go into that room and turn absolutely everything upside down. Then, involving *even more* effort was 'Christmas Life' – the same principle but involving wrapping every single one of the person's possessions in wrapping paper. Then there was 'Post-it Life' – everything covered in Post-its (and I mean *everything*) and even 'Lucky Dip Life', where all your drawers were filled with those little styrofoam balls so getting to your pens was like lucky dip – I think you are getting the picture – hilarious, juvenile and *very* irritating when it happened to you.

For our everyday uniform we had to wear these old-fashioned tweed jackets over our blue shirts and grey trousers. They were hideous. We looked awful – imagine a 16-year-old wearing a bloody tweed jacket that had been passed down from student to student so they were all old and smelt of wet dog when it rained. It was so uncool but in the end we decided to love the look ironically. Probably because it was a mark of belonging.

Welbeck Abbey had an interesting history. It had been built by the Old Duke of Portland, who was a wheelchair user. He was also an engineer and, because he didn't want people to see him getting around, he built this entire tunnel system under the estate with rails for his wheelchair. For the most part they had just become underground corridors you could use to get around when it rained, but some further out in the grounds were walled up, so we would find the old air vents and lower ourselves in wearing headtorches, giving us a whole secret labyrinth to explore. It was like being in some kind of Enid Blyton novel. So much adventure and fun and friendship. There was a general rule that if you bumped into anyone in the corridor, you always had to say: 'Hello, how are you?' It was a small thing but it fostered this sense of friendliness and manners that I really responded to. I still consider those things important and can see how much my experiences there shaped who I am today.

Our family would come up and visit at weekends a couple of times each term. I remember on the first visiting weekend Mum and Dad came with my aunt, Margaret. I'd always been quiet and somewhat uninterested in family members who I didn't have much of a relationship with, but as soon as I saw my aunt I greeted her: 'Hello Margaret, how are you, what have you been up to?' Mum said it was like I was a different person, so much more confident and outgoing. Being at Welbeck even just for a month had brought me out of myself.

There were girls at Welbeck too, but they had a separate accommodation in a building up the road from ours. We spent our days together though and I became close with Alexandra, a petite, fun, outgoing, extremely nice, open-minded and very funny girl. She ended up as the maid of honour at my wedding – but more on that later!

Alexandra was the first person I came out to as gay at Welbeck. It was midway through the first term and we were sitting next to each other in the library one day – this massive, high-ceilinged wood-panelled hall next to the chapel – and she innocently asked if I fancied anyone and, being the ultra-nerd that I was (still am), I responded that I wasn't really into her species. Her initial snort of laughter over my sheer ridiculousness was soon replaced by a sweet 'oh cool, what's your type?' And I felt instantly at ease. It was the beginning of a very close friendship.

Over time, I really found a groove at Welbeck and being open with Alexandra began to put me at ease to the point where one evening, on a whim I decided to tell Raff.

In hindsight, Raff was the worst person I could have told. It wasn't that he wasn't accepting, because he was very chilled about it, but it was just too much gossip for him to contain. He was a super popular guy. He was good-looking, funny, good at all the sports, extremely fit and he had this really infectious Northern laugh. People just gravitated towards him. I suppose his charm drew me into a false sense of security. Before I knew it, however, he had told a few people I was gay and then it snowballed from there, until the whole world knew. I felt betrayed and hurt. He was apologetic and realised what he had done, in outing me, was totally wrong, but the cat was now out of the bag.

In lots of ways, even though it wasn't my choice, it was a relief to be out to everyone, and, thankfully, nothing changed and no one was weird about it. I owned it, and was the first one to take the mick out of myself about being gay. Self-deprecation was disarming and made everyone relax, so my sexuality never really became a 'thing'.

I forged some real, deep relationships at Welbeck, so when I went off to university in Newcastle I had a social circle already. Part of the deal of getting into Welbeck is that you'll go on to study at one of the UK's military-affiliated universities, Newcastle among them. We were given a bursary to help with the fees, coming with a commitment to join up afterwards and complete the initial Officer training, otherwise that money needed to be paid back.

We were all in it for the long haul, whether we liked it or not.

* * *

In Newcastle, I lived in a house with six guys, two close friends from Welbeck in addition to a couple of dentists, a medic and an engineer whom we'd met in our first year. It was a really fun place to be, at a uni renowned not just for its good education, but its vibrant nightlife. With so many close friends from Welbeck there at the same time, Newcastle had quite the party atmosphere.

My brother, Jeff, was at Cambridge University, and we would go and visit each other on weekends and, as one of his visits was pending, I decided it would be a good time to tell him I was gay. On the Friday night we went to the student union and inevitably got quite drunk. Maybe it was my mates around me – I didn't have to come out at uni as I went with so many people I knew and it was common knowledge among our friendship group – or maybe it was the bright green 'Skittles' cocktail coursing through my body, but sitting next to Jeff that night I felt really safe. So, about midnight, the loud music pulsing, I leant over and said, 'You know I'm gay right?'

He shrugged his shoulders and shouted, 'I kinda guessed' back at me, before giving me a big bear hug. It was a complete non-event to him. It's just who Jeff is. He had nothing but love and support to show me. But maybe because he'd had a few drinks too, he continued: 'Do you remember that time when I saw you in Mum's bedroom?'

I felt a familiar panic wash over me. 'Yes...'

'Do you wanna talk about that?'

'Nope, I don't,' I replied as warmly as possible, not ready for *that* conversation yet.

It's one thing to tell people you are gay, but trans? Even among educated and open-minded friends and family, it still felt like something I shouldn't... *couldn't* let anyone know.

And once again proving his character, Jeff smiled kindly, nodded and headed to the bar to get the next round.

As the years went by, my friends who so openly accepted me as gay started to wonder why I never had a boyfriend; after all it's not like there weren't gay guys in Newcastle. Two of my mates, Glynn and Harry, both of whom I'd lived with in Welbeck, convinced me to hit the Pink Triangle, Newcastle's gay village. It was sweet. They wanted to be my wingmen and give me some support and go for a night out somewhere they thought I would be happy and maybe have a chance to meet someone... they could not have been more wrong.

Harry has always been fantastically eccentric, starting to go grey at 18, questionable fashion choices and couldn't care less what anyone thought of him or what he did. We loved him for it. Glynn was a tall, second-row rugby player who, while ferocious on the pitch, was reserved and kind off it, a real gentle giant with a quick, witty sense of humour. As with so many of my friends from Welbeck, they both had such an inner confidence and security in their own identities, so when we entered Powerhouse, one of the bigger gay bars, with a dance floor lit like *Saturday Night Fever* and sticky carpets, they were first to be in the middle busting out the moves. But as was usual for me in these places, I hung back.

For me, being out as gay was just a mechanism to distance myself from the expectations of being a straight cis guy. It was a label that allowed me to be more myself, but never fully myself. Hence my awkwardness in gay male spaces. I didn't belong. So that night, I remember connecting eyes with a man at the bar. My friends were egging me on: it was all such a novelty to them. *I'm supposed to be interested in this guy. I'm supposed to go over and talk to him, see where it might go, but...* I wasn't feeling it. I'd kissed a handful of guys by this point in my life, but intimacy had never felt right.

So, throughout uni, while my friends were starting to have their first serious relationships, being overtly themselves and enjoying life away from the shackles of school and parents, I carried on living the lie. But while my identity in public life was subject to the same constraints as before, in private that wasn't case. Being at uni was the first time in my life that I had my own room, with a door that had a lock, for which only I held the key. No worries of the repeat of what happened with Jeff all those years ago.

I also had my own money and, while I didn't have the confidence to walk into high street shops and buy the clothes I wanted, the dawn of internet shopping gave me the ideal way to shop in the privacy of my bedroom. I just had to hope that the packages of makeup I bought didn't arrive on the doormat of my shared house in bright pink bags with the brands emblazoned on them, but I learnt to shop at places like Boots, which sold so many things that the packages would go unnoticed. Thus, it was at this time of my life that I started to buy my own clothes, my own makeup and spend evenings locked in the privacy of my room.

There was still a sense of shame to what I was doing, but I was no longer sneaking into my mum's room or worrying about someone coming home, so the experience was much more relaxed. Oh, and the absolute best thing about uni was the sheer number of opportunities there were for fancy dress. There was a running joke among my friends that every single time there was a fancy dress party I would rock up as a girl – they weren't wrong.

Aside from the fact the Army has a long tradition of cross-dressing for fancy dress, being out as gay gave me an excuse for that to be totally acceptable. Whether the theme was 'school' or 'Disney', I'd always do my makeup to high level when I dressed up for a party. My bedroom was tiny – there was just enough space for a single bed, a wardrobe and a desk – but I had a long mirror on the wall and spent hours staring at my own face, reproducing techniques from watching YouTube videos, as I learnt to enhance my feminine features, while concealing the masculine parts. I got a lot of tips from drag queens as they're very good at feminising their faces, even though they were a bit over the top for the look I wanted. I learnt how to use Pritt Stick to conceal my unplucked eyebrows, use orange lipstick to counteract the colour of stubble before foundation and contour my jaw line.

I was relatively young and baby-faced so with enough practice, even with a cheap wig I could make myself fairly feminine. It was exciting to transform the way I looked, but something deeper was happening too. As I've always said, the makeup, the clothes – they were fun ways of expressing myself, but they weren't the root of it. When I looked in the mirror and saw myself as a woman, I felt right, and complete in a way I never had before. I would take pictures of myself to validate this feeling – they were all saved on my laptop, buried deep in encrypted folders.

By this time, in 2008, there were some examples of trans women in the media – still, they were few and far between. There was a growing community online and I was experimenting with posting my photos on chat sites and talking to people in my female identity for the first time. That didn't always go to plan because, while part of me enjoyed feeling attractive and desired as a woman, it didn't take long for me to recognise that there are a lot of people out there who fetishise and sexualise trans women and aren't necessarily interested in us as people. A lot of these men were creepy and offensive so sharing my female identity online wasn't exactly an uncomplicated experience.

But my understanding of myself as a trans woman was pretty well formed at this point. Every time I made up my face or took a picture, I sat with the feeling I had while doing so and I recognised that beneath the shame foisted upon my actions by the world outside of my little sanctuary of a bedroom, there was a joyful truth being uncovered.

I was happy at university. In some ways it felt that I was leading a double life, but no real trauma or distress came with that as I was so lucky to have great friendships and a close, loving bond with my family. When I think of the countless trans people who go through what I went through without that safety net, without knowing that they were loved, it breaks my heart.

My biggest worry was: if I'm trans, what does that mean for my military career? Ever since getting into Welbeck at 15,

I'd known that after uni I would have to go to the Royal Military Academy Sandhurst to complete my training. If I didn't go I would have to pay back over £16,000 in fees, money I just didn't have. So at the same time as I was finding out who I was, I was also very aware that the freedoms that I had enjoyed at uni were facing an abrupt end at Sandhurst. Even if I got through it, what lay after? Being openly trans in the Army didn't seem possible and I was left with an uncomfortable feeling that I had slowly been digging myself into a hole. Had I really devoted seven years of my life to a career where I couldn't be me?

CHAPTER EIGHT

From Brighton to New York

Jake

Pain, sharp as a dagger, woke me. I groaned in agony, grabbed my stomach and writhed, twisting in the sweat-wet sheets on the mattress where I slept. *It must be a bad hangover*, I thought, as a wave of nausea crashed over me. I ran to the bathroom, just about making it, and vomited black bile. I was in an agony like nothing I had ever felt before.

It hurt to breathe, to move, to stand.

I was terrified and utterly alone in the little dump of a room that I rented for £50 a week above the Lanes in Brighton. My flatmates were certainly not friends, and were out of their minds on drugs most of the time, certainly not the kind of people I could expect help from in an emergency. I reached for my mobile and called the only person I knew I could rely on: my mother. As I lay there, waiting for her to answer, every breath making me feel faint with the pain, I genuinely believed that I was about to die. Not for the first time, I wondered how I had got here.

* * *

When I'd arrived, 12 months earlier, my Brighton life had felt new and at least a little hopeful. I'd lasted about two weeks in the squat, before moving into a room in a B&B populated by Polish builders. I'd found work in a pub in Kemptown, The Jury's Out, and held court for a colourful band of largely alcoholic pensioners who appeared as the doors opened and staggered home as the sun went down. Once again, I had some routine and stability and, while there was little room for ambition or advancement, it wasn't taxing work.

Away from the pub, I was making a whole new circle of friends and as I was mildly attractive and always up for a good time I quickly became a popular fixture on the gay scene. The problem though with bar and pub work is that alcohol is everywhere. From the on-shift half-pints bought by the regulars, to the post-shift shots bought by the manager, an old guy called Alan who loved a lock-in, it was hard to avoid the lure of booze, and I would wake up most mornings filled with guilt and disappointment at yet another night of over-indulgence.

After several months behind the bar and far too much unwanted, drunken attention from some of the patrons, I was told about a woman called Caroline who needed help taking care of her three kids, a two-year-old, eight-year-old and eleven-year-old. I'd always loved being around kids and for years had helped friends' younger siblings with homework, doing school pick-ups, park trips and so on. Kids were simple, drama-free and had always loved me. I gave my notice at the pub and threw myself into being the best possible nanny for the three kids.

When I arrived at Caroline's small, run-down house, on the outskirts of Brighton, it became clear that she was struggling and, while she loved her kids, she wasn't able to give them everything they needed. I thought about my big house in

London, the holidays, the nannies. I had always known how fortunate I was, but the fact that despite all of that priviledge I had still been so miserable jarred me, adding to my feelings of guilt and self-loathing. But from the first meeting the kids and I clicked. Their energy and innocence was such a balm compared to everything else in my world at that time.

Working for far less than minimum wage, I quickly became close to the children, especially little two-year-old Chesney. It was a job I took very seriously, as I always had when left in charge of kids. It felt like the most important job in the world to have young people dependent upon you, looking to you for comfort and guidance. I loved spending time with them – we'd run along the seafront, building castles out of pebbles on the beach, jumping in the cold surf, fighting off seagulls that swooped for our chips or ice cream. I tried to give the children stability and teach them some French, talking to them about a world beyond the one that they knew. There I was, trying to be a role model for these kids, yet I was just about functioning myself. The irony was not lost on me. Yet the stakes were different now – the children were all that mattered, and their trust in me meant the world. We also had fun together and I know I helped their mum manage during a particularly tough time.

I only realised a few months in that Caroline was involved in some shady behaviour, selling knock-off gear and the odd bit of weed. Eventually the law caught up with her and she was put in prison. The children were taken into care and I was heartbroken once again, having lost both my little friends and my new sense of purpose.

I bounced around between jobs, painting and gardening,

picking up bar shifts here and there. I had a close group of friends, mostly women, and the occasional relationship that lasted more than a few weeks. Honestly, I was just living day to day, devoid of ambition, plans or dreams.

I was still very uncomfortable in my own skin, still unable to look in the mirror without feelings of discomfort. Intimacy was hard unless I was intoxicated, and my own body still felt alien to me. I was perceived as a butch lesbian and that identity felt as close to the truth as I dared to go. The image of the trans man in *Boys Don't Cry* being hounded and murdered was never far from my mind. I had no other examples of people who were living in a gender other than the one they were prescribed at birth. I felt male but I had no way of knowing how to act on this – I was just lucky that among the community being a butch lesbian gave you permission to present in a masculine way.

My mum and I were still barely speaking after I'd turned my back on my education, and I missed her badly. I felt untethered, lost, hopeless. Days blurred. I drank and partied and sat on the beach looking wistfully out to sea, often choking back silent sobs. I'd watched the old boys at the pub, their only care finding a few extra quid for their next drink, and felt a growing despair that I would never make my way out of this mess.

* * *

'Mum, I don't know what's wrong with me. It hurts to breathe. I can't really get up,' I cried, the blood pounding in my ears, my vision blurring.

My mother took a sharp breath. 'You need to get to a

hospital immediately. Is there anyone you know with a car? Or call an ambulance?

'No – I...'

Then I remembered Amy – a sweet girl who I worked with in a bar on the seafront and who, for whatever reason, had a bit of a crush on me.

Amy came straight over and bundled me into her car, where I lay on the back seat in the foetal position until we arrived at the hospital. The nurse took one look at me, brought over a wheelchair and rushed me past the waiting crowds at the Royal Sussex A&E, a busy little spot at the best of times. A doctor came to speak to me and they took some blood, then informed me that I was throwing up my stomach lining. The pain was so intense I couldn't concentrate on what they were saying. Amy repeated it back to me.

'Acute pancreatitis.'

My mum and sister drove straight down to see me and sat at my bedside while the doctor lectured me about my lifestyle.

'You're drinking yourself to death here,' the doctor said pragmatically. Chloe turned to look out of the window, too angry with me to engage, but my mother took my hand kindly, perhaps starting to realise just how serious things had become.

'— which is a direct result of alcohol abuse and if you carry on like this you will die.'

All I could think was, *how the hell am I going to get through life if I can't drink? What am I going to do? I can't function without alcohol.*

It's crazy now to look back and recall that reaction given

that Hannah and I barely drink nowadays, but at the time I honestly couldn't imagine a sober life.

A lot of friends came to see me, though few wanted to acknowledge the reasons why I had ended up at death's door. Most were party animals, though none as desperate for oblivion as me. Honestly, drinking had long since ceased to be 'recreational' for me. It was now about trying to escape from the daily discomfort, dysphoria and utter self-contempt I felt for myself.

What it did make me realise, once again, was how many people genuinely cared for me. I remember a friend came to see me and we lay on my bed together for a whole afternoon watching episodes of *Friends*. It felt so normal and safe that it was almost foreign to me.

My mum would visit every other day. She'd bring me magazines, even one day doing her best to show how right on she was by bringing me what she thought was a lesbian magazine. What she didn't realise was that despite it being positioned on the top shelf next to *Diva* magazine, the similarly named *Diver* magazine held little of the same thrills and pretty young things that I had hoped for. I did learn a lot about deep sea fishing and scuba suits though. Her mistake really tickled her and we chuckled about it, although laughter was still excruciatingly painful for me. Her presence reassured me that she still loved me, would love me no matter what, and that in itself was a balm.

I felt so sick with shame for what I'd put her through, and spent a long three weeks lying in that bed overlooking the sea, pondering my next steps. I had scared her, my friends and my sister, but I had absolutely terrified myself. I couldn't see a way out of the drinking and drugs that had by now blighted nearly a decade of my life, but knew that I needed to make a serious change.

*   *   *

The first couple of months after that fateful morning, life improved, at least superficially. Terrified to drink, I was more lucid than I had been in years, a novelty at first, but one that soon waned as I had to face my dysphoria, my social awkwardness, my shyness, my discomfort. The clarity only made it harder to feign happiness, and the day to day became darker and then unliveable once again. Within a few months of leaving hospital I had a little sip of beer, then a half, then a pint and before I knew it I was drinking again every night. The difference this time was if my stomach started hurting, I'd stop. I knew that I needed something to give, that if I stayed in Brighton, barely living, things would end badly. I would walk home at night and stop on the beach, and spend hours staring out to sea, the waves crashing down against the shore, feeling utterly hopeless. When you can see no future, every day feels like an eternity.

I knew I had to get out of Brighton if I had any hope of survival. I missed my family and hated the chasm that existed between us. Losing my father and beloved nana had nearly broken me and I spent a lot of my time yearning for my mum, who, out of sheer self-preservation, was keeping a distance. I needed a change of scene, a new focus.

An old school friend, Adi, had moved to New York with her two-year-old daughter. She was working for a human rights charity out there and, hearing about the hospital and my steady decline, offered me a lifeline. She said if I looked after her daughter after school every day I could stay in her apartment and try to find my feet. She is another friend that I will always be thankful for.

After a week or so of weighing up my rather limited options, I decided that little could be worse than my current situation. I packed my limited possessions into two wheelie cases, had a rather emotional leaving party with the Brighton girls and headed off to the Big Apple, another leap into the unknown. I called my mother before I left, my heart breaking at the worry in her voice as we said our goodbyes. I hoped the distance might give her some respite.

*   *   *

New York 2003. Winter. As soon as I stepped outside the airport into the freezing air, everything felt different. People were louder, lights were brighter. I took a taxi to Adi's house north of Central Park in Spanish Harlem. From the open window I stared up at the towering skyscrapers, steam rising from potholes in the street just like in the movies – Manhattan was big and dramatic, especially when covered in thick snow – Brighton suddenly seemed tiny, and a million lifetimes away.

When the cab pulled up in front of her house I realised it wasn't quite the New York of *Sex and the City* that I'd found myself in. As I nervously paid the driver, I wondered, not for the last time, what I had got myself into. So desperate to get out of Brighton and make a fresh start, I hadn't asked where Adi lived, or, indeed, any other details other than how to get there from the airport. The old mantra of 'look before you leap' was clearly lost on me.

I stood outside the flat in the middle of Harlem, my quick-ening breath swirling around me in thick white clouds, taking in this foreign landscape. There were bins burning under the bridge just down the end of the road with guys warming their hands around them, broken windows in several houses in front of me, and an old smashed-up car abandoned on the corner. I was in the ghetto proper, looking conspicuously queer with my matching luggage and a rucksack on my back.

'What up, white boy?' shouted a kid, riding past me on a bike.

Adi buzzed me into her actually rather nice apartment, all wooden floors and open-plan kitchen, and I was introduced to three-year-old Zoe. We hit it off instantly. She was like a breath of fresh air, funny, cute and bright beyond her years. Adi was so glad that I had rescued her from a childcare nightmare, I was warmly received and had a real sense of usefulness, which went a certain way towards rebuilding my shattered pride.

I took Zoe to school in the morning and picked her up at 4 p.m. every day. I made dinner and we danced around to Stevie Wonder and Linkin Park, watched TV and hung out until her mum got home from work around eight. Then the night was all mine. Within a week, I had discovered the lesbian scene and within it a whole new world of women and adventure.

My ongoing recovery from pancreatitis coupled with the fact that I was living with a professional person and her small child curtailed my nihilistic instinct for a short while. But I only needed to hang out in a lesbian joint for a night before I'd befriended the bar staff, snogged a regular and been named karaoke champ. I got a lot of attention as a new face on the scene – an 'English girl' at that. And the more attention

I got, the better I felt about myself. Meow Mix, Henrietta Hudson, Cubby Hole – I was a fixture at all these dyke bars by the end of my first month in town. I started knocking around with the cool set – the girls who ran the club nights. New York living was intoxicating and as fate would have it my old friend, Pavlo, the first person I'd come out to, was dating an American girl and had moved out to be nearer to her, so I found some grounding familiarity in having such an old friend, someone who knew me so well, in the city.

New York was like a rebirth for me. I loved Manhattan, the bars, the restaurants that catered to every taste imaginable. Pavlo had a job in Soho managing a high-end furniture store and so at least once a week I would venture downtown to see him, and we would spend hours walking through New York's grid system, bar hopping but also taking in the culture, the people, the pace. I loved that strangers would greet you with an amiable 'How you doing?' pretty much anywhere you went.

It was only a few years after 9/11 and New York felt like a united, kind city, its people welcoming and warm. The women I met were from all different walks of life and I dated tough-talking Staten Island medics, Puerto Rican artists, New Orleans dancers. They were all there, and all had a story to tell, some even as chequered as my own. I fell completely in love with New York and with all things American, a love that has never waned.

The situation with Adi and Zoe worked well, and kept me away from the bars during the week and provided me with a sense of responsibility and purpose. After school pick-up, we would go to Central Park and play in the vast green areas, chewing Twizzlers and singing the songs she loved.

I had a big group of friends and a very real sense of community and if I wanted to go out for a drink, there was always someone who'd be up for it. After a few months, I noticed this young guy always at the same joints we went to. He was friends with my lesbian friends and seemingly always had a gorgeous girl, or boy, on his arm. The gay girls all seemed very close and protective of him.

'That's Nicco,' said my friend Tracy. 'He's trans.'

Nicco was smaller than me, and absolutely beautiful. He had peroxide-blond hair that he wore in short spikes and a handsome face with a short, well-maintained beard. I was transfixed. We got talking and Nicco saw something familiar in me instantly. A wired, edgy discomfort in myself. We sat in the corner of a dive bar, ordered beers and spoke all night. He was six years older than me and very wise and calm. He was really educated about gender and opened my mind to a whole new conversation. He talked me through his transition, explained what top surgery was, told me about hormones and dysphoria. He never once suggested I might be trans but just knowing that he existed finally allowed me to admit out loud what I had known since I was two years old.

'Nicco, I'm a man too. I always have been.'

He gave me this great big brotherly hug and said 'You're OK, it's going to be OK.'

With those few words, he saved my life.

CHAPTER NINE

An achievable goal

Hannah

After 20 hours of digging with no sleep, I'd become zombie-like in my relentless task. I'd pushed through tiredness and physical exhaustion and came out the other end as a collection of limbs that existed simply to move earth from inside the hole, to outside of it. The dull thud as the shovel hit the earth time and time again became the metronome to a song from Disney's *Pocahontas* (yes, I am a massive Disney fan) that had lodged in my head many hours previous.

'*Dig and dig and dig and diggity dig and dig and dig and diggity...*'

'Orders in 10 minutes!' A shout from a fellow Officer Cadet stirring me from my sleep-deprived trance. At five that autumn morning, we'd been dropped off in the middle of the Norfolk countryside with our Bergens and folding shovels, for what is notoriously one of Sandhurst's most challenging exercises, Exercise FIRST ENCOUNTER, affectionately known to the Cadets as 'worst encounter'.

The exercise begins with digging a six-foot-deep trench for your section of eight people, complete with corrugated iron supports, camouflaged by the displaced earth and grass. It forms part of a wider dug-in defensive position, completed in the knowledge that an enemy will shortly follow, so there's no stopping until the trenches are finished – then the cries of '*Gas! Gas! Gas!*' will fill the air, a signal to don your gas mask to deal with the staged chemical warfare and to engage in a firefight.

It was cold, but the work was so physical we were drenched in sweat beneath our uniforms. The hours slipped by and progress was slow but steady. We were used to functioning on very little sleep – three hours a night wasn't unusual during the first five weeks at the elite Officer academy that I'd been preparing for since I was 15.

*   *   *

For the first five weeks, the days would start at 5.30 a.m. with Colour Sergeant Baird, my instructor (and a very intimidating Yorkshireman), shouting down the corridor for us to get out of our beds and line up. I'd rush out into the corridor in my underwear and stand to attention alongside the other Cadets in my platoon before singing the National Anthem at the top of my voice, and cracking on with getting my room ready for inspection. At Sandhurst, you are observed constantly – your physical performance, your mental performance, your character – everything is under review at all times. On an average day, I might go for a team run or do a heavy gym workout, conduct training in fieldcraft, marksmanship or radio communications, have swimming sessions, attend classes on military history, lectures on leadership and then, at the very end, have to get my uniform and room ready for inspection the next day. My duties usually finished at midnight and it would take an hour or more to prepare my room. In drawers, T-shirts had to be perfectly pressed and folded to A4 size and neatly piled on top of each other. Next to them were my five pairs of socks, all neatly rolled up together. Exactly the same, all in a line.

Everyone knows it's ridiculous. But the point is, they're putting pressure on you and pushing you to your limits in every sense. Did I enjoy it? No! It was hideous. Absolutely hideous. But what kept me going was a steely drive to succeed. I wanted to become an Army Officer, and this was a means to an end.

*   *   *

After about 36 hours, our trench was dug, the metal supports in place, and all that remained was the turf to be relaid on top so it blended seamlessly into the environment. I fell asleep carrying a big, heavy square of grass and didn't wake up until I walked into somebody, jolted back to reality. I had to push through, but not because I knew that a simulated chemical attack was inbound, but because that is how you demonstrated to the instructors that you have what it takes.

If you watch films about the Army, you often see soldiers being shouted and screamed at, suffering the wrath of their Sergeant, and it's true, you do get shouted at a lot in training. Perhaps what is less understood is why. It's not because they want us to be miserable, but rather that in the heat of battle the world is incredibly noisy, complex and stressful, and leaders need to be able to make life-changing decisions in those moments. Pushing us to (and beyond) our limits is the only way to simulate that in training. It also brings people together as a team, which is foundational at the beginning of any military training. There are times when you are so exhausted, you can't think straight and you doubt whether you have what it takes. And it is in those moments that you rely on the teammate next to you to pick you up, tell you a stupid joke, offer you a handful of Haribo or whatever it takes to get you back on your feet and moving again, in the full knowledge that there will be plenty of times when you will do exactly the same for them.

The mental resilience I learnt at Sandhurst has given me the armour I need to protect myself from the nonsense that is thrown at me as a trans woman in today's world. For one thing I know how to accept the support of those around me when I need it, and for another I have a willingness to keep fighting, even while under relentless attack. However, perhaps the best thing the Army has given me is a sense of perspective. I have known good people who have lost their lives, have stood at a service in the middle of Helmand Province, Afghanistan, and mourned the death of a fellow soldier serving their country. *They* matter to me, not some idiot insulting me on Twitter.

If you pass out of Sandhurst, you are confronted with your first Platoon Command position at a fairly young age, leading a team of 30 men and women, and within that team is a whole wealth of experience, including a Sergeant with 15 years of experience and probably several years your senior. This is why it's tough. Going through that level of training is what makes you credible in that position, although it is vital that you maintain enough humility to know that you still have a lot to learn from those you command.

The training was surprisingly broad: we did the obstacle courses, 30-mile treks carrying 40 kilograms, and learnt how to win firefights, but we also did courses in War Studies, Communication and Behavioural Science and Defence and International Affairs, learnt how to organise expeditions abroad and even had classes on hosting and dining etiquette. And at the core of everything we did was leadership. At the end of Sandhurst, you are given the privilege of commanding other soldiers, soldiers who you could potentially lead into battle. It's seriously hard preparation for a seriously hard job.

There were no quotas for how many women Sandhurst should accept, it was just a matter of how many had applied and succeeded in being selected for that intake. There was one female platoon and eight male ones. When I was there, women trained separately to men, a bit antiquated since we don't work separately when we are qualified. Thankfully Sandhurst is now mixed and there are better provisions for female recruits – one of the many changes the British Army has grappled with during my lifetime. But back then, it was the most gender-segregated environment I'd been in – even Welbeck felt more mixed – and this solidified my sense of myself as not being male.

My body dysphoria and being trans weren't things I really had the time to contemplate at Sandhurst. Five miles into a weighted run when I was struggling to keep going, my gender identity was not front of mind, yet it was always there. And in those rare, quiet moments alone, I would daydream of a future where I could be my female self and still be in the Army. I was a trans woman and it was a secret I carried with me like my rifle – always by my side – dangerous and life saving in equal measure.

*   *   *

I was very unhappy with my body. One of the by-products of such intense physical training was bulking up; broadening shoulders, growing biceps and so on, and this was something that the guys around me revelled in. I lived with them 24/7 and saw how completely at ease they were with their bodies, but, despite being the fittest I'd ever been, for me it simply didn't feel right. I had no desire to get into a relationship with a man, partly because there wouldn't have been the time or the headspace to do so, but mainly because I didn't want my male-presenting body to be the thing someone desired about me.

Telling people I was gay meant no one asked me about girl-friends and it was justification for anything that was even remotely feminine about me. It was the lie that covered the deeper truth, a defence mechanism to protect myself from people finding out that I was trans.

One of the biggest challenges we find as an LGBTQIA+ community is that people make assumptions about us based on stereotypes, and the media tropes that exist. But when someone spends time with us, all that stuff gets broken down and we connect as individuals. In some ways it was easier for me: I was at Sandhurst in a platoon with several friends from Welbeck and university so I didn't really need to 'come out' as most people already knew or quickly found out about me. No one had a problem with it. We all lived and worked together, and I was one of the team. With the constant pressure we were under there were more important things to worry about than someone's sexuality.

*   *   *

Colour Sergeant Baird walked into my room. It was late in the evening and he was checking in on us as we polished our boots for the following day's drill practice.

'Is it true that you're gay?' he asked in his thick Yorkshire accent, as he eyed my Disney Princess duvet cover – the whole platoon had agreed to get children's bedding as a joke and I couldn't resist it.

'Yes, Colour Sergeant,' I replied. After six years of telling people I was gay, I was fairly confident about discussing the subject, but this was the first time I'd talked about it with a military chain of command, and as my instructor he had every opportunity to make my life very hard.

After a long pause that had begun to feel slightly awkward, he said simply, 'Fair enough,' before adding, 'doesn't change anything,' and walking out. It was hardly the most enthusiastic response, but I'd guess he'd never really known anyone gay in the Army before and, considering his background and experience, I was actually quite pleased. I didn't want any fuss, I wanted to be treated the same as everyone else and prove to him that I was worthy of being an Officer.

*   *   *

Despite our differences we all had the same goal – to receive a commission from Her Majesty The Queen and to serve our country as Army Officers. The commission itself is a simple A3 certificate, signed by the reigning monarch, co-signed by the serving prime minister, with details in cursive script about your appointment and responsibilities as an Officer in the Armed Forces. For the most part it is simply a keepsake to have on your wall, symbolic of the achievement of passing out of Sandhurst, but also a reminder of the huge honour and responsibility bestowed upon you to serve those whom you lead.

As I progressed through Sandhurst, that responsibility weighed on me as I wondered if it would mean sacrificing any opportunity to truly be myself. The thought that continued to rattle through my head was that the Army was certainly a hypermasculine environment and, despite much of the progress within its ranks, I had never heard of anyone coming out as trans who hadn't had a really tough time, before eventually leaving the service under a cloud. So even as I focused on the goal in front of me, I knew that every day closer to passing out was a day closer to an impossible choice.

Being gay in the Army had been legal for nine years at this time (it was against military law before 2000 and individuals were hunted and prosecuted in military courts, lost their pensions and were handed criminal convictions, with life-long consequences that still exist today). However, there's always a lag between policy change and inclusion, and so there weren't many openly gay soldiers around. The Army is built around men and, while there's a rich history of women being in service since the First World War, it wasn't until 2018 that every role was made available to women. This means the traditions, culture and even clothes were all grounded in the experiences of men. A case in point: the 'unisex' uniforms were designed for men, and ponytails have only been acceptable since 2021! There are now, of course, many strong female leaders across the ranks and a growing female community, both of which are innovating and challenging these traditions – yet old habits die hard.

The one time anyone messed with gender binaries was on nights out. Sandhurst was full of young, very fit, confident men and Army Officers love a party. Fancy dress was pretty much par for the course, so we all had a fancy dress box that we could dip into at a moment's notice and it was quite common for the guys to have the odd dress or crop top stashed in there. Weirdly (or perhaps not?), much like you might see a men's rugby team dressing as women for a night out, it is the more hypermasculine guys who are first to grab the skirt and lipstick – the Royal Marines are famous for it!

There was a thriving social scene at Sandhurst. After the initial weeks, when we had to work seven days a week, we started to get some Sundays off, so we were able to let our hair down and decompress. Sometimes that was a formal three-course, silver service dinner, but more often than not they were informal affairs. During my second term, we had organised a circus-themed night in one of the Sandhurst bars. I had decided to go as a mime artist, as it not only fitted the brief, but also gave me an excuse to 'enrich' my fancy dress box with items that, out of that context, might simply be seen as female clothes. I also used the opportunity to buy some red lipstick, the sense of justification giving me the confidence to peruse the local Boots. The night itself was fairly typical; music, games, dancing and, of course, more than a couple of drinks going down range (to coin a military phrase).

The next morning, I woke up feeling pretty rough and rose to look in the mirror, my pale face reflected back at me.

Juxtaposed against it was the red lipstick... What little colour I had left drained away from me and I scrambled to find the lipstick I had bought, only to discover it was actually a 24-hour lip stain. Panic washed over me as I imagined Colour Sergeant Baird's response to seeing me standing at attention with bright red lips – I was due on parade in 30 minutes! Digging the packaging out from the bin, I frantically read the small print, which referred to using an 'oil-based product' for removal. I looked around my small room. There had to be something. And there it was. Resting next to the mess tins on my top shelf was my rifle cleaning kit, complete with gun oil. Yep, I wiped off my lipstick with gun oil. It was actually very effective. I can think of no better visual metaphor for being secretly trans in the Army.

By this point I'd been living this double life for five or six years. In the privacy of my room I was inhabiting my female identity whenever I could, and outside of that I was convincingly 'one of the guys'. Thanks to all the fancy dress parties over the years, there was always a good excuse for having 'women's' clothes and makeup lying around. If anyone found something and questioned it, I'd be quick to brush it off and have any number of believable answers up my sleeve. That being said, there wasn't a lot of time to relax at Sandhurst and you have to take your education seriously. The simple fact is, you are being prepared to fight in a war.

No one who joins the Army is ignorant to this fact, and I was in training in 2009 against the backdrop of operational conflicts in both Iraq and Afghanistan where casualties were making the newspapers on a regular basis, but this awareness only served to focus the application of your training, rather than acting as a deterrent. Indeed, there was actually an eagerness to be deployed and play your part.

I know some reading this may have political or ethical objections to both those conflicts and perhaps conflicts in general, but as a soldier you come at it from a different angle. Carl von Clausewitz, a Prussian General, famously wrote, *'war is the extension of politics with other means'*, illustrating that the Army is simply a political tool, used to advise and support the foreign policies of a democratic system. I am not saying that those policies are always correct but, to me at least, to be a soldier is to be willing to make the ultimate sacrifice in order to serve your country and the people it protects. I did, as it happens, deploy to Afghanistan shortly after commissioning from Sandhurst, and felt the fear for my own life for the first time, providing top cover for a vehicle as it drove down an alley that we knew had 12 Taliban explosive devices that had been identified in the previous week. Thankfully for me, I came home from that mission and deployment without injury. Others weren't so lucky.

My parents lived in a dual state of pride and fear. They supported what I was doing and understood why it was important to me. But at the same time, on a human level, they were scared that their child was preparing to deploy somewhere very dangerous. They watched the news and saw that people were dying out in Afghanistan, but they never stood in my way. I wondered if they'd have had the same attitude if I told them I was transgender. It was something so far out of our frame of reference as a family, I couldn't be sure.

*   *   *

After the final, gruelling three-week exercise in Scotland (I honestly felt like I would never be dry again), and just two weeks before the end of the last term, I got the nod that, along with the rest of my platoon, I had proved myself to be worthy of being an Officer. Just 14 days of polishing boots, ironing and drill practice was all that stood between us and commissioning.

The commissioning day itself was fairly manic and began with a light run to shake out any cobwebs before the parade – at least that's what we thought it would be. In actual fact we only ran a short distance to the parade square, where none other than Mr Motivator was standing atop the iconic white steps of Old College, clad in his brightly coloured lycra and leg warmers! One of the Cadets had organised for him to come along and so we all exuberantly jumped into an 80s' aerobics routine among fits of laughter.

Just a couple of hours later, though, on a warm summer's morning, all the Cadets in Sandhurst gathered for our pass-off parade, dubbed the 'Sovereign's Parade', nervously removing specks of dust from each other's uniforms before we were brought to attention by the Academy Sergeant Major. The band struck up, the big bass drum pounding the beat as we began the march to the parade square, where gathered on the stands were the then prime minister, David Cameron, senior Officers, royalty from the Middle East and, most importantly, our friends and families.

The parade itself was pomp and ceremony at its finest, full of complicated choreographed marching, award presentations, the inspection by David Cameron (involving a lot of standing still and waiting) and eventually the culmination of the parade, where the Cadets who'd finished their course slow march up the stone steps of Old College, symbolising stepping into life as an Officer. Once inside, the clatter of hobnail boots was deafening as we jostled with each other, hugging, cheering and backslapping. We'd done it and we'd done it together, through physical and mental exhaustion – we had finished our training.

The rest of the day was a slightly more relaxed affair, time for photos and gathering together with family, a formal lunch and then a few hours in the afternoon for packing things up before donning our new Mess Kits for the Commissioning Ball. A 'Mess Kit' is an evening uniform worn by Officers, each specific to the Regiment or Corps to which we belonged – I had been selected to join the Royal Electrical and Mechanical Engineers and so the uniform consisted of tight black trousers, with a red stripe down each leg, and a red waistcoat and fitted black jacket fixed with brass buttons over a shirt and bow tie. Atop each shoulder were epaulettes fixed with 'pips', representing your rank. For me, a single pip on each shoulder indicated the First Officer rank, Second Lieutenant, but at this point they were both covered by a strip of fabric.

The Commissioning Ball itself was just a big party. A 30-metre-long bar that pretty much only served champagne, live band, dance floor, fairground rides and fireworks, it was simply an opportunity for us to celebrate. As midnight approached however, we pulled away from the partying to find our loved ones, which for me was Mum, Dad and Jeff, and we stood together as the clock tower ticked down. Midnight is the official moment when you cease to be a Cadet and become an Officer and Dad grabbed his camera to catch that moment, as Mum symbolically removed the fabric from my rank slides, revealing the pips. It's tempting here to write some glib comment about transitioning before my mum's eyes and how that was a foreshadowing for my future. The truth is this was the one of the proudest achievements of my life and, in that moment, my gender seemed irrelevant. I hugged my family, joy mixed with relief, and they toasted to my future as Second Lieutenant Winterbourne.

The next morning, we were woken by Colour Sergeant Baird for one last duty at Sandhurst – clean-up. It's hideous. We were all feeling worse for wear, but we still had to get up and restore the academy to its pristine glory. This involved picking up rubbish, dismantling the marquee and – my personal favourite – crawling on hands and knees across the rugby pitches to collect all the debris from the firework display.

Some two hours later, and feeling slightly better for being out in the fresh air, we gathered in our platoon lines with our bags for one last ritual. Colour Sergeant Baird came to each one of us in turn and, when he reached me, I handed him my military ID, which still held the rank of Officer Cadet. He snapped it in half, before handing me a new ID with my new Officer's rank across it. Shaking my hand, he wished me luck for the future and, in the final act, saluted me as I now held a superior rank. As he was the man who had shouted and screamed at me over the last year, and taught me so much as he drove me to my limits, I cannot say I felt superior in any way, but his gesture of respect hit me hard as I realised that Sandhurst was really over. I picked up my bags and left.

CHAPTER TEN

A star ascendant

Jake

On a tropical summer's evening, Tracy and I sauntered through The Village, every sidewalk alive with buzzing restaurants, past the overspill from the noisy bars and tourists enjoying the heat. As we entered Beauty Bar, Katie was already there, sitting at the bar after her shift. She was what we would have called a lipstick lesbian in the UK, but in Manhattan she was just considered smoking hot, with long, wild blonde hair, a gym-toned body and a killer smile. Her Jewish background was also appealing and we had already discovered a lot of shared history, always a boon.

The scene back in London and Brighton had been so binary, so rigid – you were butch, like me, or femme, like Katie – there was no space for anything in between. But here, at the white-hot centre of early-millennial Manhattan, where Samantha Jones was eating men for breakfast on *Sex and the City* and dating was a sport everyone played, the word 'queer' was being tossed around in a way I'd never heard before.

Gender was fluid, so was sexuality. People were exploring the corners of their identity right out in the open – sleeping with girls, guys and – as I was learning – trans men and women too.

Katie had picked me up at karaoke at Meow Mix a few weeks before, after I had jumped in with the rap section to TLC's 'Waterfalls'. She was so forward, so clear about what she wanted, it was hugely attractive. She was exploring this new world much as I was, and she decided that I was someone she wanted to experiment with, which was fine with me. I told her that I identified as trans and explained what that meant, a learning curve for her too, but she seemed utterly unfazed by most things.

The next few weeks were a blur as I tore through the city with Katie on my arm, feeling more and more myself. It was as if suddenly this future had been opened up to me. My internal and external worlds were aligning in a way that was euphoric compared to the battles I'd been fighting these past three decades.

Katie accepted that I was trans and in the really early stages of a social transition, and, like Nicco, she made me feel safe, like everything was going to be OK. She had never dated anyone other than cisgender men before but was clearly very open to me and my own journey. And after all, this was New York – many of her friends were queer and together we were learning how to give form to a new kind of relationship for both of us.

Nicco, Katie and this crew of LGBTQIA+ (and everything in between) friends talked to me about the practicalities of taking testosterone and having top surgery, but also about gender as a construct and the fluidity of selfhood. It was the first time I'd ever had the headspace to really think deeply about biological sex, gender and sexuality. Suddenly the weight that I'd been carrying – a burden of social expectation and inherited ideas about who a person could be – was untethered and my mind set free. Transitioning would be expensive, and a huge undertaking in every sense, but it could also offer me a content-ment that I'd so far been lacking in life.

Don't worry, it's going to be OK.

You can be who you want.

You can be the man you know you are.

Had someone said these words to me earlier in my life it really could have been transformative. These were all affirm-ations I wanted or needed to be told. Now I try, through my roles with Stonewall and Mermaids, to be the person who says these words to as many young people as I can, whether they're gay, trans, lesbian or gender fluid. When you're surrounded by fear and rejection, those few reassuring words can be truly life saving.

Nicco was such a great influence on me. I was still what Americans call 'a hot mess', but for the first time in my life I felt a glimmer of hope, of a future where I might one day feel complete – completely happy. Nicco and I would meet a couple of times a week and sit in the pizza joint across the road from Meow Mix, talking, until three or four in the morn-ing. I had so many questions. Nicco seemed to have his life together and I really looked up to him. He was working, his parents were supportive, his friends championed him. A whole new way of living authentically was opening up to me.

Trans people are made to feel so ugly and so unworthy of love. My biggest fear about transitioning was that no one was going to be attracted to me. But Nicco was dating a guy *and* a girl. He was a catch. Meanwhile, Katie was a sweet, caring woman who validated me completely as a boy (I didn't feel grown-up enough to call myself a man yet!). I dared to wonder if maybe this life could be mine. There was one problem though. My tourist visa was coming to an end and my time in New York was nearly up.

In those last few weeks in the city, I felt I was carrying a ticking time bomb around with me. Knowing I had to leave filled me with fear and dread. The thought of going home to England and having to slot back into that old world after the epiphany I'd had terrified me. My gang of lesbian friends were far from as fluid and open-minded as their New York counterparts. I didn't know how I'd even begin to tell them I was trans.

I had to say goodbye to Katie, which felt like the end of something very important for me. It had been a casual relationship and mutually beneficial as we both figured out a lot about ourselves while we were with each other – her as a queer woman, and me as a trans man – and it had completely altered my self-perception.

On the eve of my departure, my New York gang organised farewell drinks for me at our favourite club night, Snapshot. As I said my goodbyes, I clung onto each of them, thanking them for the love and hope and warmth that they had offered me when I was utterly lost, Katie and Nicco and all the other magical new friends who I had met out there. I fully expected to never see them again. That night was heartbreaking and the flight home filled me with dread.

Several hours later, I landed at Heathrow hungover and alone. The stage was set for the next few months of my life back in Britain.

*   *   *

I returned to a cold and wet Brighton, the city appearing to cower under a grey blanket, flat and lifeless. I called my mother to tell her I was home and she promised to visit soon. The old gang was waiting for me, and I was offered a place to live in the hotel that I'd helped renovate before I left.

Depressingly nothing there had changed – the same people worked the same bars, still seemingly more interested in what they were going to do on Saturday night than what they were going to do with the rest of their lives. I slipped back into my place on the scene, but I wasn't the same person I'd been before I left.

'So, in New York I kind of came out. As trans. I'm not really a lesbian... I'm a man,' I told my friend Carly as we walked along the seafront, clutching take-away black coffees in paper cups and kicking up pebbles.

She looked at me and laughed as though it were a joke. 'What are you talking about? Of course you're a woman. Don't be crazy.'

'I've known for a long time, but I finally saw someone like me. Another trans man. And in New York, people were calling me "he" and it... it felt right.'

I was feeling good about myself. I'd been joining Katie in the gym for intense evening workouts and New York had given me biceps and bigger shoulders. I was still hiding my chest under baggy T-shirts but often with cut-off sleeves to show off my arms. My hair was cut in a 'short back and sides' barbershop style. But it took one look from Carly, one raised eyebrow and dismissive comment to bring me crashing right back to self-loathing all over again.

'I don't get it. Is this some weird trendy New York thing?' Carly shook her head. 'What's so wrong with being a lesbian? It's who you are. You can't just suddenly waltz back into our lives saying you're a man now and expect us all to just accept that. I think we all know you better than your new American friends.'

Carly gave me a lacklustre hug before leaving me on the beach. When she pulled away she stared at my face as if looking for answers, and I saw all the confusion and shock and maybe even a hint of betrayal in her eyes. It was a look I would come to know well.

Of course Carly told the girls and soon enough I was fielding 'concerned' phone calls and text messages from people asking if it was true I 'thought I was a man now'. I knew that if I lost my lesbian friends over this, I'd be alone. And there was nothing I feared more. So within a few days, all the positive progress I'd made thanks to Nicco in New York was undone and I played down my gender and said it was something I'd just been thinking about but realised now how silly it was.

Once again, I was living a lie. And it felt awful.

Lying in a single bed at night in the cold, windowless basement of the hotel, terror would engulf me. It was worse even than that nadir I'd hit after my hospital stay – at least then my mother was by my side. Now I'd seen a glimpse of light, the darkness was blacker than ever. I went out each night to stave off the loneliness and dreaded being alone with my thoughts. Once again, I drank to oblivion and worked hard to forget those feelings of burgeoning happiness that I had felt in New York, now another lifetime.

How I managed to maintain any friendships or relationships is beyond me but I suppose I was well practised by then. It was clear to anyone I became even fleetingly intimate with that I was not OK. Having finally acknowledged why I had always hated my body and felt so utterly ill at ease in my own skin, it was hard now to slip back into dating and intimacy.

I recoiled from people's touch and hid myself away even further. I was seriously depressed and on a self-destructive path to annihilation. A few of these women I dated tried to save me. I met Caro a couple of weeks after getting back and she asked me to move into her nice flat in The Lanes in central Brighton and make some kind of normal life work. But like many of the women who fell for me, she soon came to the conclusion that I was beyond saving, only echoing my own feelings of despair.

Despite the rejection of my nascent trans identity by my lesbian friends, and my own best attempts to bury it, the seeds that had been planted in New York continued to grow. Top surgery and hormones flickered like a lighthouse on the horizon as the only things that might possibly save me. After a year living in Brighton, and in unquestionably the darkest place I had been, I took the train back to London.

It was December and Christmas lights sparkled every-where, happy faces filling the city's pubs and bars, and a sense of merriment in the air that only served to deepen my feelings of isolation and despair.

From Victoria Station, I travelled a few stops on the District Line to Notting Hill and walked the familiar route from the tube to the front door of my family home, feeling a weird disconnect. Although so much inside my head was in a kind of radical state of flux, on the outside nothing had changed, and to my mother I'm sure it must have felt like history repeating as I arrived miserable and sullen on her doorstep.

As I rang the doorbell, I didn't really know what I was doing, I didn't know what I wanted or needed from my mother. I just knew I had to see her. She'd rescued me so many times before, but now I really felt that I was drowning.

When she opened the door she took a step back almost in fear. I must have looked grey, strung out, underweight and wretched.

'I'm so sorry,' my voice cracking as I spoke.

I'd barely made it over the threshold before I broke down crying. She guided me to the living room, sat me in a chair and sat opposite me, waiting for me to speak, imagining God knows what, given my history,

'Try to calm down. It's OK.' She spoke soothingly and, in between sobs, I attempted to speak.

'I've been so unhappy,' I ventured. 'I've *always* been unhappy because... because—'

Mum looked at me kindly, as if to say *go on.*

'—Because I've always been a boy. All my life. And I told you when I was little. And I just can't do this anymore.'

My eyes were blurry with tears so I couldn't see if a flicker of horror had registered on her face or not. She sat down next to me and pulled me in for an embrace. I was so relieved to have told her.

The first thing she said to me was not in any way what I had expected.

'Right. So... what are we going to do about this?'

Those few words changed everything. I knew then that everything was going to be OK. I didn't know how, but, for only the second time in my life, I felt real hope for the future. Mum didn't challenge me, or imply that what I was feeling wasn't true – instead she was ready to help me figure out a solution. I couldn't believe the depths of her love and her compassion – after everything I had put her through. Now I'm a parent myself, I understand this absolute, unconditional love. Her reaction changed everything and set my transition in motion. I told her I'd already contacted a therapist and had an appointment booked.

'Would you like me to come with you?'

'Yeah, please.' I was terrified at what that doctor might tell me, and I needed my mother with me. 'Thank you.'

That night I slept in my old room, which felt conflicting, both comforting but also a reminder of the wasted years of my childhood and teens, by now nearly three decades of misery. I stared up at the ceiling, terrified about what was to come. Would I look freakish and unattractive as a man? Would I lose my friends? Would I ever find a partner? Yet my mother's supportive reaction made me feel like in spite of all of these unknowns, it was the right thing to do – for me and my family. Maybe then I could be the good son to her I'd always wanted to be.

Determined to prove myself worthy of my mother's kindness, I got a job working as a waiter at a very trendy, upscale restaurant in Knightsbridge so I could make my own money and get a home of my own. Suddenly, I was living this very mainstream life, and although my band of boys from school was still always there on the periphery with tireless support, my lesbian community was slowly drifting away. I won't deny that it hurt to lose friends who had meant the world to me for over a decade, but I also fully understood why many of them simply couldn't reconcile my new male identity. I just didn't belong anymore, and that was that.

I moved into a houseshare with three people, which was a real struggle given what an antisocial, insular person I still was. Embarking on a medical transition is difficult enough, but surrounded by strangers who had no desire nor drive to understand what I was going through made home life pretty uncomfortable. So despite the constant presence of other people, I still felt a crushing sense of loneliness as I prepared to start my transition.

My therapist had warned me that taking testosterone could potentially lead to me feeling quite aggressive, having mood swings and depression, the prospect of which worried me greatly. My old school friends, as ever, were as supportive as they could be, they just had no real knowledge or understanding of what I was going through. I'm not sure they took it too seriously at first, except Pavlo, who had witnessed the genesis of it all in New York and knew Nicco. He told me he'd always be there for me and simply wanted me to be happy. He was one of the first people who really made an effort with my new pronouns and, eventually, my new name.

'Of course, man,' he'd said when I told him I'd started testosterone and was using new pronouns over a beer in a Soho pub. 'You know, you've always been our friend. That's it.'

*   *   *

I was a terrible waiter. I was far too sensitive and prickly to be any good with the customers and I hated the way they spoke to me. But the owner of the place, a lovely man called Nick, took me under his wing, becoming somewhat of a father figure to me at this pivotal time in my life. I begged him to let me work the bar instead of waiting tables and he agreed.

I had to ask for the day off to go to my first counselling appointment so I made up some excuse and headed off to meet my mother, who I'm guessing felt as sick with nerves as I did.

Within half an hour of seeing that first therapist with my mother, they said, *'Well, you've obviously got gender dysphoria.'*

Hearing these words after so many years of self-doubt and other people's dismissals felt like such a relief. I broke down in floods of tears. 'Are you sure? So, there's nothing wrong with me? It's a real medical thing?' I asked, desperate for some kind of affirmation that I wasn't the 'bad' child that I had always felt myself to be.

They referred me to a gender specialist. Thankfully I was able to access treatment privately rather than navigate the NHS – where waiting lists for trans people to receive the treatment they need can be up to five years. I'm not sure I could have lasted that long. Many don't.

* * *

After getting that official validation of my gender, and a second opinion from the specialist that confirmed gender dysphoria, my mum was on board and willing to pay to expedite everything.

'Right, let's just do this,' she said firmly and reassuringly, and soon all the wheels were in motion for my top surgery and the start of testosterone therapy.

Often, trans people have to prove they've been 'living in role' (whatever that really means) for a period of time before being able to medically transition. I felt like I'd been living a role all my life. It wasn't like I had been wearing dresses all these years and was suddenly going to have to cast them aside to start living as a man.

I'd been referred to a doctor called Richard Curtis, who also happened to be transgender, and went along to his clinic just off Harley Street. It was great to have a consultant who was able to say to me with first-hand experience, *this is the effect of this and this is the benefit of that.* He helped me move the process on and was also the first trans person other than me that my mother had ever met. I think it really helped her to see this bright, successful doctor living happily as a trans man, and get to know him as a real person.

Through all of it, I had a huge amount of respect for my mother because so much of it must have been totally alien to her. I think at that point she realised I'd been miserable my whole life and finally understood why. She actually told me she had come across some of the many birthday and Christmas cards that I had made as a child, and that I had signed from Charles or Tom or Michael, back when I was seven or eight, and she realised – *being assigned the wrong gender has plagued my child their whole life.* As soon as she started hearing doctors saying, 'Yes, this is what's wrong with your child,' it made her feel like it was OK to support me and it was the right thing to do. She never faltered and was unwaveringly there for me. She never tried to talk me out of hormones or top surgery; she was just very practical and pragmatic.

As I readied myself for the first steps of my medical transition, I won't deny that I was filled with doubt, mostly as to whether I would ever find love again. The media and film representations of trans people that I had seen were filled with sadness, pain, rejection and humiliation. We were ridiculed, the butt of the joke time and time again in all of the popular TV shows from *Frasier* to *Friends* to *Little Britain.*

Undesirable.

Ugly.

Freakish.

The stigma attached to actually dating a trans person seemed to be so insurmountable that I couldn't imagine anyone ever wanting to be with me again. I worried about how I would look once I masculinised, how I would behave, how I would feel. After nearly 30 years of forcing those feelings down, finally confronting them was terrifying. Nicco, the only trans friend that I had, was thousands of miles away. I felt alone and riddled with worry, but for the first time in my life I knew I had to face those fears head on. I never for a second doubted that it was the right thing, the only thing that stood even a chance of making me happy, but it felt a lot like falling into the unknown.

The bar I worked in was in one of the flashiest parts of London. Customers were young Eurotrash types who parked their Ferraris or Bentleys outside. I was presenting very much as a lesbian behind the bar there, and enjoyed flirting with all the straight girls, many of whom flirted right back. I let Nick know about my transition; he agreed that the bar wasn't the right kind of environment for me to be working in while I went through it.

'I absolutely love you,' he told me before my shift started one night, 'but none of these people will get it. It's not going to get a good reception. And it's not going to be good for you.'

As a gay man, Nick knew better than most that the world we were in could be a very hostile place for people like us and simply wanted to protect me. The stares I had endured as a 'queer woman' were hard enough, never mind physically transitioning in front of their eyes. I was grateful for the escape. So I handed in my notice and Nick gave me a card with £300 as a very generous leaving present and a trip to the tattoo parlour, where he paid for me to have my forearm inked: 'New Dawn, New Day'.

And a new dawn it was.

*   *   *

I had my first shot of testosterone on 5 May 2007. I remember the thrill of it and thinking: *This is it. The start of living. Here we go.*

I hated needles but as I stood in Dr Curtis' surgery, his nurse readying the syringe, the anticipation was huge. The thought of male hormones going straight into my muscles was beyond exciting, but absolutely terrifying. There's no instant effect, in fact it felt like a huge anti-climax after all the build-up, but over the course of a few months my voice dropped a few octaves and I started to grow a little facial hair. The mood swings and depression that I had been warned about never materialised, much to my relief. I just felt so incredibly lucky that I was finally becoming me. Nothing else mattered.

I had moved in with a lovely French guy from work, Morgan, in north London and he was an absolute rock to me. He was supportive throughout and vowed to help me post-surgery, when I would be largely bedridden. Things hadn't

Jake aged three on holiday in Malta.

Aged ten at the Lycée Français Charles de Gaulle, London.

Aged 13, hiding his body under a baggy shirt as puberty began to kick in.

Jake and his father, Luc Graf.

Jake aged 16: smiling on the outside.

Aged 21, and very much entrenched in London's lesbian nightlife.

As a newborn in South Wales, 1987.

Hannah aged five, at home
in Cardiff, 1992.

With brother Jeff on holiday in Corfu, 2004.

Feeling nervous on the first
day of Welbeck College, 2003.

Hannah and mum at the
Welbeck College AGI, 2004.

Hannah preparing to skydive out of a helicopter, 2008.

Celebrating becoming an Officer at the Royal Military Academy Sandhurst Commissioning Ball, 2010.

Hannah donning her 'blues' at a friend's wedding, 2012.

Hannah and proud paternal grandparents at the Welbeck College Remembrance Day Parade, 2004.

Hannah at the Cosmopolitan Ultimate Women of the Year Awards, 2015.

With Commanding Officer, then Lieutenant Colonel Phil Prosser, receiving a special recognition award at the British LGBT Awards, 2015.

Hannah receiving her MBE at Buckingham Palace, 2019.

Hannah in front of two Challenger 2 tanks whilst serving with the King's Royal Hussars, 2016.

Feeding a baby giraffe at a wildlife orphanage in Kenya whilst deployed with the Army, 2014.

One of Hannah's favourite images of herself.

Hannah and parents, celebrating Hannah's honorary fellowship from Cardiff University, 2016.

Hannah and Lorraine Kelly on the set of *Lorraine*, 2015.

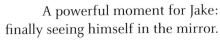

A powerful moment for Jake: finally seeing himself in the mirror.

Getting engaged on Central Park Lake.

Jake's beloved mother, Susie.

Hannah and dad on her wedding day, 2018.

The happiest day: 23 March 2018, Fulham.

This photo went viral back in 2019. Trans women are women, trans men are men.

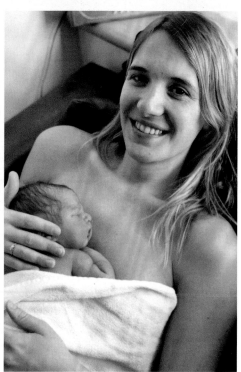

Hannah's first moments with Teddie.

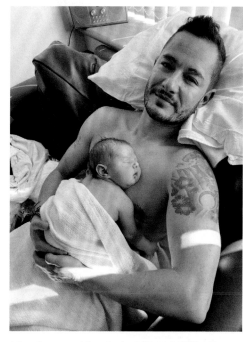

Absolute euphoria holding Millie for the first time at The Ulster Hospital, Belfast.

Starting life as a family of four.

Jake and his mini-me, Millie.

Jake's dream-come-true moment.

The first family photo in Belfast, in the second month of lockdown.

(*Left*) First moments with Teddie, back in Belfast.

Blissful days in the park as a threesome.

miraculously improved with my mother overnight – there was still a lot of resentment, residual anger and unresolved emotions so, despite the kind offer of a few days at home directly after my top surgery, we still had a lot of work to do.

She and my sister had both made it clear that they supported me completely, but those decades of burnt bridges were still smouldering, a seemingly endless list of infractions to correct. However, Mum remained hugely involved in my transition and, although we drove each other mad, she proved her love for me time and time again.

Dr Curtis had advised that I cut out alcohol ahead of my surgery and, as I stopped drinking every night and started seeing an amazing therapist, I felt more equipped to slowly start rebuilding those family relationships.

While I waited for my surgery appointment, l had a lot of time alone with my thoughts. Since tentatively coming out as trans, I felt as if the companionship of my chosen queer family, along with the women I dated, had all but disappeared. My biggest fear was that I would end up single for the rest of my life. Closely followed by, 'How would I look?' I'd always been viewed as attractive within the lesbian world at least, and there is something very unnerving about begin-ning a process that will ultimately dramatically alter your appearance.

I'd been dating a girl called Nina for nine months and I was quite into her. She had recently come out as a lesbian. She knew I was trans but when I told her I was booked in for top surgery and would be starting hormones, things started to deteriorate.

'But I'm still me. Surely it's about the person?' I'd say.

'You'll be a man. I'm a lesbian. I've dated men and I don't want to again. I don't like walking down the street and being perceived in that way,' she explained. 'It's making me feel quite uncomfortable. I've just come out and I don't want people to see me as a straight woman.'

Although we tried to work it out, my therapist suggested that attempting to maintain a relationship while undergoing a medical transition might be adding stress to an already diffi-cult time, so we reluctantly parted ways. I knew deep down that it was for the best, but at the time it really hurt and fed the growing anxiety that, post-transition, I'd be alone forever.

Around this time I tentatively started writing again, the first time since I was a teenager, and something I had long wanted to resume. I wrote a script about a trans man whose lesbian girlfriend leaves him when he comes out. I called it *X-WHY* and managed to find the micro-budget of £400 to turn it into a short film. I got my old friend, Jo, on board and we story-boarded, location scouted and went through a casting process. I also played the lead and so, groundbreakingly for the time, it was a trans character played by a trans actor. We shot it over two years so all the physical changes you see in the film are real: my voice dropping, shoulders broadening, beard growing. It's only a 17-minute short, but apparently documenting a gender transition in that way hadn't been done before and it received much acclaim, even being nominated for the Iris Prize, the largest short film prize in the world. We didn't win, but suddenly I was being taken seriously as a filmmaker and actor, and my outlook continued to improve.

During the break in filming, I had my top surgery at a private clinic on Harley Street. For some trans men this means a double mastectomy. In my case it meant a periareolar surgery to remove my breast tissue, a process where the surgeon cuts around the nipple and removes tissue through the opening. It meant that my scarring was minimal, which felt important to me. I remember the feeling of euphoria as they removed my bandages and I examined myself in the mirror. Rather than feeling shock at the bruising and stitches, my body for the first time felt like my own. My mother was by my side when I woke up and saw the joy and relief in me, which hopefully reassured her that she was doing the right thing by supporting me. The operation was a success, and I spent hours standing side-on in front of the mirror, admiring my flat male chest. I worried that my new nipples were slightly too big and had a couple of minor revisions, but the utter relief I felt that I could now, finally, stand tall and proud was incomparable. The utter euphoria I experienced when I first wore a slim-fit T-shirt almost brought me to tears. I spent a few days back at home recovering, with my mum looking after me, which meant a lot. It brought us closer together.

As she fussed about me in the bedroom, we discussed what my new name should be.

'I really like Chad,' I offered as an opening gambit.

'Oh darling, that's a country,' she quipped, rolling her eyes.

We went over countless options, with Mum vetoing most of them. I really wanted her approval.

I liked Milo – *'Milo Graf? Milograph? Sounds like an instrument.'*

Otto? Same thing, and the punchline of a joke my father used to tell.

It felt important that Mum sign off on the name because I

was her child and she'd named me originally, so I needed her to feel comfortable with it. She liked Michael. We talked about Tom. We talked about James. Jamie.

Then she suggested Jake and it instantly resonated. I liked the fact that a lot of people think it's short for Jacob, which felt like a nod to my Jewish heritage. So we decided this was my new name. And while I waited to change it by deed poll, I typed it into the opening credits of my film.

Starring Jake Graf.

My real name.

It had only taken 32 years.

*   *   *

BFI Flare takes place in March, so on a sunny Saturday spring morning my mother and I took a cab to the Southbank. After everything, it felt very important that she be there to see this. Her firstborn wreck of a child now screening their first film to an audience of 450. My mother was always glamorous but she'd made a special effort for the occasion and I was wearing a white shirt with a black blazer and jeans. As we picked up our festival lanyards, I once again reeled that I had made it this far. I was so nervous. Mum reached her hand over to mine and gave it a reassuring squeeze.

In the foyer before it started, Mum met all my queer friends for the first time, all of whom were warm and welcoming. Two decades of my life that she had never known. Seeing these two worlds collide filled me with pride. My loyal school pals were also there, Pavlo and Alex among them.

Once the audience had taken their seats, all of the

film-makers in the programme stood up on stage and introduced their films. I'd never done anything like that before – it was really early in my transition and I was still physically quite unsure of myself. Getting up on stage was a really terrifying prospect. As I waited for the directors and producers ahead of me to finish, my nerves built and I imagined I must be shaking as I stood there, rooted to the spot.

I was handed the microphone and I looked out at this room of hundreds of people. I took a deep breath and I saw my mum there in the audience, smiling encouragingly, and perhaps a little proudly, across at me. I babbled away about the film and then I introduced my mother, pointing over at her: 'She's here supporting me today. Mum, give us a wave.'

Mum looked a little awkward but, as everyone started clapping her, several even standing to applaud, we both realised then that she was one of the few supportive parents in that room, in that crowd. And people were giving her a mini standing ovation. It was an incredible moment for both of us.

Wow, I thought. *I've actually done something positive, something of which I can be proud.* It was a very pleasant feeling and one that I wanted to repeat.

Some months later, I put *X-WHY* online and began to receive messages from trans men across the world who told me that they'd finally seen themselves on screen. I was hearing from people in Afghanistan and Poland and Russia, sharing their stories, telling me I'd helped them, that they now didn't feel quite so alone. It really opened my eyes to how lucky I was to live in this cosmopolitan, accepting city and left me determined to continue to share those stories that clearly mattered so much.

Around this time I got a job with a small creative enterprise that travelled around schools in London running photography workshops, where I ended up working for four years. I loved showing the kids how to use a camera, how to pose, how to take great pics of themselves. It suited me, working in a different school every day, seeing kids from all walks of life and discovering more of my home city. It meant very early mornings, early nights and stability. It was exactly what I needed. I also began to notice a culture of acceptance and tolerance in these schools, murals for LGBT Pride month or 'Famous LGBTQ People'. There would even be the odd trans child, supported and championed by their teachers, and that felt truly hopeful.

It was a strange time in my life, because I was given the opportunity to completely reinvent myself. Finding your place in society again after a gender transition can be terrifying. On the tube, walking down the street, in restaurants – people just stare, trying to work out what you are. It's a truly unsettling time, but after 30 years of being uncertain of myself I knew exactly what I needed to do, and I was redefining my place in society as Jake.

And just where did I belong now? The Candy Bar had been my enclave, my safe space, yet I quite simply had no place there anymore.

I had a very close friend who always said we'd end up getting married. When I told her I was trans, she said, 'What are you talking about? You're my girl. You'll always be my girl.'

'But... we've never even dated!'

'Why are you doing this? You'll never be a man. Don't I mean anything to you?'

Sometimes, it was just easier to walk away. I did get some truly odd reactions and lost a good few friends, sadly.

By then I looked very different. I had a male torso, and a little 'chin strap' type beard because my moustache hadn't quite come in yet. My appearance jarred because after years of plucking my eyebrows in my futile attempt to fit in, they were thin and slightly patchy. It was quite the contrast, as you might imagine, and leaving the house during those first few months I was riddled with anxiety.

When I would venture into the Candy Bar, out of habit, I did get some bad reactions. Girls would say, 'This is a women's bar. You don't belong here.'

One September evening, after a day running a photography workshop with kids at a comprehensive school in Wandsworth, I was feeling good and proud of the work I'd been doing there, and still riding high on the continued success of *X-WHY*, which was now touring the world's festivals. I wasn't there to get drunk, I just wanted to feel a little less lonely, to feel part of something again. So when a girl I'd never seen before came up to where I was sitting at the front by the window and challenged my presence in the bar I said, 'Yeah, actually, I used to work here.'

When pushed, I reluctantly told her that I was transgender, but she wouldn't believe me and grabbed me between the legs to prove it. That was the first but not the last time someone had done that to me, and I was livid.

'What the hell are you doing?' I said, pushing her off me. She went to punch me, but I jerked away and instead she reached over and spat in my beer.

'You don't belong here, freak. Get out.'

The bouncer ran in as it was clearly getting heated, but she took this woman's side. 'Well, you're not a real man, are you?'

I was so upset that even in a queer space my masculinity was being doubted, it really knocked the wind out of my sails and I faltered. Luckily, the manager, Lisa, an older, no-nonsense Northerner, saw what happened and intervened. She had taken over when the old owner had finally been ousted, and ran the bar kindly and professionally. She had been welcoming to me every time I'd popped in and had taken me under her wing.

'Don't ever talk to one of my customers like that again,' she told the bouncer, and fired her on the spot.

*   *   *

Life was still challenging because my physical appearance lagged behind my identity, and wider society seemed lost as to what to do with me, but at least I was on the right track. I had met a girl at a dinner with friends and we had tentatively started dating. Sam was the first person to show me any interest post-testosterone and top surgery. She was laid back, funny and bore a strong resemblance to Natalie Portman. She had only ever dated cis men but wasn't even mildly fazed about dating a trans guy. She was an architect and had been over here for a few years, with ambitions to use her skills to make positive societal impact. Needless to say, my mother and sister adored her, quickly deciding that she was a good influence on me. We spent a really comfortable and easy nine months together before, bewilderingly, my attractions suddenly began to switch and I began noticing men in a way that I never had before. Honestly, I found that as terrifying as my transition. Since I was a child I had liked girls, and all of my adult life had dated women. Now, after a year or so of testosterone injections, I was suddenly completely disinterested in women. Reluctantly and after much soul searching, I ended things with Sam, but our closeness and connection allowed me to be completely honest with her about the reason why. She was naturally hurt but as understanding as I could have hoped and things ended amicably. We remained close, even dating again a year or so later, but realised that we were better as friends than partners. Nine years later, and despite a move to Australia, she is still one of my best friends.

So, my switch in attractions was more than a little unsettling and I began to research as much as I could find on this unexpected new development. It's hard to imagine how confused I was. I looked like a pretty boy, with shaped eyebrows and wisps of facial hair. Gay men would hit on me a lot, sitting on the tube or walking down Old Compton Street. It was interesting, but also terrifying. If I was a gay man now, I had even less of an idea how I'd ever fit in.

CHAPTER ELEVEN

Facing truths

Hannah

I'd never driven as fast as I did that day. Tearing down the autobahn at 110 miles per hour in my struggling Renault Clio, Guns N' Roses playing at full volume, the German countryside sped past me. My trusty ironing board poked into the back of my head and all my worldly possessions were stuffed into the boot and across the seats, with just enough space for a cup of coffee. My bags were full of uniforms and clothes, a handful of DVDs and books and, of course, my 'fancy dress box'. I was rushing, excitedly, towards my new life.

Just a handful of months after I left Sandhurst and after some role-specific (and much less intense) training I was posted to Bad Fallingbostel, a small town between Hamburg and Hanover in Germany. I'd be commanding my first platoon of roughly 30 soldiers within 2 Close Support Battalion, the Royal Electrical and Mechanical Engineers, known as REME for short. In the REME, our role is to maintain, recover and repair equipment. To quote Field Marshal Montgomery, we 'keep the punch in the Army's fist'. Whether it is Land Rovers, tanks, helicopters or rifles, if it has a mechanical or electronic component then we fix it when it's broken.

The camp itself was pretty big, split across a main road and housed multiple military units. My battalion was situated at the northern tip of the camp on a sizeable, concreted area with several large hangars and office buildings, but the Officers' Mess was located on the southern side of the road, about a kilometre away. For those who don't know, an Officers' Mess is simply the accommodation building for the Officers in a unit, somewhat like university halls in the sense that each Officer is given a single room. It has a communal dining room and bar, usually fitted out with Chesterfield sofas and decorated with military paraphernalia.

With space for a double bed and sofa, my room had an ensuite bathroom and, though modest, it was the most space I'd ever had – and, unlike at Sandhurst, there would be no threat of surprise room inspections. After a long year, I finally had some privacy back. I'd be lying if I said I wasn't looking forward to the freedom of being able to be myself, albeit behind a locked door, but, with an all-male platoon to command, the pressure of earning their respect weighed heavily on me.

The younger and unmarried Officers who lived in the mess (known as Livers-In) would gather for breakfast in the morning before cycling to the hangars shortly afterwards. My office was a tiny box up a metal gangway that I shared with my Staff Sergeant, but I tried to spend as little time in there as possible, preferring to be out on the shop floor getting to know the guys. With the exception of the handful of junior soldiers, they had all been in the Army longer than me, some of them considerably more so, but the role of any young Second Lieutenant is to lean on and learn from that experience. It's a tricky line to tread, and I certainly didn't think that being openly transgender was going to help, so then more than ever before I decided to create a persona and try to embody the 'male' Officer I thought they needed to see.

As a young Officer you have to have a thick skin. The more senior Officers mock you because you are green and don't know what you are doing half the time, and the soldiers do the same. None of it was malicious, just part of the game, and the most successful players were the ones who could make themselves part of the joke and laugh along, but also give as good as they got. I quickly told my soldiers and the other Officers that I was gay and did so almost with sleight of hand; it was out in the open, but blink and you'd miss it. I was light-hearted, and made it the least important thing about me.

There's a common misconception that soldiers who join up at a young age are somehow unintelligent and perhaps less progressive in their views, but that doesn't stack up from my experience. My soldiers were bright, funny, motivated and the thing that they really cared about me was that I did a good job. I was responsible for their reports, discipline, welfare, and so the fact that they perceived me as a 'gay man' didn't matter so long as I looked after them, listened to them and was honest with them. That being said, I just didn't think that would stretch to being transgender. It was practically never heard of and the more I embodied that 'laddish' culture and through that earned their all-important respect, the more I felt like I couldn't undo that work. I cared about my soldiers a lot and if they felt alienated from me, how could they trust me to lead them?

*   *   *

There's a time-honoured tradition between the Officers' Mess and the Warrant Officers' and Sergeants' Mess (essentially all the non-officers who were Sergeant and above), when Christmas rolls around, where each one takes it in turns to host the other for a party, usually with (drinking) games heavily stacked in favour of the host. It was our turn to be hosted that year and as I am a deeply competitive person, I threw myself into it. Halfway through the evening, the hosts announced that there was to be an obstacle course in the pouring rain outside and so the teams had to dress appropriately. The four Sergeants taking part were led away to don boiler suits and boots, whereas I, together with three other young Officers, were led into a room where the female sergeants were waiting with a collection of dresses. They proceeded to do our makeup. As much as the situation was somewhat comical, I felt the familiar rush of shame, but I brushed it aside (as well as the indignity of having such *terrible* makeup applied) as we were all led back out to general hilarity all around.

Just a few minutes later I was handed a towel to dry off and headed to the bathroom to wash my face. As I stood over the sink, I saw a movement behind me as one of the NCOs (Non-Commissioned Officers) walked in behind me. He'd had a few, which is perhaps why he stepped towards me as I turned to face him. He mumbled that he thought it was 'pretty cool' that I was gay, and that, while he wasn't, he would still

164

be 'up for it'. I froze for a second before self-preservation and training kicked in.

'I don't think that's a good idea,' I replied calmly, in the full knowledge that he was married with kids and that there are certain regulations that prevent relationships within the same chain of command so as to avoid any conflicts of interest. He looked crestfallen and actually a bit surprised. There's an assumption often held by 'straight' people that if they proposition a queer person, the queer person should be somehow grateful for the interest. Aside from the fact that I had no interest in him, I actually felt quite sorry for him. It was totally inappropriate behaviour for sure, but I wondered if this was simply a one-off drunken desire, or maybe something more deeply rooted? Perhaps he was another queer soul living half a life and feeling alone? But I had enough to deal with myself. Shrugging it off, I once again pulled on the façade, walked up to the bar and ordered another drink.

Constantly putting on this hypermasculine act would have really started to get me down, if it weren't for the fact that in Germany I was able to enjoy the company of women. Sharing our Officers' Mess were some female doctors from the Medical Regiment and some civilians who worked for the Army as teachers and physiotherapists. They hadn't been indoctrinated into the military way as my other friends had and they brought a much-needed gentleness to the environment. They changed the dynamic for the better, and although they really got stuck into the culture, drinking and partying like the rest of us, they were responsible for a new, more chilled energy during my off-duty hours. I really gravitated towards them.

Now I wasn't in training, I was starting to move away from

the group mentality that had been instilled in me since Cadets and was able to be myself a bit more. In the evenings when I was with these new female friends, my own femininity started to become more obvious.

If the girls were having a rom-com film night, I was always invited and I struck up a close friendship with two beautiful women, Vanessa, a bright bubbly physio from Leeds, and Sarah, a very lovely doctor from north London. We'd go to the German spas together on the weekends, padding around the pool, and relaxing in the sauna and steam rooms (I cannot recommend salt and honey scrub enough) and talk about life, love and (God forbid!) emotions. It was fun to do those things with them, but more than anything I took great comfort from how effortlessly feminine they were. One of the barriers to my coming out as trans was simply believing I wasn't, or couldn't be, feminine enough. I had been taught unwittingly by society that being feminine meant being a 'typical' woman, such as you might see on the cover of a magazine, and that felt unobtainable to me. But living among these women (something I had never had in my life before) taught me that femininity isn't about how you look or sound, that it's something so much more inherent and nuanced – and it planted the seed in my mind that maybe I could be like that too.

It's safe to say that after a few months in Germany, I found a groove. I'd begun to earn the respect of my soldiers in work and I was enjoying the parties, but I also had female company and my own private room, where on quiet evenings I could wear whatever felt natural and play around with my makeup or simply kick back and chill on the sofa.

However, just a few months later, I deployed to Afghanistan.

* * *

A tannoy cut through the hustle and bustle of camp life, announcing Operation MINIMISE. It meant all non-operational communications back home were being cut, although there wasn't that much to begin with. We were allocated a phone card that we could use in specially provided booths and a 15-minute daily internet limit to be used on our personal laptops (mobile phones were banned). The reason we'd gone dark was because someone had suffered a life-changing injury, or worse. There's a strict procedure for informing families back home and making sure they have the support needed, and this comms blackout ensures that no unofficial message gets to them first. The familiar drone of a Chinook helicopter sounded overhead, its twin rotors buffeting the roof of our tent, and I wondered if it was taking that injured soldier to the camp hospital. This was just another night in Camp BASTION, a city in the sand, situated in the desert, and the main hub for all the Coalition Forces in Afghanistan's Helmand Province, and it served as a reminder of the very real dangers of the deployment. I was very excited to be out there – it was what I'd trained for and a rite of passage, after all. That doesn't mean there weren't things I worried about, and I knew my mum was beside herself with anxiety, but you have to put that stuff to the back of your mind, and focus on getting the job done.

My role there was to make sure that all the newly arrived REME soldiers were given on-the-ground training in

maintaining vehicles in Afghanistan. They had already under-
gone training back home, but these lessons were taught by
soldiers who were coming to the end of their deployment and
had five or six months' experience in Afghanistan. They had
handy tips like where fine sand gets built up or how certain
engines manage (or not) with the extreme heat.

The training I delivered required me to move around the
Forward Operating Bases (FOBs), which were situated among
the populated areas around the Helmand River. Before each
movement, we'd be briefed on the route and any intelligence
about enemy activities in the area. On one trip, we were moving
down a road where more than 10 improvised explosive devices
(IEDs) had been planted in the last week and so I was a little
more nervous than usual, wondering if any slight discoloura-
tion of the road or handful of rocks were hiding the trigger to
an explosion. I was very fortunate that I never experienced an
IED explosion, nor did I have to fire my rifle in conflict, but you
always live with the idea that it might happen at any moment.

I lived in one of a series of pods that branched off one
central tented corridor. Most of the pods were simply accommodation, with the exception of a couple that housed showers
and sinks. The pods were big enough to house 10 people, 5 to
each side, and you had just enough space for a camp cot with
sleeping bag, a Bergen, a lockable plastic box and some hanging storage for personal possessions and reminders of home.
That was it – my little area. I shared the pod with the male
REME Officers, and the guy sleeping next to me was only
about two metres away. The showers had cubicles but they
weren't far off being communal. There was no privacy,
anywhere.

When people think of being on an operational deployment, they tend to think of the movies they've seen featuring
high-adrenaline battles, and while those do of course happen,
there are many more times when life is quiet and monoto-
nous, with only very limited access to the world back home.
As a result, I spent a lot of time in my own head in introspec-
tion. I thought a lot about my gender, about where I was in
life and how it made me feel. Without the distractions I had
hidden behind for years, or the ability to be myself in the
confines of my room, I found that what it made me feel more
than anything was pain, and it took me to a very dark place.
For so many years I had lived a double life, but in Afghanistan
I could only live one of those lives, and it wasn't the right one.
Yes, it was exciting to be there. Yes, I was proud to be there,
and I was glad that I did it, but being there also made me
realise that if I wanted to be truly happy I had to make a
change. Although it left me riddled me with fear, out there in
the dusty heat of Helmand Province, I allowed myself to
genuinely consider coming out as trans. What it might mean.
The impact on myself and those around me.

*   *   *

When I returned home safely, I quickly fell back into my old
routine and was of course particularly grateful to have my
own private space back, yet there was a nagging sense of
unease. I'd felt so far away from my true self while deployed
and I had made a promise never to put myself in that position
again. Equally, though, I didn't have the first idea of how to
find the courage to fulfil that promise. So, for several months
more, I lived my double life, relaxing on the sofa in my room,

in the clothes that made me comfortable, watching TV and surfing the internet. And that is how I found myself one Tuesday evening in the summer of 2011 tuning in to a BBC documentary called *Jamie: Drag Queen at 16.*

Just as I had when I was a kid, I consumed any TV that was even vaguely queer or 'gender bending', and this show followed the story of Jamie Campbell, a 16-year-old boy from County Durham, who wanted to be a drag queen, and the challenges he faced from family, friends and his school. He was being bullied, his dad refused to talk to him and the teachers refused to let him wear a dress to the prom. The documentary really brought to life his struggles and culminated in Jamie attending his school prom, wearing a stunning dress, immaculately made up, only to be denied entry by the teachers. In a very moving show of support, his fellow pupils and friends protested until the teachers finally relented, to much celebration and teenage dancing under a glitterball.

It hit me hard.

Here was a young kid, without many of the privileges I had, radiating his inner strength and self-belief, regardless of the consequences. I had an entire inner monologue that went something like this:

'You are a fraud. As an Army Officer you are supposed to embody courage, integrity and selfless commitment. People say that you are brave because you jump out of planes or have been to Afghanistan, but it's all a lie. That young kid in northern England has shown more courage than you have ever done.'

At this point, I needed to be harsh with myself. This had gone on long enough and it was the jolt I needed to get me into action.

I jumped onto Facebook and scrolled down the messenger to see who was online. I paused when I saw the name 'Lucy' with a little green dot next to it. Lucy was one of my best friends' girlfriend and was always very lovely to me. We were quite friendly, but we weren't that close, which kind of made my next step much easier. If she freaked out then it wasn't like I saw her every day...

I began to type:

Me: Hey Lucy, can I tell you something?
Lucy: Sure! What's up?
Me: So, I've never told anyone this before, but I'm not
    really gay, I actually just feel like I am a woman.

I held my breath for an eternity, as I waited for her to respond.

Lucy: OK, there's nothing wrong with that.

My heart pounded as relief flooded over me, and I followed up quickly:

Me: I haven't told anyone before – please don't tell Andy!
Lucy: Of course not, you can talk to me about stuff if you
    want. I feel very honoured that you confided in me—

Honestly, I can't imagine what was running through her head in that moment, probably something like: *What the hell? I certainly wasn't expecting THAT on my Tuesday evening at home...*

Whatever she thought, Lucy was very sweet and kind to

me and a couple of weeks later I received a card from her and a little makeup palette in the post. I'm very grateful to Lucy because she didn't treat me any differently. She supported me and we discussed it a little bit here and there and, each time I had a kind reaction, I felt a little bit of the shame ebb away and found a little more self-belief. I was a long way off coming out in everyday life but I had told someone and they hadn't treated me like a freak. I know it's a pretty low bar to set, but it was all I needed to get a foot in the door, even if it was only open a tiny crack. Those first steps made it easier to gradually open it more and much harder to ever close it again.

*   *   *

Telling Lucy gave me a bit more confidence to start talking about being trans with the people I was living with in Germany. Vanessa and Sarah were both relaxed about it. They had lots of questions, naturally, but my biggest worry – that they'd think I was some kind of deviation – was totally unfounded. As with all the little moves I made towards being more open, each one felt a little more exposing than the last, and the next step was to allow Vanessa and Sarah to *see* me. Now you have to remember that while I had become more comfortable with myself in private, no one else had ever actually seen me like that, so I was extremely nervous to allow them into that world. It is an unfortunate reality that most trans women have to really battle with their physique and I'm certainly no different. I have broad shoulders, big hands, a deep voice and, at the time, had a short back and sides haircut and facial hair. Even though I had learnt some of the tricks of the trade from watching drag tutorials on YouTube, there is only so much one can do, and I was terrified they would just think I looked like a bloke with a wig on. If they did think that (and I hope they didn't!) then they never let me know it, and it felt quite novel having the external validation of my female self.

Buoyed by this experience, I found the confidence to start to tell some of the guys in the Officers' Mess, although I played it down somewhat, making it about 'crossdressing' for a bit of fun. They were a pretty open-minded bunch, but still quite 'laddish', so I thought it would make it more palatable for them if it was seen as a thing that I did once in a while as a laugh, rather than anything deeper about my gender, or wanting to transition. But even this allowed me to be just a bit more *me*. And because people were kind and supportive, I felt I could push open that door just a little more each day.

*   *   *

There were tons of social events while I was stationed in Germany. Some were fancy dress, which I always embraced with unmatched enthusiasm, but others were black tie formal dinners. Part of the fun was getting ready – and I loved being in the girls' rooms with them as they did their hair and makeup. But now I was more open about my identity, I allowed myself to admit that I was jealous. At a formal event, often with external guests, I was expected to wear a black suit and bow tie, and it was quite depressing watching all the girls get ready, doing hair and makeup and choosing dresses and all that kind of stuff and not being fully part of it. It was one of those moments of being so othered that even though I was

173

more open about myself, it was a stark reminder I was still not who I wanted to be.

In the end it was Sophie, one of the teachers who taught at the camp's primary school, who came up with a fairly pragmatic solution: 'Well, just get ready twice.' And so that's what I did.

At the next function I got ready with everyone else, makeup, dress, heels, wig, the whole shebang. We had a few glasses of champagne, chatting and laughing until about 30 minutes before the start of the event. I then left, jumped in the shower and washed all the makeup off. I put on my trousers and dress shirt, each button a dagger to my heart, before tying my bow tie neatly and slipping the dinner jacket over my shoulders. Checking myself in the mirror before I left, I rubbed at the last of the eyeliner that was stubbornly lingering and headed downstairs to perform the role I knew so well.

It was miserable, and, even though I put a brave face on it, so as not to spoil the fun, the girls could tell I was unhappy. The next morning, to make me feel better, Vanessa asked if I would like to plan a shopping trip. I felt simultaneously excited and terrified. This was a big step. This wasn't just presenting as female in a safe place with friends, this was doing it in public, but excitement won out and I agreed, planning to go to Hamburg the following Saturday.

The morning came and I woke early to get ready and dressed in some simple skinny jeans, T-shirt and cardigan (and a wig of course), and waited for Vanessa to pull her car up outside the mess. When I heard the beep of the horn I furtively checked my surroundings before running down the stairs and jumping into her Mini, as she took off for the autobahn.

It felt different to any experience to date because there was nowhere to hide from any stranger we might meet. No room to retreat to, no convenient fancy dress excuse, no explanation other than the truth. The Officers' Mess had grown to become a place of safety for me, and what had started off only taking place in a locked room had expanded beyond that to the people who lived there and supported and looked after me. I was widening my circle of comfort, but it was still relatively small. This was the first time I was taking my female self out into the real world.

During the drive, Vanessa asked me what she should call me while we were out. I pretended to think about it, but I already knew my name – I'd been using it online for years. *Hannah.* 'I like it,' she said. 'It suits you.'

It was summer and a busy Saturday morning in Hamburg. I was absolutely terrified. I'd never felt more exposed in my life. I didn't present too badly, but I was still obviously wearing a wig and probably obviously trans.

We did some clothes shopping, Vanessa very encouraging and patient with me (especially when I was about to make some terrible fashion choice – you have to remember I didn't have much experience at this point), but I remember the scariest thing was having to go to the loo in a shopping centre. There was a big queue for the ladies' (I swear most public toilet facilities must have been designed by men) and I had to stand there for five or six minutes, surrounded by strangers, just waiting to be found out. My imposter syndrome was through the roof and I honestly felt more stressed in that moment than I had at any point in Afghanistan. I came out of the bathroom shaking and said to Vanessa: 'I need to go home now.'

It was just too much. Yes, it was exhilarating and amazing, but my heart was pounding and I needed to be somewhere calm. I'd gone too far beyond my comfort zone. Vanessa got it; she drove us home and I began to relax a bit in the car. Once I had calmed down, I started to 'defeminise' myself, which was a logistical necessity as I had to show my military ID to get back into the camp, so I removed my wig, wiped off my makeup with a pack of wet wipes and put on the baggy hoodie that I had stashed in the car. I was still very much living a double life at this time, but the life where I was true to myself was growing quite fast, so fast in fact that having to switch away from it was becoming harder each time.

After two and a half fantastic, life-changing years in Germany I was posted back to the UK to take on my next role. Moving around is just part of Army life. You get used to it, but I'd made such good friends and had the security of being able to be out, in different ways, as my true self there, and it was rather heartbreaking to leave it behind.

*   *   *

Now in north-west England, commanding a Regional Army Recruitment Team, it was like having to start all over again. Being openly trans and transitioning medically felt like less of an impossibility, but it was still a long way off. There was a major thing on my to-do list before I could even begin to plan for that – and that was speak to my parents. I hadn't even told them I was gay – while it wasn't the truth, it would pave the way to it. So, as the Christmas holidays beckoned, I travelled home to be with Mum, Dad and Jeff. My brother, of course, knew, so having him there for moral support was great, but I still waited until after Boxing Day so it wouldn't 'ruin' Christmas. With the plates washed up after dinner, and a much-needed glass of wine in hand, I broached the subject I'd been dreading. I didn't know how they'd react.

'I've been meaning to tell you both something for a while now.' I steeled myself for the next step. 'I'm not attracted to women. I'm actually attracted to men.' If I didn't actually say the word 'gay', this felt closer to the truth.

'I can't say it's a big surprise.' Dad choked slightly, then got up to give me a hug. 'When your good-looking, successful, confident son never brings a girlfriend home, or even mentions anyone, you do start to wonder.'

My mum has always been the emotional one and she started to cry, even as she hugged me and told me that she would always love me. It was tough on all of us – a sad fact of reality is that anything other than 'straight' is still seen even by many of the most open-minded of families as a disappointment, less valid than the norm. And despite their reactions, I felt like I was letting them down. But we brushed ourselves off, refilled our glasses and settled in to watch a film. We were perhaps half an hour into *Thor* when Mum piped up:

'Well, what do you think of him then?'

I laughed. 'Chris Hemsworth? Oh, he's *definitely* my type.'

It was forced, but the intent behind Mum's comment meant a lot to me. We were going to be OK. At least for now.

*   *   *

My new role was very different and I had a much smaller Officer community: there were just four of us in total. With fewer opportunities to build friendships, those old nagging thoughts resurfaced and I was starting to feel a bit depressed again, wondering if transitioning was something I'd ever be able to do in the Army.

While I was in this quieter posting, however, I took the opportunity to speak to a GP about being referred for a psychiatric appointment. At this stage all I wanted was to get some medical validation of the way I was feeling, but, when I requested that I be referred without it being put on my medical records (a piece of 'evidence' that would be impossible to remove once entered), I was told that wouldn't be possible. So that was that and I went back to my quiet life a little crestfallen, and lonelier than I had felt in some time.

Later that year, I agreed to support an expedition to Malta, where I would lead a handful of soldiers for 14 days of scuba diving. It would be a two-week trip in the sun, letting off steam and enjoying the serenity of clear blue waters. One of the massive benefits of the Army is that expeditions like this are still classed as 'work'.

I had planned leave for the two weeks prior to the trip and I had driven to visit Lucy up North. We had gone to a mall and over a coffee I mentioned that I'd always wanted my ears pierced. In typical Lucy fashion, she said, 'Just do it, let's go now.' The issue was that while there was nothing against a 'male' soldier having their ears pierced, the dress regulations made no allowances for wearing earrings, and they needed to be kept in for a month when first pierced. I was at the start of two weeks off before travelling to Malta, where I wouldn't be wearing uniform for another two weeks, so I had just enough time. Off to Claire's Accessories we went.

I had chosen the smallest, most subtle studs that were on offer and was very pleased with the result (once they had stopped bleeding, that is) and had got quite used to them by the end of my leave. However, as the Malta trip came up I knew that I had to come up with some sort of story for the lads on the trip as to why I had earrings. I concocted a story that I was wearing the earrings for a bet, and if I kept them in during my whole time in Malta I'd get a case of champagne from one of the other Officers in the mess. They seemed to buy it, but I hadn't accounted for the Officer who had organised the expedition. I had never met him before and it turned out he was an ex-Special Forces Major who had come up through the ranks. He cornered me very quickly, telling me to take them out, a look of disgust on his face. I was embarrassed and did as he said and tried not to think about it for the rest of the trip.

Back in the UK, just a few days after the expedition, I was busy organising the Christmas party. My then Commanding Officer travelled down from his office about an hour away for the day's festivities. I greeted him when he arrived. Shortly after, he asked to speak to me in my office. I followed him in and he sat behind my desk in a clear positioning of authority.

'Is it true that you wore earrings on the expedition to Malta?' he asked without any preamble.

'Yes,' I admitted, my heart falling through my stomach, full of terror.

'You will report to my office in full service uniform at 06.30 tomorrow morning.' His order was laced with anger and disapproval.

'Yes, Sir.' Stupefied, I watched as he stormed out of the office.

Had I pushed it too far?

Had my comfort zone grown too wide?

Suddenly, I thought of everything I had done to get here.

Was my entire military career about to come crashing down around me?

CHAPTER TWELVE

Making my mark

Jake

The incoherent thud of dance music reverberated through my body. Strobes flashed like a storm of lightning, illuminating the euphoric smiles on the faces of the men around me. Skin, chests, sweat. Six packs. Bodies writhing, moving together to the beat. I was in the middle of the throng and yet so separate from it. I hated dancing but if I just stood still I'd be moved by the crowds as if by the waves of the sea. Gay men, en masse, were so much more overt in seeking sex than lesbians. Nightclubs like Heaven, GAY Club, these were the new after-dark haunts that I would be dragged to by my old flatmate, Morgan. Places where I passed as one of the guys, even if I felt totally out of my depth.

In one of the strangest and most unexpected twists of fate in my story so far, I was now attracted to tall, handsome, bearded men. I was essentially going through a second puberty and so my hormones were all over the place and I found myself filled with a near constant physical desire that was entirely unnerving. Now I was more fully inhabiting my own maleness, I was attracted to stereotypically 'manly' men and had absolutely no idea how to navigate this new world.

Gone were many of the subtleties of the lesbian scene. The vibe on the men's scene reminded me of the women I'd met in New York. Open, unashamed, direct and heady. Here though, I didn't have the confidence that I had built up over two decades of flirting with and dating women. Also, my transness held me back and filled me with self-doubt. In the last eight or so years, there has been such an increase in trans visibility and endless discussions around dating as a trans person, but back then I had no idea how a gay man might react to me. Would anyone be interested at all once I told them I was trans? As it turned out and much to my surprise, the answer was most definitely yes, but I didn't know that then. There were a couple of trans clubs and online trans chat groups but Instagram didn't exist yet and it was much harder to connect with like-minded folks. I don't think we even had WhatsApp, so if I wanted to chat to Nicco we had to email or arrange a phone chat. I had found the FTM (female to male) community on YouTube and the men who shared every aspect of their physical transitions became an invaluable resource at a time when we just didn't have a visible community in the day to day. Still, it was a far cry from the intimate one-to-one chats that had helped me find myself in New York.

I was living in a small flat in beautiful Barnes, just by the river, in a lovely, leafy part of west London. Overall, life was immeasurably better, but at times I felt so lonely that I'd take a bus into Hammersmith and walk the aisles of the 24-hour supermarket just to be around people.

While grappling with my evolving sexuality, I was inspired to write my next short film, *Brace,* the story of two men who meet in a gay club and don't realise the other is trans. Focusing on getting this project off the ground really helped shake off the anxiety and isolation that was building in me. I produced and starred in it, and being able to express so much of what I was going through – all the fear and loneliness of transitioning and finding my place again – through writing and acting was key to rebuilding myself and my confidence.

Meanwhile, my old school friends, Pavlo and Alex, had really got on board with my new name and pronouns and would both leap in if anyone got it wrong. It takes a minute to rewire your brain when you've referred to someone for almost 30 years in one way. They made the effort and that's all that most trans people hope for. Certainly, I didn't get upset with anyone for making a mistake or tripping up on pronouns in those early days. I've made mistakes myself when friends have come out to me as trans and slipped up, which as a fellow trans person always feels particularly horrifying! My dear mum, who never missed a beat in her support of me, would still until recently unthinkingly refer to my sister and me as 'the girls', despite me being Jake for over a decade. Pavlo and Alex were also unfazed that my attractions had shifted, as they were about most things, and I think slightly relieved that I had cast aside the women's bars that I used to drag them to. Now, we could all go down the pub together, like 'normal lads'.

And so here was a whole *other* experience of recalibration and finding my feet. Because finally I was presenting as male, but I'd walk into these bars, where most guys are around the six foot mark, and feel tiny. I'd get jostled around at the bar and try to be assertive. Often some big guy would push in front, not even acknowledging my existence.

'Sorry mate,' I'd shout above the music, smiling. 'I was queuing there.'

The looks I'd get made me realise quite quickly that as a man around other men, a smile and cheeky wink would not get me anywhere. I quite often just about dodged getting thumped, so quickly learnt the laws of the jungle, that bigger and stronger often gets served first. Matters escalated to violence now far more quickly than they ever did when I presented as female and frequented lesbian bars. Whenever we went out together, Alex, who is quite a big boy and not afraid of a scrap, would often jump to my defence and de-escalate one situation or another. There were even a few times, once I learnt the lay of the land, when I was able to return the favour.

Most men would rather not fight, and I quickly gleaned that you can talk down most situations. I've never been physical. I'm not a fighter. I'm not good like that and I wouldn't want to be. In a straight bar where everyone's a bit boozed up, there can be a real atmosphere of aggression. The boys are on the pull and often, so are the girls, but it doesn't necessarily feel as mutual, as equal as in the gay clubs. There was just a lot of bravado to wade through, a lot of posturing, and it was a lot to get used to.

And even just out and about, moving through the world as male was a big adjustment. For example, a bigger guy sits next to me on the tube and they spread their legs, I'd say: *'Mate, sorry, do you mind?'* Unless they were real macho idiots, they would, more often than not, pull their legs in a bit. I never experienced that when I was being read as 'female' and, in fact, would probably just have taken up less space to counteract that.

As my self-esteem grew, so did my creativity. I was on a bit of a roll and shortly after the premiere of *Brace* I made my next short, *Chance*, about an elderly widower who falls for another man later in life. It caught the attention of the British Film Council, ending up on their international LGBTQ short film package, a real thrill and more validation for my filmmaking.

I was starting to find my voice and build my confidence. I was being asked to host Q&As and appear on panels, I'd done some magazine interviews and photoshoots and my profile not only as a filmmaker but also as a trans advocate was building. Running the photography workshops had been good for four years, but I wanted something more stable. My love for the childcare profession had never waned, so I registered for my DBS, did a first-aid course and began looking for work as a male nanny, or 'manny'.

Drugs were a thing of the past by then and I've never missed them. I simply had no use for them anymore. Fifteen years of abuse, and I stopped over the course of a few months. It certainly wasn't easy, but the fact that I was able to slowly wean myself off them felt like confirmation of the self-medication that I had implemented since age 15, and testament that they had only ever been an extreme form of pain relief. Also, they hugely impacted my creativity. I literally had zero desire for any of it, and have never again felt the urge.

I joined an agency and worked ad-hoc with different families, but never came out to them as trans. It seemed irrelevant, and almost like an over-share. I didn't tell them who I was dating either, it just wasn't important. When I was offered a full-time role working with five- and seven-year-old boys in

St John's Wood, I happily took it. I met the family and we really hit it off. A few days before my contract with them started, the father phoned me early on a Saturday morning, which seemed strange.

'Hi David,' I said as breezily as possible.

'Look, Jake, when you told us all about your films we thought we'd have a look, so, um, Gaby and I... Well, we've Googled you.'

My heart sank. This was it. I'd been found out. I'd been naive thinking it wouldn't happen sooner. By now there was quite a bit of press about me and my films online. I was so anxious I couldn't make words come out of my mouth so I stayed silent. David continued, obviously also a little out of his comfort zone.

'Well, I mean, it's not a problem, of course, just... why didn't you tell us?'

Did I just hear that right? Did he really say that me being a trans man was *not* a problem? Relief flooded my body.

'I'm so sorry, I just didn't know what to say, so...'

'You don't need to apologise but... Well, is there anything else we need to know? We want you to be in our circle of trust so please don't hold anything else back.'

We were on the phone for about an hour, as I gave him an abridged version of my transition story. He was so kind and understanding and made it clear that it wasn't an issue for the family at all. After we hung up, I felt like I was walking on air. I was so encouraged that someone who I barely knew – this lovely Jewish father – had been so kind and accepting, something I'd not really experienced so far.

The whole family ended up being extremely supportive of

me, even their lovely grandparents. The boys didn't know until much later, when they both in fact also Googled me (the joys of the internet!), and they were equally accepting, having been taught well by their parents. They were all at our wedding and their eldest, Guy, 11 at the time, was one of my best men. He gave one of the sweetest, funniest and most moving best man speeches ever heard. His younger brother, Raf, then nine, played 'Under The Sea' on his viola, which floored the room. I was with them for three great years and they've remained very close friends.

Working with the boys was an absolute joy. We absolutely clicked and would laugh together for hours, talking about everything from their favourite football team (Arsenal) to the minutiae of my friendships and family life. We were the best of pals. Moreover, seeing the closeness of their wonderful family made me even more determined to follow my dream of one day becoming a father. There was no way I could ever contemplate carrying a child, although many trans men do. I did some research and, although there was very little information out there, I learnt that if I stopped taking testosterone for a few months there was a chance that I might be able to have my eggs harvested. That would enable the possibility of me creating my own biological children in the future, although there were no guarantees.

Despite the fact that I was now financially independent and stable for the first time in my life, fertility treatment would only be possible with the help and generosity of my mother. Our relationship had been slowly improving and I was able to start being a helpful and supportive son, rather than an angry, resentful daughter.

I went to the London Women's Clinic, a very smart and upscale place in Harley Street. There were no provisions for anyone like me to undergo fertility treatment on the NHS at that time and the LWC were openly supportive of LGBTQ parents and families. Obviously going somewhere called the Women's Clinic as a single transgender man felt awkward, but I focused on the end goal.

I asked my mum to come with me to my first consultation. She was 65 at the time and she's always been very glam. As we sat in the waiting room, we wondered why people were staring at us and whispering. It was only as we caught a glimpse of ourselves in the mirror in the corridor that we realised how we must look together, that I was the toy boy and that my mother was going in for fertility treatment. After that I left her at home.

'We've never worked with anyone like you,' the doctor said. 'We can't tell you if it will work or what will happen or if anything will still be viable after six years on testosterone, but we'll give it a go.'

I was to come off testosterone for six months, allowing it to fully leave my body before they would start treatment. It was a big challenge but one that I was determined to get through to realise my dreams of one day being a father. My friends worried about me, scared of how I might react. *Are you feeling OK? Call us anytime, day or night*, they'd say. One of them had read about trans people becoming suicidal when taken off their hormones and feared the worst. But by then I was completely confident and comfortable in my masculinity. Had I not been, I'm not sure that I could have gone through with it. Stopping testosterone wasn't pleasant because things started happening within my body again that I really didn't want, but I understood the science. The nurses were sympathetic throughout, and not without a degree of curiosity as to how my body might react. I think I even asked: 'Is there a way to do this without this monthly thing happening?' Of course there wasn't and that was probably the hardest part of the whole thing.

My muscle mass dropped dramatically. My face really slimmed down again and a lot of the jaw muscle I'd built up that masculinised my face dropped off, so I looked a lot softer. My beard didn't stop growing, which helped.

I think it's true what they say, that boys don't cry. Certainly for me and for many of my trans male friends, testosterone treatment dammed up the tear ducts. I remember one guy saying: 'All I want is to really cry and let it all out, but I just can't.' Once I stopped the hormones, however, the floodgates really opened!

Before the egg collection procedure, I had to inject myself with different hormones by sinking these very fine needles into my tummy. Not pleasant but nothing compared to the bi-weekly testosterone shots I had been giving myself for the last six years. Going into fertility treatment, I still found it hard to believe that I'd ever find anyone who would help me have a baby, but I had hope, and that was enough for me to continue on this difficult journey.

I was then informed that any pregnancy would have a much better chance if rather than just freezing my eggs I also fertilised them, freezing the resulting embryos. So next on my to-do list was choosing a sperm donor.

I sat in my flat going through all the donor profiles at the

London Sperm Bank. This certainly felt like one of the bigger decisions in my life and worth taking my time over. For a start I wanted someone tall, as I'd always wanted a bit more height. I also wanted to balance my own 'right side of brain' thinking with someone logical and who excelled at maths and science. I looked for a family history of good health, no allergies and so on, wanting to tick as many boxes as possible. I eventually found a donor who was a tall, brown-eyed engineer, which funnily enough doesn't sound far off the description of Hannah.

The next morning, I went over to my mum's to show her the chosen donor.

'He sounds like a good choice. How exciting!' she said as we sat sharing chocolate eclairs from her favourite, M&S, at the kitchen table.

It was remarkable how much calmer and at peace I now felt with her, and Mum was far more relaxed in my company now as well. We were approaching the kind of easy back and forth that she'd always enjoyed with my sister. For her to just sign off on a sperm donor to fertilise her transgender son's eggs was a major thing to get her head around but by this point I don't think anything I did could have shocked her.

They put you to sleep for the procedure, and when you come round the nurse tells you how many eggs were collected. I got 19, which was pretty decent. At the end of my IVF journey we had created five viable embryos which I paid to freeze for an initial two years. My dream future was quite literally on ice. All I needed now was a partner to share it with.

My initial loss of interest in women had now returned, but I was still attracted to men. It left me with the realisation that I'm quite simply attracted to the person regardless of their gender and I would now describe myself as pansexual. I'd started dating guys and girls who I met on apps. It was easier to get the whole '*Hi, I'm trans*' thing over with online, rather than having to drop the bombshell in person. Encouragingly and surprisingly, it didn't put many people off and, once I got back on testosterone after all the fertility stuff, I started to really feel at home in my body.

In October 2017, my second film, *Brace*, was also nominated for the Iris Prize. At the film festival in Cardiff, I was at the cinema balcony bar with my friend, Alicya, when a tall, bearded and very handsome guy walked in.

'He's cute. What do you think?' I asked.

Alicya just strolled straight over, said something in his ear, pointed at me and led him back to me. His name was Danny and he was there volunteering for Stonewall. I'd had a couple of drinks so was showing a bit of Dutch courage, but as we began speaking I started to spiral: *he's cute, he's obviously gay, he's going to have an issue with trans guys.*

As all these anxieties were spinning round my head, Danny was asking me questions about my film and seemed genuinely curious and engaged. He was a hairdresser and lived in Cardiff. He was sweet, a little shy but apparently interested. There's no point in dragging this out, I thought, so I found a way to drop into conversation that I was a trans guy and, to Danny's credit, he barely faltered. We just carried on talking.

'Do you want to get out of here?' he asked. 'There's a good place around the corner.'

We sat and chatted in a bar for much of the night before he headed off in a taxi around 3 a.m. The following day, I invited him to be my guest at the awards lunch and we made plans for him to come and see me in London soon. We got on well and, despite it being the first time I'd really connected with a man, it felt very easy. As with most of my relationships, I still very much took the lead, but he didn't seem to mind that. It was our dynamic and it worked. He would drive to London to see me at weekends and we'd go out on the town and I'd show him the city.

Going to the men's bars as a couple actually felt very natural, but I also noticed the marked difference in how people treat you and look at you when you are part of a male couple as opposed to a lesbian couple. I'd also experienced dating as a straight man, having dated a few girls post transition, and the realities were worlds apart. Being openly gay certainly felt more perilous, more judged, more threatening. On the London tube, for example, if I put my hand on his knee people would look and make comments or laugh. If I held his hand or kissed him we got even more negative attention.

Early on we found it safer not to show affection beyond the protection of the West End, if only to avoid the barbs and occasional perceived threats of violence. He was a big guy but more of a gentle giant and wanted to avoid any kind of confrontation. We got very used to not showing closeness unless we were right in the heart of Soho. Being out as part of a lesbian couple in the past, I had never experienced half as much scrutiny, nor overt comments. That's not to say that lesbians don't experience hate crime or bullying, merely that I perceived and felt it much less potently. With Danny, there was this real latent sense of threat around us being out together in public – straight men didn't like it. Once we were in the safety of Soho we could relax. We were just two gay guys snuggling in the corner of a bar. People left us to it.

I've always introduced partners to my mum quite early on in a relationship. I hold her in such high esteem that her validation really matters. Danny was no exception. We met in October and he joined me for a birthday dinner with my family in January. They seemed to like him. He's a very sweet man and Mum appreciated his good looks and charm.

My old friends also easily warmed to him, but I think they could all probably see, because they knew me so well, that he was a little bit too sweet for me, too nice. He was a really great guy, but it just wasn't a match.

I was happy though for the few months we dated and I don't regret any of our time together, I just knew that it wasn't right for me. I feel bad to this day, for not recognising that Danny's feelings ran deeper than mine. Maybe I still didn't feel worthy of that love. We ended things and I asked if we could be friends, thinking he was fine about it. I realise now I hurt him by being so flippant with his feelings and for that I'm truly sorry.

After Danny, I went back to my single life in Barnes, writing seven days a week, loving the productivity, the sense of achievement, the attention that I was seeing for my filmmaking and my advocacy. I was starting to feel confident, comfortable and, if I'd ever dared to admit it without thinking the rug was about to be pulled from under me, I was happy. I was working as a manny for that lovely family, I was making a film every year, doing some acting and things were steadily improving with my mum. Life started to feel lighter somehow.

My drinking had also seriously slowed as I relished the pride in my accomplishments much more than the rush of another shot of tequila, and a hangover just meant a wasted day. When Hannah and I first met she was very used to the Army's drinking culture, and on a weekend we would often have a session and wake up a little bleary, but we've now got two little girls who need us. Millie makes no allowances for hangovers and we've every reason to wake up feeling fresh in the morning and ready for a day with them, so neither of us drinks that much.

So life was on this slow, steady climb upwards. I started to be invited to give the odd talk about trans representation in film and TV. Something that I could never have done before. The fact that I was able to stand in front of rooms full of people and speak from my heart about an issue that mattered so much to me was a sign of how far I'd evolved. Life had changed immeasurably and I barely recognised the person that I used to be.

*   *   *

On a bright July morning, not long after I made this speech, I was heading to St John's Wood to spend the day with the boys, walking with my back straight, my head high, feeling what I can only describe as an unfamiliar kind of inner calm. My phone rang in my jeans pocket: it was a call from an agent I'd just employed to handle the various requests I was getting for speaking and panel events.

'Jake, you're not going to believe this but casting director Nina Gold has been in touch. She wants you to read for a part in the new Tom Hooper movie.'

I stopped walking. People pushed past me but it felt like the world was standing still.

'Tom Hooper? Oscar-winner Tom Hooper? Seriously?'

'It's for the new Eddie Redmayne film, based on the life of Lili Elbe—'

'—The transgender pioneer. Oh my God – this is amazing.'

'They want you to go in and read tomorrow. 11 a.m. Don't be late!'

*   *   *

The audition was at Nina Gold's house. Even though I didn't read with her as she was out on another job, it was the stuff of dreams. To get an audition of this calibre was huge, and, as I had only really read for student films so far, felt pretty terrifying. I knew full well that I was only being given this opportunity because I was trans, but I was absolutely fine in that knowledge. I read several times, for two different parts, and several days later got a call from my agent. 'Are you sitting down?' she said. 'Yes,' I lied as I walked along Ladbroke Grove. 'The producer loved your tape, you've got the part!' It all felt absolutely surreal. My life had changed so drastically in just a few years, none of it felt possible. I guess in many ways I still didn't think I deserved it.

The preparation for the film was almost as exciting as the shoot itself. Costume fittings at Elstree studios, being picked up and dropped off in my own private car. Makeup tests in central London, and the thrill of being dressed in a wig originally made for Eddie Redmayne. I received the contracts and was blown away to discover that my scenes would be shot in Belgium, so an international trip to boot. The whole experience of working on a big feature film like that is just unlike anything you've ever seen. Chauffeured cars, being flown business class to Belgium where another car awaits. A huge hotel room where your scripts are dropped off the night before by a runner. I made some good friends on that shoot, one in particular who I've worked with since, several times. We stood on set in our period costume, watching as Eddie and Alicia Vikander ran their scenes, directed by Tom Hooper, and I absorbed every wonderful second. For me, it was an opportunity to watch and learn from some of the masters, and I took it all in. My long conversations with the producers about trans representation were also apparently taken into account during the edit, which meant the world.

Sadly, my scene was mostly cut from the film, which, although pretty crushing at the time, now hurts a lot less as I've had to cut friends from my own films. Honestly, the experience was priceless and, despite not seeing much screen time, the publicity team were still keen for me to be involved in promoting the film, as one of its few trans actors. Suddenly, I was an expert on trans casting, being asked repeatedly whether I thought Eddie was the right choice for the role. Although times have changed and I now firmly believe that only trans actors should play trans roles, in 2014 and with very few mainstream transgender actors to choose from, I thought that Eddie did a great job. His profile brought a huge amount of attention and visibility to an extremely important figure in our trans history and meant that Lili Elbe's story reached across the world. Following the shoot, Eddie became a good friend to Hannah and me, even executive producing one of my films. He was and remains a strong ally to our community, so I was happy to speak in favour of his casting and incredible performance. I was asked to write op eds for newspapers, and was interviewed on panels and on morning television. I was even invited on the press tour with the cast. Not bad at all considering my 'blink and you'll miss it' moment!

I took my mum to the premiere. We walked the red carpet together and as she held my arm she whispered, 'I'm so proud of you.' I don't think winning an Oscar could have made my heart soar in the way it did then. After everything we'd been through together, all that pain, for her to say those words felt like the only plaudit I'd ever need. Before we sat down to watch the movie there was a Champagne reception. I turned my back for one minute, and there was my mum holding court with Eddie Redmayne and Alicia Vikander, as though this were a regular Thursday evening on the town!

Six months later I got an email:

You have been invited to the White House.

Ha ha. Nice try, I thought, assuming it was some kind of catfishing scam. My finger was hovering over the 'delete' button when I got a call from the other trans actor in *The Danish Girl*, Rebecca Root. 'Did you get the email?' she asked.

'It's a joke right?'

'No Jake, I've had it confirmed – they're flying us out to Washington. They want us to attend the first ever trans event at the White House.'

The next person I called, of course, was my mother.

A sleek black Mercedes picked me up from home and drove me to Heathrow, from where I was flown business class to Washington, DC. They put us up in the grand old hotel, The

Hay-Adams, opposite the White House. It's where many visiting dignitaries have stayed over the years and is all chandeliers and plush soft furnishings. Myself and a gaggle of fabulous LGBTQIA+ people, including the editors of all the major gay magazines in the US, the cast of *Transparent*, Alicia Vikander and Tom Hooper, and many of the top filmmakers in America, all welcomed as though we were royalty.

The night before the big event I went for a drink in the hotel bar with the boys from *Out* magazine. With polished wooden floors and red velvet banquettes, soft lighting and a grand piano tucked away in the corner, it was the perfect intimate spot for cocktails. We all got swept up in the moment and the guys got the shots in. We had a phenomenal evening, excited and incredulous that us queers were going to the White House. Luckily I only had to stumble upstairs to my sumptuous king size bed as the bar closed. The next morning, fuelled by room service pancakes and several hot coffees, we all rocked up hungover to face the rather stringent White House security. Standing in the blazing winter sunshine it all felt rather momentous, and an important moment in our LGBTQIA+ history.

The PR team running the show were flawless and knew who everyone was. 'Ah Jake – the film director,' they said, as they handed me my security lanyard. I can't explain how good that felt. I tried my best to act as though this weren't one of my life's highlights, that a morning spent in Washington, DC, rubbing shoulders with some of the world's biggest queer producers and writers wasn't a big deal, but inside I was reeling.

We were at the White House for about five hours (President

Obama was in Paris at the time, sadly). Young intersex advo-
cates, trans elders, gay pioneers, were all welcomed and celebrated. It was an unimaginable honour to be there, and as I
was introduced around the room it truly felt like I was living
someone else's life. After several speeches and panels, we
were given a private tour. As we moved through wood-clad
studies and past oil-painted portraits of previous US presi-
dents, we would occasionally catch each other's eye, once
again marvelling that we had made it here.

After the White House it was a quick change before we
headed to a screening of *The Danish Girl* downtown, during
which the cast and crew were taken out for a dinner at one of
the city's top restaurants. We were whisked back as the film
ended and the event was concluded by a panel made up of
Alicia Vikander, Tom Hooper, Rebecca Root and myself.
Again, the stuff of dreams. I held onto every second.

Afterwards, there was a big party back at the hotel. Trays of
tequila shots were handed around, with Champagne on tap
and the most amazing canapés to keep the night going.

As the evening ended, I walked slowly back to my room,
every molecule in me buzzing from the last few days'
wonder. As I prepared for bed, I felt overwhelmed with
emotion. Checking the time, I called my mother. She
answered quickly, probably assuming something was
wrong.

'Mum,' I said, through some of the happiest tears I'd ever
cried, 'I just can't believe I'm here.'

CHAPTER THIRTEEN

Transitioning

Hannah

My fingers ached as I layered polish over and over again on the shoes and belt of my service dress uniform. Typically, it takes a few hours to get them to the mirror shine expected for an inspection and so, with an appointment with my Commanding Officer at 06.30 the following day I had left the Christmas party early so as to prepare my uniform. That was, of course, one of the desired effects of the early inspection, to punish me by taking the evening away from me, and it worked. Working into the evening, knowing that my colleagues were all having a great time at the event that I'd organised was pretty miserable, but nothing compared to the prospect of the next day's meeting. Somewhere around midnight, with my uniform pristine and hanging on the door, I lay down to sleep, although it never really came.

I arrived at the camp in Shrewsbury at 06.15, grabbing my last bits of uniform from the back of the car before heading to Lieutenant Colonel Turner's office. In a weird twist of fate this was the very same camp I had first interviewed at for my Welbeck selection. As I strode into the main building I wondered if it was to be the setting for the beginning *and* end of my career. Steeling myself for what was to come, I knocked on the door and was instructed to enter. I marched a few steps in, threw up a salute, then remained at rigid attention. My Commanding Officer sat behind his desk in his own service uniform, silent for a short moment – before the barrage began.

I won't go into the detail of everything that was said and shouted at me in that moment; suffice to say that the air turned blue as my integrity, ability to command soldiers and position as an Army Officer were all called into question.

It was horrible.

Aside from the fact that I had barely slept, the admonishments cut deep, as he doubted the very things that I truly prided myself on. I felt a jumble of emotions: misery, frustration, anger. However, the one overriding them all was a huge sense of injustice. How was any of this fair?

My entire life, I had put the Army first. I had hidden my true self in service of my country and my soldiers, and it was all crashing down because I had done something to try to make that sacrifice even a little easier to bear. I found an unexpected steel forming within me and when the tirade finally came to an end, I uttered into the silence: 'I can explain.'

A look of indignation crossed his face as he responded through gritted teeth, 'You can try.'

My eyes shifted focus from staring into the middle distance to looking him directly in the eye as I stated three not-so-simple words: 'I am transgender.'

Silence.

An interminable silence where even the birds outside in the twilight seemed to be holding their breath. Our eyes still locked, his face unreadable, something suddenly seemed to give in the room. He visibly relaxed and, in a much calmer voice, he invited me to take my hat off and sit down. A simple gesture, but one that totally changed the dynamic of the situation.

'I didn't know that. I'm sorry. I wouldn't have dealt with things in this way had I known.' From the tone of his voice, I could tell his apology was heartfelt. I could hear the regret in his voice. 'I don't know much about being transgender, could you explain it to me?' he added.

Now it was my turn to sit quietly. I hadn't intended to come out to him and the whiplash from his sudden U-turn had thrown me, but a few deep breaths later I started to talk. I honestly can't remember what I said, but it was, certainly, more than I had told anyone in any position of authority over me before. Amazingly, given how the morning had started, it seemed that he was sympathetic to my situation.

'Thank you for sharing with me,' he responded when I had finished, pausing before adding, 'Did you know that I am gay?'

I stared at him in disbelief. 'I didn't.'

'Well, I actually find that a bit frustrating as I do talk about it openly because visibility matters, but it also means I am part of the Army's LGBT network. Have you heard of them?'

We spoke for another hour and I learned a lot about his

experience, as he did mine. I emerged from his office with LGBT support contacts, an invitation to an LGBT conference and his personal commitment to supporting me on my journey. I sat in my car for some time as I processed the morning's events; in a strange turn of events, I'd done what I had feared I would never be able to do. I had come out as trans in a semi-official capacity. It was only a beginning but a pivotal moment in my journey to my true self. I breathed deeply as I watched the dawn light break the across the sky.

Buoyed by my experience, I returned to the GP and this time followed through with my referral to a military psychiatrist. At that time gender dysphoria was considered a psychiatric condition by the World Health Organization and so it was an important step to get a diagnosis. Although modern medical understanding has moved away from classifying being transgender as any type of mental condition, at the time for me it was also quite a validating experience. As I've mentioned, I've always had this worry that I'm not trans enough to be trans because I didn't fit the stereotypical model of what many people might perceive a woman to be, and so to find out that a qualified psychiatrist objectively agreed with me was very comforting.

Aside from the diagnosis I took two other things away from my appointment: a referral to one of the national Gender Identity Clinics (the NHS specialist clinics for people with gender dysphoria) and a promise from the doctor that he would ask one of his previous transgender patients if they would be willing to speak to me.

*   *   *

Ayla was beautiful. Tall, slim, with long auburn hair and a sweet smile. She was an RAF Officer and helicopter pilot with impressive military history, including serving as a Search and Rescue pilot with HRH Prince William. She was also transgender and, while not in the Army, as part of the military she was an amazing role model to me.

She had reached out via email at the request of the psychiatrist, but we soon started talking on the phone and I had *a lot* of questions, some practical, some more emotional and others downright neurotic. She answered them all with the same patience and kindness. She became a real confidante to me over the coming months as I prepared to come out fully and, perhaps inevitably, I developed something of a 'girl crush' on her. Nothing sexual of course, I had only ever been attracted to men and she was happily married, but Ayla embodied everything that I was hoping for in my own life and I really admired her for who she was. It was the beginning of a friendship that we maintain to this day and some years later, when I received my MBE from Prince William in Buckingham Palace, we had a brief chat about Ayla, both agreeing what a lovely person she is.

After a year with the Army Recruitment team, it was time for me to pack up once more and move to my next role, which was based in Catterick, North Yorkshire. Once again, a new role meant hitting the reset button and working with a whole new group of people who know nothing about you (this is a challenge that LGBTQIA+ people face all the time – you never come out just once – as long as the 'norm' is to be straight or cisgender, we have to come out every time we find ourselves in a new environment), but I had come a long way in the last few years and I wasn't about to retreat into my shell. On the first day of any new posting for an Officer, there is always an interview with the Commanding Officer and, in good old-fashioned military style, I went in prepared.

One of the best pieces of advice Ayla had given me was reminding me that even the best people in the military are very unlikely to know anything about what it means to be trans, or that there is a policy that supports your transition. She told me that even though technically it will be me that needs the support, the trick to a smooth transition was to provide the support back to the chain of command, who in that initial moment probably won't know the first thing to say or do. With that in mind, I planned for that first interview like I was planning a military operation; I knew my first move, I had my resources ready at hand and knew how I intended to respond to any reactions or questions.

In stark contrast to my previous coming out, my new Commanding Officer and I sat across from each other in comfortable sofa chairs in the corner of his office set aside for interviews. He, of course, led the conversation, asking questions based on my letter of introduction that I had written in advance but also talking a little bit about himself and his expectations of me as one of his Officers. It was a very pleasant meeting, and we had a lot in common: he, too, was from South Wales and had attended Welbeck College several years before me. As the interview was coming to a close, I took the opportunity to explain my somewhat unique situation.

'There is one thing I would like to let you know about, which is that I am transgender,' I stated confidently, before giving a simple explanation of what that meant. I received that subconscious wide-eyed stare that I have now seen so many times and watched as he processed the statement. He soon explained, with quiet confidence, that he didn't know much about the experience but he was willing to learn and that he wanted me to have the same opportunities as everybody else.

It was a far better response than I could have hoped for and so I added that I had been under the care of the military medical system and that I was on a waiting list for a local NHS provider to transition, and, while nothing would be happening imminently, it was something that I would like to plan for with him. Pulling out a folder from my bag, I handed him the Armed Forces Policy for Transgender Personnel, highlighted in a few key areas.

'Colonel, the main thing I want you to know is that I am committed first and foremost to my job, to my soldiers and to you, and I will do everything in my power to make this as smooth a process as possible for everyone involved.'

'OK – well, let me take a look and we can work something out.'

'Thank you, Colonel.' I stood before saluting and left his office to begin my new role.

It was the beginning of a great relationship and, of all the leaders I have worked under, he is perhaps the one I looked up to the most. As it happens, he is now one of the most senior Officers in the Army and headed Operation IRON VIPER, which was the operation for all the UK's military-administered COVID vaccines.

A few months later, my transition really kicked off. I approached it in the same way I would for any other aspect of my job. In the Army you are constantly planning – working out what to do when something goes wrong, accounting for every eventuality, thinking about people and rations and transport, equipment, timings, training etc. I put the same mindset to work on my desire to transition, asking myself: what are all the things that have to happen for me to do this? What have I got to do? Who have I got to speak to? What diagnoses have I got to get, what support do I need from which different part of the military? I knew the policy and that process inside out so that at each step and with each person I was engaging with, I was telling them what their part of that process was and specifically what they needed to do.

There were still gatekeepers though, people I had to get things signed off by to get to the next hoop to jump through, and it wasn't always easy, least of all navigating the NHS system, but I was determined. There was a running joke among the close friends that I had made in the mess that I burst into tears at 22.30 every night. And it wasn't far off – on the nights when we were enjoying a drink or two, the combination of alcohol and the emotion of being so close to my dreams coming true but not quite there was often just too much to contain. My friends were very supportive though and, when the floodgates opened, they'd come and cuddle me and tell me it'd be OK. Then I'd brush myself off and go in to work again the next day.

While on the waiting list for an appointment at the Gender Identity Clinic in Leeds, I was fortunate enough to be able to afford to see a private doctor in London, who after several more assessments and repeat diagnoses eventually gave me a prescription for testosterone blockers and oestrogen. It is a momentous moment for any trans person who wants to have hormone therapy and I was very excited, but what made it even more special was the Officers in the mess actually threw me a party! As I got closer to the big day, I had been much more open with the Officers I lived with and as the oestrogen came in these sticky patches they called it my 'patch party' and they all came to the bar covered in plasters to celebrate.

So I had it all mapped out and, while asserting that degree of military control over planning didn't alleviate the fear or the enormity of what would happen next, it did at least provide a welcome distraction. However, for all my planning, there was one milestone on my roadmap that I still hadn't met – my parents. I had told Jeff the last time we were in Cardiff together. He was predictably fantastic about it and, aside from the fascination of how orange lipstick can be used to counteract the blueish colour of stubble, his main concern was how overwhelmingly hard it must have been for me. (There are not enough superlatives to describe my brother's kindness.) It was comforting to know I had an ally in the family, but I obviously had to tell Mum and Dad before I came out publicly and that wasn't far away. With the Christmas holidays looming, I knew it was my last chance and I was dreading it.

The drive down to Wales from Yorkshire was about five hours, so I had plenty of time to think over the situation that was ahead of me. Having told them I was gay the previous

Christmas, I was confident that their love for me was unconditional, but I also knew I was about to unleash something hugely
challenging into their lives, and I felt really bad about it. Don't
get me wrong, coming out as gay can be a really hard thing to
do, and there are many who suffer really nasty consequences
from doing so, but, for my fairly open-minded, middle-class
family, they knew and liked several gay people, so it was at
least in their frame of reference and they had many years of
considering if that was the case for me. Coming out as trans,
though, was going to be a complete shock for them and I wasn't
expecting a particularly positive reaction.

Fairy lights twinkled at the window as I pulled into the
driveway. I knew Dad would have waited for me to buy the
tree. It was our tradition. Ever since I was a kid, we'd go and
choose the Christmas tree together, always opting for the tall-
est, bushiest one we could find (much to Mum's annoyance).
Jeff arrived shortly after from London, where he was working
as a geologist, and we settled into our traditional Christmas
routine, which, much like the previous year, I intended to
allow everyone to enjoy before hitting Mum and Dad with
the news.

Christmas in our house had remained somewhat unchanged
since we were kids; Mum and Dad still gave us stockings with
silly little presents, followed by my mum's fried breakfast
with Bucks Fizz, presents under the tree and culminating
with turkey and all the trimmings for dinner. (We had to
move it from lunch as we were usually all too full from breakfast to eat it!). Boxing Day was a much more relaxed affair
and as I've always acted as Dad's sous chef, I found myself
alone in the kitchen with him. He was preparing leftover

turkey while I was at the sink washing up, looking out over the garden where I had so many childhood memories. I realised it was now or never.

'You know that last year I told you I was gay?' I began. 'Well, that's sort of true, but there's more to it. It's more that I am transgender. That I feel like I am a girl.'

Dad paused where he stood, lost for words.

'I haven't told Mum yet,' I rushed on. 'I was going to do it later.'

It had clearly shaken him and I think he asked some fairly simple questions, which I tried to answer in the calm manner that I had become so accustomed to doing with people in work, but my voice still quavered slightly. I don't think Dad really knew what to say – I certainly didn't. Something deeper than words found him, though, and he pulled me into a tight embrace, conveying what I knew to be true, that he was finding this hard, but would always love me, whoever I was.

*   *   *

Later that evening, almost a year from the day since we'd sat in the exact same chairs and I had told them I was gay, I once again broke the quiet by letting Mum know that I needed to tell her something. She looked nervous as I reeled off the same words I had said to Dad just hours earlier. She was, understandably, quite emotional; inevitably there were tears. She didn't say much, and I honestly can't remember much of it as it is a moment I have all but blocked from my memory. I mostly remember the hurt I caused her that day. But the one thing I will always remember, as they are etched on to my heart, were her simple words: 'I will always love you.'

It was hard for both my parents. You must remember that their experience of transgender people was non-existent save some sensationalised newspaper story describing us as freaks, deviants or worse. Of course, they didn't see their successful, decorated Army Officer son coming out as trans as a good thing, and, even if they could understand that being trans wasn't inherently bad, the worry set in. Would I be bullied? Would I be an outcast? Would I ever find love, have kids, even just be *safe*? These are all fair questions to this day and ones that I know would have kept them up at night.

In the days that followed my announcement and before my return to work, we all tiptoed around each other. We did our best to pretend that my news hadn't shaken the family at all, even though Mum and Dad were processing the news and I was obsessing about how much I had hurt them. Jeff was an amazing comfort, the least fazed by my coming out and always around with a hug for anyone who needed it. That isn't to say we didn't discuss it though. There were moments, usually one on one and while engaged in some other distracting task, where Mum or Dad would pipe up with the odd question. I would respond as honestly as I could and we would talk for a few minutes, before emotions started to build and we would move away from the subject again. If I'm honest, I was looking forward to getting back on the road.

Being back in the Officers' Mess in my own room gave me the space to relax as I threw myself into work, which provided me with a welcome diversion from the emotions back home. I was only able to compartmentalise it for so long, and so one evening when everyone else had gone home, I decided to check in and call my dad. He answered promptly, but his cheery greeting was betrayed by a deeper note in his voice. I asked him how he was and after some back and forth it transpired that he'd had to take a few days off work because of the stress.

I was surprised, not because it was so unlike my dad (which it was), but because I have always thought of my dad as the ultimate pragmatist and I hadn't really understood the emotions he was going through beneath the surface. In the years since we've talked about it and a lot of it had to do with feeling embarrassed by me, a reaction that I now know to be one of his biggest regrets and one I do not blame him for.

Not really knowing what to say, I simply stated the truth: 'I'm sorry, I never wanted to hurt you.'

He began to cry and I joined a moment later and it took us both several minutes to gather ourselves, reaffirming our love for each other before hanging up the phone. I sat still in that quiet office for some time before I could brush myself off and head back to the mess.

I do not blame my parents one tiny bit for any negativity they may have felt about my coming out. They were victims of societal conditioning as much as I was. Yet to their absolute credit – and to my huge benefit – they put any such feelings aside and held my hand every single step of the way. I am not a religious woman, but I give thanks to any higher power for giving me such loving parents.

*   *   *

A few short weeks later, I was sitting down with my Commanding Officer, finalising plans for my official coming out. The quartermaster had been made aware a couple of weeks previously and had ordered in my female uniform (although mostly it was unchanged), my new military ID had arrived following my name change and all that remained was to tell everyone and get on with it. The Commanding Officer was going to brief all the Officers, the Regimental Sergeant Major (RSM) was going to brief all the Sergeants and Warrant Officers and the message was going to be cascaded down to all the remaining solders by their Platoon Commanders – all coordinated to happen in the same morning.

I had also been doing the rounds, calling all my friends who I hadn't been able to tell in person, which was like some sort of queer Groundhog Day, but, as much as I had to have the same conversations over and over, there was also a little rush each time as I took another step to towards my future. Most of my friends (but not all) were fine if not a little taken aback by the news and we laughed and looked back at the signs they might have missed (*umm, fancy dress anyone?!*), but the point I reiterated to all of them was: I didn't want anything about our friendship to change. I was changing clothes, and yes my body was changing too, but I was ultimately the same person – which brought me to the sticky point about my name.

Since Welbeck I had always been known as 'Winty', a simple nickname from my surname 'Winterbourne', and several of my friends delighted in the realisation that 'Winty' was neither male nor female and came from my surname so they could just keep using my nickname. I knew however, that to them 'Winty' would always be a guy in their heads and so I asked them all to leave the nickname behind and use 'Hannah' from that point on.

'Hannah' was a name that I chose firstly because I liked the sound of it, but also because it is inherently feminine with no real male equivalents. To my mind its femininity is also understated rather than overt, which particularly appealed to me. I chose my name by myself, but wanted to give a nod to my parents, who had chosen the names I was leaving behind. I settled on 'Rose' as my middle name as it was the name my parents would have given me had they (knowingly!) had a girl.

With the benefit of hindsight and with confirmation from several of my friends, I know I became a little myopic and self-obsessed during that time, fixating on every detail of my transition. I will be forever grateful to all those who stuck with me during that first year, who put up with my endless self-discovery and analysis while dealing with their own emotions and education without ever letting me see it. I hope they know how much that meant to me.

Then, finally, it was time. All the preparations made, everyone informed and the plan in place. I stood on the precipice of my new life, took a deep breath and... leapt.

The next morning, I went to work as Captain Hannah Winterbourne for the first time. In many ways it was a complete anti-climax, particularly in appearance. The day-to-day uniform is the same for both men and women and there wasn't much I could do about my hair at this point as I had the regulation short back and sides. It would take some time for it to grow out, and wearing a wig wasn't practical when you consider the physical life of a soldier. It was important to me that no one could say for a second that anything about my transition made me less effective as an Officer, and that meant putting my vanity to one side.

The unit got the hang of my female pronouns pretty quickly. The first time one of the soldiers saluted me and greeted me with a 'Good Morning, Ma'am', I nearly cried with joy, although I held it together as I returned the salute. Yes, people got it wrong and called me 'Sir' by mistake, but they usually corrected themselves shortly afterwards. That never bothered me and I always did my best to put them at ease when it happened. However, the novelty wore off for everyone pretty quickly as the nature of the job takes over, and hearing 'Good Morning, Ma'am' loses its shine when you realise it is usually accompanied by a stack of paperwork or a problem to resolve. I also found myself more determined than ever to prove that my transition hadn't changed me or my ability to do my job, that I was no 'lesser' for this change. I would stay later, work harder and take on more responsibility – I wanted to be bulletproof – as I knew that there would be some out there looking for me to fail. And that simply wasn't an option for me.

I'd been taking hormones for a few months by this point and was warned that I was likely to go through mood swings and high emotions, not dissimilar to a 'second puberty', but honestly, I didn't experience anything as dramatic as that, although I certainly found that I was a little more outward with my emotions. For me, it just felt like a natural alignment with my inner self.

There were, of course, physical changes, which were gradual but built up over time, particularly my muscle drastically reducing and the fat redistribution on my body, resulting in a much more feminine shape and facial features. I became obsessed by every tiny change and spent a lot of time staring at my face, wondering if others were noticing and wishing those changes would speed up. However, there are some things that hormones cannot fix, most notably body hair, which meant many excruciating hours in the chair getting laser hair removal. Once a month, for 18 months, I would drive down to Leeds and have my face, chest, stomach, arms and legs zapped for two hours. It's the most physical pain I have ever endured, and I emerged each month red and blotchy from head to toe, but ultimately, joyfully, free of a beard and hairy chest.

Eventually, when my hair had grown long enough, I went all out on a full head of high-quality extensions and, combined with facial changes and my body realigning, I started to see a woman looking back at me from the mirror. Words cannot convey how exhilarating and life-affirming that image was.

Throughout this time, I was still going home for the holidays and staying with Mum and Dad, but, because I only saw them after fairly long intervals, the changes in my appearance weren't as gradual for them. If they felt any discomfort at the changes they saw, they hid it well from me and they always made the effort to comment on how lovely I looked, or how certain clothes suited me. They also, over time, began to relax and we fell back into our normal routines. Mum and I would go to a coffee shop, do the crossword and chat about *Strictly Come Dancing*, my dad and I would go to the rugby and chat about sports (and also *Strictly Come Dancing*!). I think we all took comfort in enjoying each other's company in the way we always had, reinforcing that while my appearance and name had changed, I was still the same person they had cared for all their life.

I've no doubt that as I was acclimatising to life as a woman, they were going through a huge emotional journey of their own to get to that point, and that included keeping painful experiences away from me. Again, that is something I will be forever thankful for.

*   *   *

After a year of hormones and as all of the physical changes settled, I finally began to feel like the woman I had always known myself to be. I began to consider what surgical options were available in order for me to feel fully comfortable in my body. I had been slightly disappointed in my breast development through hormones, and, as a taller woman with broad shoulders, I felt that the resulting proportions were not particularly feminine. After jumping through multiple hoops, including yet another independent psychiatric assessment (I have lost count of how many of these I have had over the years), I checked into a private hospital in Manchester one Tuesday morning, ready for a breast augmentation. I didn't tell anyone: it just felt too personal, so I went down on the train by myself early in the morning, had surgery in the afternoon and got back on the train home the following day after being discharged. I had definitely been a bit 'gung ho' about the recovery and it wasn't the most comfortable journey home, but I was lying on my own bed just a day later, feeling much happier about myself.

I thought that after my transition I would settle quietly into my new identity. I continued to push myself in my military career and strived to live an unassuming but happy life. Everything was coming together, both personally and professionally. Not only had I been accepted by my friends and family, I was still serving as an Army Officer. My career was progressing and I was now the Second in Command of a company of soldiers, as well as an active member of the Army's LGBT network, advocating for further inclusion in policy and culture. This was everything that I had ever hoped for and more.

'Excuse me, Sir, is Captain Winterbourne available?' An admin clerk had just interrupted a classroom lesson on Strategic Warfare Planning, of which I was a student.

As Army Officers, we have continuous training and development throughout our careers, and I was on a two-month course in the south of England. We had been briefed at the beginning of the course that we would not be pulled into any work back at our home units, so it was unusual for me to be excused from a lesson. I was taken to an office where I was handed a phone and was introduced to the Army's PR team.

'Hannah, the *Sun* have approached us, intending to write a piece about you as a serving transgender Officer.' Clearly someone had decided to make a quick buck from selling my story, and I was speechless as I tried to comprehend the repercussions. 'Ultimately, you have two options: you can ignore it, they write whatever they write, it becomes tomorrow's chip shop paper and you get on with your life. Or, second, you give them an interview, let them take some photos and you have a chance to influence the article. We will support you in whatever you choose.'

Both options were terrifying and I had no idea what to do. I couldn't possibly have imagined just how deeply that decision would change the course of my life.

CHAPTER FOURTEEN

The media vs reality

Jake

The outing of trans people in national newspapers is so last decade. When the *Sun* ran their story about Hannah coming out in the Army, it was almost a given that crudely exposing a transgender person's existence on their front cover would be enough to sell papers. The personal cost to Hannah, the loss of her anonymity and privacy, the sleepless nights and worry in the run-up, would most likely not even have factored in their decision to make her front-page news. To them, she was just a means to an end, the ramifications on her life utterly irrelevant. More recently, however, with more trans people in the public eye than ever before, the 'first trans xxx' trope simply doesn't shift papers like it used to. Although clearly a sign of progress for trans visibility, the media, undeterred, quickly reinvented its approach to trans coverage, now implementing a far more cynical and infinitely more damaging way to profit from trans people, and one which, today, pervades the daily life of everyday Britons.

If you walk into a newsagent's on any given day, you are likely to pick up a newspaper that contains at least one article about transgender people, but more likely several. In fact an

IPSO (Independent Press Standards Organisation) report from 2020 identified a 400% increase in coverage of 'trans issues' over a five-year period – rather impressive considering our tiny little community makes up around 0.1% of the population. In your morning paper, you are likely to find articles claiming that trans women like Hannah are a threat to cis women, that trans kids are being handed hormones like Smarties, that parents are pushing their kids into transition or that we are simply mentally ill, confused gay people who have just gone that step too far. The coverage is usually sensationalised, biased and inflammatory. At best these publications are neglecting to provide readers with the full facts and context and at worst, seem content in printing unchecked, outright lies.

The world for trans people in 2023 can feel terrifying. Some of you may snort at that, arguing that we have more rights now than at any time in history, and in many ways we do, but we also have a government, here in the UK, that is disproportionately focused on rolling back and removing those rights. As an example, the government pressured the Equality and Human Rights Commission to withdraw its guidance resource for schools on supporting trans students, and our so-called equalities minister, Kemi Badenoch, urged the Financial Conduct Authority to drop its trans inclusion policy, which it did just weeks later. When Scotland recently passed a self-identification law that would allow trans people to be legally recognised in their correct gender, without having to be vetted by psychiatrists or provide evidence that they are woman or man 'enough' (a law that, incidentally, already successfully covers 350 million people and exists in countries such as Ireland, Portugal, Denmark, Malta and Argentina, to name but a few), the UK government took the unprecedented move to veto a law passed in Scottish Parliament, sending a clear message as to their stance on trans equality. These and countless more examples have seen the UK drop in Europe's LGBTQIA+ rights, falling from first to seventeenth, and paint an ugly picture of how the current media coverage of all things trans has now been weaponised for political gain. Money and power, delivered at the expense of our already vulnerable trans community, just trying to live our day-to-day lives.

In the last few years we have seen authors, actors and politicians publicly and proudly sharing their disdain and suspicion for transgender people in the press and on social media, as though perhaps we do not feel and think and hurt in the same way as everyone else. To be constantly maligned, attacked, doubted and torn apart is saddening, exhausting and scary. There are of course many marginalised sections of our society who experience daily prejudice and systemic inequalities, but the level of open 'debate' into our rights or even our existence is disproportionate and arguably serves to raise the acceptability of the hatred that we face. In what world would we accept a debate into the rights of people of colour, Christians or women on mainstream morning television, as we so often do the trans community? That acceptability stems from the most common argument against transgender rights: that transgender rights are in direct conflict with (cis) women's rights. Transphobes and bigots have succeeded in fooling large swathes of impressionable readers of the press that this is the case, and we hear, again and again, 'But surely women's rights should be protected too? I mean, women have fought so hard . . .' It's an emotive statement, pulled straight from the fearmongering playbook that has been the go-to of bigots for centuries. Whether it's defending the racial segregation of bathrooms, buses and sports in 1960s America, or arguing that gay men wanted to infiltrate bathrooms to predate upon heterosexual men in the 1980s, the reasoning is the same – those who differ from you must be feared, controlled and contained, lest they harm you and your loved ones. People of colour and gay men posed no threats to you then and trans women pose no threats to you now. Mankind has a shameful and repetitive history of bigotry and division, yet appears incapable of learning from it.

I grew up in the 1980s when trans people were all but invisible, and so know full well the detrimental effect that lack of presence can have. This current explosion of anti-trans coverage, however, and the impact of seeing people like ourselves torn apart and vilified in the mainstream press and across social media, can't help but have a devastating effect on the mental health and safety of our community. I shudder at the fear and anxiety that it must be instilling in our trans youth from such a young age, making an already tough existence infinitely harder.

Looking further abroad to the US, it's a truly horrifying landscape. In just the first four months of 2023, 533 anti-trans bills across 49 states have been introduced seeking to block trans people from receiving basic healthcare, education, legal recognition and the right to publicly exist. Trans healthcare is being criminalised. Trans teens are being forced by law to detransition. Doctors fear for their licences and freedom if they continue to treat their trans patients. And all of this under President Joe Biden, a proud and vocal ally. The Republican alternative is too terrifying to contemplate. Many trans Americans and other members of the LGBTQIA+ community have already left for Canada and elsewhere – and while the figures have dropped from those leaving during Trump's era, they've quickly risen again in the wake of restrictive legislation such as *Dobbs v. Jackson* that historically overturned *Roe v. Wade*. It is a stark reminder to us all that hard-won rights can easily be removed.

*   *   *

Hannah and I live with that fear, that anxiety, every single day. There are nights when we lie in bed, frozen, angry, lost for words as to why we – why any of us – should be made to feel this way by our government, our press, our leaders, in 2023 Great Britain. Doubted, debated and dismissed as lesser.

We venture out into the world each day, worried and mindful that someone in the swimming-pool changing room might scream hateful obscenities at Hannah as she takes our nine-month-old to swim class, or that someone at nursery will recognise us and say something cruel in front of Millie. So far, no one has.

We'll occasionally quietly celebrate that someone, after one of our talks, in Hannah's office or simply walking down the street, has felt compelled to stop and share a kind word, to tell us we've changed their opinion or, occasionally, that we've given hope to them or their families. Those interactions, those words of kindness and shows of support are the ones that keep us going, that make us wonder if all the nonsensical hate and rage that the media amplifies is just that: noise. That the world is, despite it all, a kind place.

What we see, largely, is acceptance and some understandable curiosity, which we welcome. Anyone who is open and keen to learn about our experience feels like a step in the right direction. We are more than eager to help allay any fears and dispel the myths perpetuated by the media, extremist groups and the misinformed. If the kindness and openness that we see out there is at all representative of the general feeling towards our community, then there is cause for hope.

Life is worrying, and we know that we are more fortunate than most. Hannah and I have the support of our families and our friends. We are hugely privileged, white, middle class and employed. Many trans people are not so lucky, and have more to endure than we could ever imagine. Life can already be hard; being trans makes it harder.

What gives us strength and fortitude is knowing that there are more and more of us every day, emboldened to come out and live happy lives, despite the challenges. That more and more parents are supportive of their trans children, and will fight until their last breath to protect them. And that, while we are aware that there are many people working to eradicate us, there are so many more who are fighting for our safety and our happiness. As Hannah always says, 'Most people are good.'

CHAPTER FIFTEEN

Stepping out into the light

Hannah

I rocked up at the Park Plaza Hotel, just by Waterloo Bridge in London, with my military holdall on my back and a sequinned dress in a suit carrier over my arm. I'd taken the day off work to attend *Cosmopolitan* magazine's Ultimate Women of the Year Awards, a slightly unusual leave request for my Commanding Officer. I might as well have been going on a mission to Mars as far as he was concerned. This was such a different world.

I had eventually, after a lot of soul searching and taking advice from Ayla, decided to engage with the *Sun* and give an interview. I had come to the conclusion that it was going to be terrifyingly exposing either way, but the prospect of them writing whatever they liked risked a really negative article. Reading negative stories of others had such a damaging effect on me pre-transition, and I hated the idea that my story would do that to some other trans person out there. So, after a sixty-minute interview and a handful of pictures, my fate was sealed and I waited nervously for the news to hit.

On 19 January 2015, emblazoned across the front page of the *Sun* was the headline *'An Officer and a Gentlewoman'*, accompanied by a 'before and after' with a picture of me pre-transition in Afghanistan on the left and a more current one of me wearing a ballgown on the right. As predicted, it was terribly exposing to see my life reduced to a couple of sensationalised pages for all the world to see, but while the article was littered with poor language and overly focused on my physical transition, what it didn't say (much to my relief) was that I was a freak who should be kicked out of the Army. It was, in a roundabout way, a positive article.

At this point, my life became a little bit crazy as I was overwhelmed by requests for all the daytime TV shows, news shows, magazines and other newspapers, many from abroad. The Army's press team stepped in to help me manage it as I had very little experience with the media. Ultimately, I turned most of it down, but we agreed to do one TV interview. I had the pick of the bunch, and choosing *Lorraine* was an absolute no-brainer! A staunch military and LGBTQIA+ ally (as well as all-round legend), Lorraine Kelly was the perfect fit. I was incredibly nervous to be interviewed on live TV but, on the day, Lorraine came to see me in the green room to put me at ease, and I couldn't have been in safer hands as I shared my experience with the nation.

What I didn't realise immediately, but which began to dawn on me as the days went on, was that I had accidentally become some sort of role model. For many trans people, my story was the first positive representation of a trans person that they had seen, and I received a huge outpouring of love and support. I did predictably get the trolling as well, with many a thread and distasteful comment made about me, but I chose not to focus on them – it served my mental health well and is something that I try to maintain today, although it isn't always easy.

I do think it's important to mention that when it comes to my life in the public eye, the stars really aligned for me. Trans people have existed forever and there are many courageous trans people who have been through as much as me and more, but who were never afforded the visibility that I have had. Simply put, I was in the right place at the right time, at a moment in our society when the mainstream media was willing to publicly support a trans woman for the first time. Had that timing been different, someone else would be writing this book. That isn't to say that I haven't worked hard at supporting individuals and representing our community. In fact, given the platform that I now have, I feel a real sense of responsibility to use it to further trans equality and elevate other trans voices, but I am more than aware that many others would have done the same.

So yes, I got to receive an 'Ultimate Trailblazer' award at the star-studded *Cosmopolitan* awards, enjoy a gift box with everything from GHD straighteners to free gym memberships, and drink Baileys cocktails with Rebel Wilson and Olly Murs. But I know a lot of that is due to luck, and I have never taken it for granted.

*   *   *

However, away from the occasional award ceremony or pride event, my life as an Army Officer trundled on and with it came my new posting to the King's Royal Hussars (KRH), an armoured regiment based in Tidworth in Wiltshire and with a history that stretches back to 1715. It wasn't until 2017 that women could join the KRH, but prior to that, female soldiers who performed supporting roles (such as medics, engineers and admin staff) could serve as part of the regiment. We were few and far between, though, and when I joined I was one of about 15 women in the 400-strong regiment.

It was a huge honour to serve with them. The KRH primarily manned the Army's main battle tank, the Challenger 2, and had one of the biggest fleets of vehicles. As such the Royal Electrical and Mechanical Engineers (REME) detachment that I commanded was also one of the largest, with 80 soldiers under my command. They were fantastic – some of the best people I have served with and a team that really understood the balance between work and play – but despite the prestigious appointment, I wasn't happy.

In their history the KRH had only had a handful of female Officers and certainly never any trans Officers, so living in the mess was pretty awkward to begin with. The other Officers were quite a tight-knit bunch and while they weren't unkind or rude, they were clearly uncomfortable around me and didn't know what to say or do. Most of them were privately educated, many with a family history in the regiment and the type of guys who wear mustard corduroy trousers and go clay-pigeon shooting on the weekend. At face value I just didn't fit in and I suspect there were more than a few who were a bit embarrassed to have a trans woman in their mess.

I did my best to join in and get involved, but inevitably I found myself falling out of the conversations fairly quickly. Then one evening, sitting by myself after dinner, the Quartermaster, a Cornish guy called Paul, pulled up a chair next to me and plonked down two pints of beer in front us. Paul, in contrast to the other Officers in the mess, was a late-entry Officer, which means he started at the lowest rank and worked his way all the way up to become an Officer over his career. Late-entry Officers are known for being 'no nonsense' and so when he lifted his glass to mine, we both took a large gulp, and he said to me, 'Right, what's all this transgender stuff about then?' I laughed and started to explain a bit about what it meant for me. Several rounds later and after many questions and much laughter, Paul and I were in full swing with banter flowing across the table. He asked me frankly about everything and, yes, some of it would be viewed as inappropriate, but I didn't care. In fact, I welcomed it. My view has always been, 'If you don't mean to cause offence, I won't take it,' and Paul was a good guy who was just trying to understand something of which he had no experience. Somewhere in the wee hours of the morning we called it quits and, after a hug, stumbled back to our rooms.

What I didn't realise until a bit later was that the following day, Paul went around to some of the other Officers and told them that they needed to stop being so off with me, and that I was actually pretty down to earth and fun. It was the catalyst I needed, starting to be included more, and as I was, so my friendships began to build. I threw myself into the KRH culture, which has many traditions ranging from black-tie, three-course, silver-service dinners four times a week (do you know how many evening gowns I had to buy?!), to drinking champagne out of a silver chamber pot supposedly owned by Napoleon. I loved it. Those traditions are integral to the life of a KRH Officer and as I lived and breathed them, I formed a close bond with the other Officers.

*   *   *

Every year, all the cavalry regiments of the Army have a big memorial parade through London's Hyde Park, the soldiers marching in uniform with the Officers walking behind in pinstripe suits and bowler hats (luckily it was acceptable for me to wear a dress and observe with the wives and girl-friends!), after which the Officers congregate in a pub just off Parsons Green, in Fulham. We were out in the beer garden, a mix of Officers not only from the KRH but the other regiments, and it had the atmosphere of a summer barbeque as we drank champagne in the sun. But the vibe changed when, as I walked to the bar to buy another bottle, a much younger Officer from another regiment muttered to his mate next to him, 'That's the tranny,' sniggering as I walked by. I am not one for confrontation, so I ignored him and walked back to my crowd. Something must have read on my face, though, as one of the guys asked me what was wrong.

'Oh, just one of the subbies over there is being a bit of an idiot.' I tried to make light of the situation as I really didn't want anything being made of it, but the guys were able to gather what had happened and were having none of it. A few of them marched over to confront him before Rob, the KRH Adjutant (responsible for Officer discipline) quickly stepped in to prevent anything getting out of hand. After a quick conversation with the Adjutant from the other regiment, the young Officer was frog-marched up to me, where he gave a somewhat sheepish apology.

It was a real point of realisation for me. These guys, who had once been embarrassed by me, had stood up for me in public without a moment's hesitation, willingly defending me as a trans person. Even to this day it reminds me that when people are given the chance to understand trans people, more often than not they become strong allies. I spent more than two years with the KRH and they were the best two years of my Army career, during which I made some lifelong friends.

*   *   *

At this point in my life, things were busy but settled. Alongside the stresses of my day job, I had become the Army's Transgender Representative, which involved advising senior Officers, delivering training and education and mentoring other transgender soldiers, and all this set against the constant hum of media attention. It was a balancing act and one that often left me exhausted, but one of the values of the British Army is 'selfless commitment' and I felt very passionately that I had to find a way to give back to our community.

Also, I had by now gone through lower surgery. It is not a part of my transition that I wish to dwell on, partly because it is of course intensely personal, but also because people tend to overly focus on the physical aspects of a transition rather than the emotional ones, especially the surgeries. It is still an integral part of my transition and something that I felt I needed to truly align my body with my sense of self and help alleviate some of the anxiety and self-loathing that I still carried when looking in the mirror. It was a long and painful surgery, with a much longer recovery time, but ultimately resulted in me being much happier.

In many ways, one could say that I had by now 'completed' my transition. Physically I was happy with my body for the first time in my life, I was living as a woman in society with support from my family, friends and colleagues, and that was more than I could ever have dreamt of. But when I got there, I found that I was still missing something.

*   *   *

Romance had always been absent in my life. Having never been comfortable in my own body as I was growing up, the idea of being intimate with anyone was simply an awful prospect. When I transitioned, I genuinely believed that I would be giving up the chance to ever be in a relationship. After all, who could ever love a trans person? Sadly, transphobia runs so deeply in our society that we internalise it and end up believing the narrative that we are undesirable and unworthy of love. This is one of the reasons why so many trans people struggle with their mental health. From a very young age we are taught to hate ourselves, and it's very hard to shake that. But as I started to feel whole in my body, and with so much validation in other aspects of my life, I began to consider for the first time whether love might be an option for me. I knew from the many messages I received on social media that there were men out there who found me physically attractive, but they were often inappropriate and sometimes downright vulgar, fetishising me rather than seeing me as a real person. What I wanted was not someone who just wanted a fling, but someone who would be happy to introduce me to their parents.

Dating as a trans person is riddled with challenges. Putting aside the personal hang-ups and insecurities that we will carry with us for the rest of our lives, even in the first moments you are faced with an impossible choice: when do you tell someone you're trans? It's a real catch-22. If you tell someone before meeting in person, that could likely end the relationship before it's even begun, as a potential suitor is likely to judge you without ever really knowing you. If, however, you wait to bring it up at a later date, you might be accused of 'deception' and risk an abusive response. Even if you are lucky enough to find someone with whom you can get over those initial first hurdles, they then have to steel themselves for the judgement that they might face from their friends and family – transphobia by association. It's a real minefield – and that's just casual dating, let alone moving towards a relationship. Suffice it to say, I was open to love, but had no idea where to find it.

One cold winter's afternoon in December 2015, home with my family for Christmas and mindlessly scrolling through Facebook, I saw a friend request pop up. Jake Graf. I knew who he was as there were only a few high-profile trans people in the UK at that time and he had been all over the press, having been in *The Danish Girl*. We had never met but had some mutual friends so I knew a bit about him. I clicked through some of his photos and accepted his request a few minutes later. I decided to write him a little note to accompany my acceptance of his cyber friendship, and really tried to be smooth about it.

> 'Hi Jake. I know we have never met but I wanted to drop a quick message to say hello. Been watching your exploits with interest recently. Hope you enjoy the premiere tomorrow! Xx'

Twenty minutes later he was messaging me back and it just went from there.

It was sweet, innocent flirting. We had loads in common but also such different lives that it made for interesting conversation. Knowing that Jake was also trans was a huge relief for me. It wasn't something that we actually talked about much, but it made me feel much more comfortable knowing that I wasn't going to have to come out or face any difficult questions about my identity. It allowed us to focus on everything else, almost like I imagine other people do...!

As time went on I think we both wanted to move on from Facebook messaging as it was starting to feel a bit 'teenage', but I was reluctant to get on the phone as I've always had an insecurity about my voice being quite deep. I prefer video calls so people can see me as the woman I am rather than make incorrect assumptions based on the way I sound. Jake countered, quite reasonably, that a Skype call was an unusual first method of communication. I guess I was ahead of my time as Zoom calls have now become ubiquitous, but at the time I think he felt it would be awkward to stare at each other on a screen as we got to know each other. Finally, after about a week of online chat, I succumbed and agreed to chat on the phone.

He instantly put me at ease. He was charming, funny and clearly very bright and even on that first call I felt quite attracted to him. I wasn't, however, prepared for the bombshell he dropped just a few minutes later.

'Look, I don't want to freak you out, but I want to be honest. I've had a lot of dates and I'm kind of looking for more than that... What I'm really looking for is something that could become marriage and kids, so I kind of need to know if that's something you would be open to...'

I admit I was taken aback. My experience of dating was

pretty much non-existent but I had seen enough rom-coms to know that it was rather forward to drop that in on the first call! I was keen not to put him off, however, and after considering the question for a moment I honestly responded, 'Well, I wouldn't be against it, I just haven't thought about it much before.' Over later conversations it transpired that Jake had wanted children for many years, and had even gone to the effort of creating and storing five embryos on ice, so to his mind he was just trying to avoid wasted time and disappointment, which now seems rather wise.

Never in my wildest dreams had I ever considered becoming a parent; it just felt like too many unlikely steps for my logical brain to ever conceive as a possibility. I hadn't made any provisions for my personal fertility, a decision I made for that very reason. I was given plenty of advice and options from the NHS to do so, but in my mind, what was the point? (There's that internalised transphobia again.) Hearing about the lengths Jake had gone to in order to give him that choice was quite inspirational and, although he might have been somewhat jumping the gun, I actually very much respected him for asking. It was clearly a very considered and sensible thing to establish before getting emotionally involved, rather than starting something only to find out later that our visions for the future simply didn't align. It did pose an interesting question for me, though – could I be a mother? An intoxicating and novel prospect. I honestly had no idea.

However, before we could get too consumed by ideas of parenthood, we had to remind ourselves that we hadn't actually ever met... and so Jake did something that had never happened to me before. He invited me on a date.

PART TWO

The Road to Us

CHAPTER SIXTEEN

The first date

Jake & Hannah

Jake

We arranged to meet under the clock in Waterloo Station. I arrived slightly early and scanned the area, the towering Christmas tree and twinkling lights adding promise to a moment that already felt rather magical. It was 30 December 2015 and as everyone was saving themselves for New Year's Eve, it was quieter than usual in London. The weather was mild and sunny and tourists strolled smiling through the station, appreciating the clement temperatures.

Feeling a frisson of anticipation and nerves, I found a quiet bar in the station for a quick JD on the rocks to steel myself before Hannah arrived. I had changed my shirt three times before leaving the house, aiming for a 'made an effort but still laid back' vibe. This was my first date in some time and I was feeling slightly out of practice. Or, more likely, I just cared more than I had in a while, a rather unsettling feeling indeed!

Hannah

I'd never been on a date before and it was quite daunting, in many respects, to be on the train speeding from my parents' house in Cardiff to London to meet this guy I'd only been talking to online for a few weeks. I didn't *really* know much about him despite the weeks of flirtation but from the way he spoke and the obvious closeness to his family, he seemed like a nice guy. We had being trans in common, and that in itself was a great leveller. We knew that neither of us would have to deal with the usual hang-ups associated with 'disclosing' our trans identity. I'll never know for certain but I imagine it's how cis people go into a date – without all this pressure on their identity, which for trans people normally becomes the focus. I fully assumed that it was still going to be awkward though – from what I understood, first dates always were.

Def Leppard pumped through my headphones as I watched the countryside slip into something more urban as we approached our destination, breathing deeply to keep my nerves in check. I had decided on a grey and black bodycon dress with black tights, knee-length boots, a scarf and my brown leather jacket. I wouldn't have said that I was feeling confident about my look, but I wasn't unhappy either. I'd sent pictures of a couple of different outfit options to friends and they had all been very complimentary and encouraging.

As we pulled into the platform and I stepped off the train I had that old familiar sense of getting ready to jump. I couldn't back out now and just had to trust that it was going to be fine. I arrived first and waited nervously, texting my friends to let them know that I'd arrived safely. As I looked up, I saw Jake casually sauntering over, smiling, and my heart leapt a little, a tiny part of me relieved that he had shown up at all. After some fumbled formalities, he took the lead, which I was happy about as I didn't know London at all, and guided me out of the station.

As we walked towards the Southbank, talking in a surprisingly easy way, I was scarcely able to believe that I was on my very first date. I know it might sound silly now, after seven years together, but I can still recall that feeling – like I was in a Richard Curtis movie.

Jake

After my quick shot of Dutch courage, I loitered some distance from the clock in the centre of the concourse, so that I could easily spot Hannah when she arrived. My suggestion to meet at 3 p.m., an unusual time for a date by anyone's standard, was not without prior planning. Call me a cynic, but I think we all know fairly quickly if a first date is going well. As it was the holidays, my friends were all out on the town that evening and I didn't want to miss that if the chemistry just wasn't there. I know it was poor form, but the early kick-off meant that if things went south by six-ish, I could still go and join the gang for the evening. As Hannah had never been on a date before, the timing didn't seem to jar with her. My friend, Alex, even offered to give me a fake emergency call as backup, something that now feels pretty underhand!

Scanning the crowd, I spotted her. She was tall and slim with shoulder-length brown hair and was nervously playing on her phone. I must admit that I was very pleasantly surprised: even standing some way off, I fancied her, which was really unusual for me. I usually needed to get to know someone a bit before feeling any kind of attraction. I approached her and we smiled shyly before both going in for an awkward hug. As we pulled apart, laughing, I noticed that she had the most beautiful smile and a deep, throaty chuckle.

Strolling over together to the bustling Southbank, we chatted the whole time. The unusually mild winter's day allowed us to take in the views and the Christmas market, before I took her up to one of my favourite London spots, the top of the Royal Festival Hall, to admire the stunning views across the river and Parliament.

Hannah was a stranger to London, so everything was new and shiny to her and her enthusiasm was really sweet. At the small bar just off the large outdoor balcony terrace, she ordered a white wine and I got a tequila.

'Do you want a shot?' I asked, half joking, and when she readily agreed I warmed to her even more.

Sitting in the crisp December air, I smiled as Hannah took in the panoramic views of the city, never more beautiful than bathed in evening light. As we sat there, the other patrons melted away and we talked non-stop about everything from family to music, to kids to jobs, to the Army. Everything except being trans. It was a wonderful relief after the last few years of explanations and questions and curiosity. Hannah quite simply got it, and so the topic became irrelevant.

At 6 p.m., like clockwork, my phone rang, making me wince.

'Sorry, one sec,' I muttered sheepishly.

Hannah turned away, sipping her drink, waiting for me to finish.

'No, no we're all good here, bro.' I quickly ended the call, smiling apologetically.

'Everything OK?'

I decided to come clean, pretty sure that she could take it, and the fact that I'd confessed seemed to charm her.

'I'm just glad I made the cut and you don't need rescuing.'

'Far from it,' thinking, *Whatever this is, it feels like I've known this girl for years.*

Hannah

The time flew by that night, and at 7 p.m. Jake suggested we go for dinner at a riverside restaurant called YO! Sushi.

Yikes!

Sushi sounded like my worst nightmare. I don't eat fish – in fact, I'm a very fussy eater and don't like lots of food, but I didn't want to come across as difficult or weird so I reluctantly agreed. I spent the entire walk to the restaurant gearing myself up to force down raw fish, dreading what was ahead, but breathed a massive sigh of relief when we slid into a cosy booth in the restaurant and they handed us a menu with an extensive meat section. As it turned out, Jake doesn't eat fish either but loved it for the Southbank vibe and the hot sake.

We barely paused for breath during dinner, conversation flowing like the rice wine. Afterwards Jake suggested a drink in the British Film Institute just along the river, and there regaled me with stories of the history of the building and his various film screenings. His life seemed so fascinating and so unlike mine. Making films, writing, acting – worlds apart from Army life – and I loved hearing about it, while trying not to look too impressed by it all.

Jake

Six hours in and after much flirtation, conversation and casual touching, all I wanted to do was kiss her. For me, the first kiss is the litmus test and I badly wanted to gauge if our chemistry went beyond a good connection. Sitting in the bar at the BFI, only inches apart, Hannah casually rested her hand on my leg and the conversation led round to attraction and how to tell if it's there.

'So, do you think I fancy you?' I asked cheekily.

'I don't know,' she answered coyly.

'Well, does this help?'

I leant across the little bar table and kissed her. She had the softest, most beautiful lips. A perfect first kiss, which neither of us wanted to end.

After that, any of the last remaining 'getting to know each other' nerves vanished. As the BFI kicked us out and we walked out into the chilly night air, I took her hand and she smiled shyly. It was the first time, it turned out, that a man had held her hand like this and that just made it extra special. Neither of us was ready to go home but all the bars along the Southbank had closed their doors and I was at a loss. Anyone claiming that London is a 24-hour city is a liar.

Hannah

We walked as slowly as possible back to Waterloo to catch our train home, not wanting the evening to end, until I suddenly remembered that behind the station is an exclusive military bar that stays open late. Rather pleased that I could now impress Jake, I led him up the red brick stairs to the entrance of The Union Jack Club. Inside, after showing my military ID, we found a sofa in the corner and Jake brought over some drinks, impressed at the subsidised prices. On the wall above us hung military shields and historic portraits of various soldiers and Jake was clearly a bit taken aback by our surroundings, but there was something so poignant about me having been in his space at the cinema and now him getting a taste of my military world. And to this day, he still mentions how impressed he was that this Cardiff girl knew a late-night watering hole in London!

All I really remember from the end of that night is feeling special, part of something exciting and full of potential and drunk on the soft gentle kisses that Jake was showering me with. Our fellow patrons sat quite blatantly staring at us, the youngest people there by about 30 years, cocooned in the corner, oblivious to their curiosity.

At around 2 a.m., Jake noticed the time: our very last train was soon leaving Waterloo. We had a mad dash out into the cold night air, headed for the station. I was staying with my brother in Clapham Junction and Jake still lived in Barnes, so we shared a train and sat holding hands, looking like teenagers. As we reached my stop, I gave him one last kiss, before hopping off the train, very much on cloud nine. I was buzzing with the obvious connection we had, the intensity of our shared experience and the miracle, really, that we had hit it off at all.

Creeping into my brother's flat, I lay down on the sofa and called Jake to let him know, as requested, that I had made it home safe. Just as I was about to hang up, Jake very sweetly invited me to spend New Year's Eve with him. I assumed that it was the drink talking, but my heart still skipped a beat. We agreed to catch up in the morning and then I said, without thinking:

'Love you. Bye'.

Oh God – where had that come from?!

Any cool points I'd accrued over the evening instantly negated, I sat in bed blushing, mortified. Still, the evening had been perfect and more than I had ever hoped for on my very first date. Teeth brushed and face washed, I turned off the light, still smiling to myself.

Jake

As I strolled home at 2.30 a.m., I realised that our first date had lasted 11 hours. Not bad considering I'd doubted we would make it three! Hannah had obviously really let her guard down and relaxed with me and I rather enjoyed her accidental declaration of love. As I rolled into bed, all I knew was that I wanted to see her again, and soon.

I woke to the sound of Saturday morning football on Barn Elms playing field across from my flat, my feelings unchanged. I was also rather touched that Hannah had already texted to thank me for a lovely evening and, rather sweetly, given me a 'get out of jail free' card, saying that she could just head home to Cardiff if I'd rather spend the evening with my friends. Honestly, I had rarely met anyone who so effortlessly ticked all of my boxes and knew without hesitation that I wanted to see in the New Year with her. I texted straight back to confirm that I would meet her after dinner. Looking back, neither of us played it very cool when we first met, but if you know, you know and Hannah was clearly on the same page – we both wanted to see where this would go.

My dinner plans at The Royal China in Bayswater with my friends, Rana and Reem, quickly amended, I ALMOST managed to get away without inquisition. But not quite.

'What do you mean, you're leaving after dinner? It's New Year's Eve, darling. You can't leave after dinner. Who is this girl, anyway?' queried Rana, one of my closest friends.

'The girl that I met last night and—'

'You're cancelling on us after one date? On New Year's Eve?' they teased.

That only opened the door for more grilling, but I was happy to answer their questions and to talk about Hannah. Both were mostly curious about my dating a trans woman, never having met one, and they did ask some fairly probing and inappropriate questions, which (mostly!) came from a place of caring.

After a lovely dinner waxing lyrical about my new crush, I wished the girls a happy New Year and, armed with a big bunch of lilies, Hannah's favourite flower, set off to meet her.

Jumping off the bus, I saw Hannah walking down the street from the station, waving in this adorable, enthusiastic way. Honestly, I practically skipped down the street towards her, while trying to maintain my cool, of course.

'These are for you.' As I handed her the flowers, she visibly and adorably blushed.

'You know, no one has ever given me flowers before.' Hannah looked a bit embarrassed by the admission, so I gently kissed her on the lips and led her back to my flat, brimming with excitement, safe in the knowledge that I had most definitely made the right choice.

Hannah

I would have been pretty miffed if one of my good mates had ditched me on New Year's Eve to spend the night with someone they'd only just met, but that's exactly what Jake did that night. It still means a lot that he was willing to do that for me, as I know how much his friends matter to him. His friend, Rana, who from the start welcomed me with open arms, is now godmother to both our children.

When we entered his flat, Jake felt the need to apologise, clearly awkward about his small digs.

At the time he was still working as a manny, and, like me, despite the profile and invitations to fancy events, was of fairly modest means. So yes, his place was small, but I had lived in far smaller and quickly reassured him that the size of his accommodation meant nothing to me.

Handing me a glass of Prosecco, he rather smoothly asked if I'd like to watch any of his films. It's a move we still laugh about today, but it certainly won me over. I sat on his sofa in tears, impressed and deeply moved by his work, much of which features women just like me.

At midnight we watched the fireworks explode over the rooftops of Barnes from his living room window and then he kissed me again, with real feeling, and we both knew that this was the start of something real.

And that's how our relationship began. We sort of hit the ground running. It went from me saying, 'Should I come back to London next weekend?', to pretty much not spending a weekend apart for the next year.

CHAPTER SEVENTEEN

Finding our feet

Hannah & Jake

Hannah

Jake was never a big fan of coming to visit me at the Army barracks in Tidworth. I think he found Army life a rather alien concept and somewhere he didn't fit. Jake is fairly adaptable once he's found his feet in a new situation, I just always felt that my military life was a stretch too far for him and he would become quite insular and shy. I was also a bit different when I was around my Army friends and there was a lot of bravado and banter. I certainly wasn't the woman that I was at home with Jake, when I could let my guard down and be truly vulnerable. That was fine for work but a bit foreign to Jake and to be honest I was mostly happy keeping my two worlds apart.

So in the early days of our relationship I would drive to London most weekends, which also gave me a welcome break from my small room in camp. If there was a special event or party at the mess I might be able to convince Jake to come but luckily these were few and far between. There's a culture and a way of life that's very specific to the British Army, particularly the older and more historic regiments like the KRH, which still maintain many traditions in the Officers' Mess, from the formal dinners to requesting permission from the ranking Officer to retire for the evening when you're tired and want to go to bed. To the uninitiated, it can be quite the culture shock.

The KRH was known for holding these particularly lavish summer balls in the Officers' Mess and the grounds of the barracks. Tickets were over £100 and people would plan their costumes for weeks in advance. And yes, of course, there was a fancy dress theme! In July, six months after our first date, I invited Jake, as my plus one, to the South American-themed ball.

It was such a lovely feeling to arrive, for the first time ever, with a boyfriend on my arm. Everyone was very welcoming of Jake, and he did his best to get involved but I could tell he wasn't enjoying it. We were all so close-knit and familiar, and Jake would readily admit to feeling awkward in a big crowd, and this event was huge. The parties were extravagant to say the least, the whole mess decked out to fit the theme, which in this instance included a two-storey Aztec pyramid covering the entrance, meticulously crafted using cardboard boxes, and a 10-foot 'Christ the Redeemer' statue, which was my personal contribution. Champagne and Moscow Mules were the drinks of choice and inevitably we became somewhat intoxicated as the evening progressed, but Jake had held back and so when the mess games began at midnight, he said: 'I think I'm going to sneak off to bed.' And off he went back to my room, which thankfully was in a separate block away from the party.

Jake

Army life was pretty foreign to me, and I had a lot of precon-
ceived ideas about it, based largely on the sensationalist
depictions I'd seen in the media. Both my uncles had served
and I'd seen the uniformed photos of them dotted around
my grandmother's home when we were kids, but I didn't
know much more than that. Honestly, it had never really
entered my consciousness. What I quickly came to understand though was that it wasn't just a job for Hannah; it was
a way of life. I certainly felt some trepidation about getting
involved with someone so completely tied to the Army and
that was before we even discussed her projected career
longevity!

I remember one evening about five weeks into our relationship when we were lying in bed and both coyly admitted
that our feelings were rapidly growing. With tears in her eyes
Hannah told me: 'When I transitioned, I fully expected to
end up alone. I knew I had my friends, my family and my
career and I had to believe that that was enough for me.'

Putting aside the heartbreaking confession, what stood out
was the importance of her military life.

At the start of our relationship, Hannah was stationed two
hours from me, which, although slightly limiting, still meant
weekends together, but she warned me from the start that
that could change overnight and she might be sent further
away or even, with some likelihood, abroad, with little to no
warning. I had done long-distance relationships. My last
three relationships prior to Hannah were long distance and
had been frustrating, painful and eventually devastating, so

the thought of repeating that pattern scared me. The first months of our relationship were particularly unsettling as even as I fell for Hannah, I worried daily about losing her.

As you probably know by now, I worry about things. I fretted about her safety and about the possibility of her being deployed to somewhere like Kenya or Canada, and even the uncertainty of her next posting created a lot of anxiety for me.

It added an edge to our fledgling relationship and, while I tried not be negative about the Army being her first love, the more I got to know her and fall for her, the harder it was to be nonchalant about the future. On our very first phone call, I had been entirely candid that I wanted something real and lasting, but hadn't truly grasped the limitations already put upon us. And, of course, this was Hannah's first relationship, so everything was all new to her. I was trying to give her the romance, the magic, the care, while also trying to protect myself and stay true to my intentions.

It was certainly a confusing, complicated start!

Hannah

Jake worried a lot more than I did at the beginning, I know that. For me, never having had a connection with anyone, never having felt that bond, that intimacy, those secret moments shared with just your special person, it was all so new, so exciting. Of course, it wasn't all roses and rainbows and I knew early on that Jake wouldn't follow me across the world according to where my military career took me, but I was discovering a whole new world of romance and dinners à deux, and lying cocooned in bed laughing for hours with someone. Honestly, it all felt pretty good.

Our entire relationship is heavily documented through iPhone photos, thousands of them. We would lie in bed in the morning, overlooking Barn Elms playing fields, and take photos of the sun, the trees, the light in each other's eyes. It was less naff than it sounds, I promise! I became the Instagram girlfriend quite quickly, after realising that Jake had a burgeoning social media presence and fairly active Instagram account. I got very good at taking photos, even buying special lenses for our phones and mini tripods and things. Our weekends were punctuated with these moments of, 'Oh, that would make a great picture,' or 'You look great against that backdrop,' but also with many, many shots of the two of us.

For me, there was something quite remarkable about those images, and seeing myself as part of a couple: my boyfriend and me. I got quite involved in Jake's social media, which was another discovery to me as my own social media was pretty much non-existent. I had posted one solitary picture on my Instagram before I met Jake, the picture of a DVD cover of a film I had just watched. Jake gave me a gentle ribbing, pointing out that wasn't the sort of content that would set the internet on fire!

Jake had about 10,000 followers at the time, a large number of those fellow trans men from across the world who had seen Jake on the covers of various magazines or in short films online, and his audience was steadily growing. He explained how important visibility was for our community and convinced me to start building my own platform.

At first it felt a little counter-intuitive. I'd kept so much secret for so long, it was hard to believe I was now in this position of being able to be out and proud and share the truth about my life with people. Not just the big important serious stuff, but the silly stuff, the sweet stuff and selfies just for the sake of them. It took some getting used to but it was good practice, allowing myself to be more honest and open in my daily life.

It didn't take long to realise that people were interested in Jake and me as a couple. There were so few representations of happy trans people in relationships that I started to realise it wasn't just a bit of fun and nonsense – together we could make a powerful impact and bring a well-needed dose of joy and positivity to other trans people's lives. Jake and I had both grown up with zero trans visibility and knew how damaging that had been, so were aware of the importance of that representation. As the old adage goes, *'You can't be you if you can't see you'*, and for those trans folk who wanted to find love, get married, have kids, we were able to offer a little hope.

We knew that we were by no means representative of all trans people as our community comprises all different races, faiths, colours and creeds, but if we could put out some positivity to even the smallest section of our community, then it was important we did so. And it was a good feeling, being able to show those younger folk that our transness didn't necessarily need to hold us back.

We also realised that it wasn't just other trans people but the parents and family of trans children and youth that were following us on social media, because it showed them that a happy future for their loved ones was possible. We were dating, we had careers – I was a soldier, Jake a filmmaker – we had fun together, and we talked about families and the future. We addressed many of the fears that you might have as the parent of a trans child, by showing the lighter side of our lives. You can be trans and still be happy.

Meanwhile, from a media perspective, we were a good story.

She was 'a boy', he was 'a girl', now they're together!

It was that kind of clichéd, sensationalised stuff.

The fact that we present quite 'traditionally' in this binary world of gender meant that mainstream media responded to us better than to many of our friends who presented more androgynously, for example. We saw an opportunity to use this growing interest in us to spread a message of love and acceptance and try to change the perception of trans people in the UK. So, we embraced the media attention and found ourselves in the public eye as a couple. It added some pressure to our relationship – there was a lot riding on us 'working' – but it also afforded us some incredible opportunities. We went to events together, started being invited to do speaking engagements together and went on the LGBT awards circuit as a couple.

I think we both recognised that in terms of making an impact and changing the narrative around transgender issues, we were stronger together.

Jake

Hannah was with me every weekend and it was wonderful. We were really getting close and our world was expanding as a couple, as we met new and exciting people through all the events and awards ceremonies we were doing together. But during the week I'd miss her, gradually more and more. I wanted a life where I could take Hannah for dinner midweek or watch a film together or even just have an early night with my girlfriend watching a boxset, but none of that was possible. All of the 'getting to know you' time, the fun and the down time had to be packed into two days, and that pressure began to build. We wanted to spend more time together, to really get to know each other better, to connect. She'd drive down to London as soon as she clocked off on a Friday afternoon and would stay until Sunday evening. At first she'd head back around 5 p.m., but then it got later and later until she was leaving at 10 p.m., normally in tears. It was during one of these emotional goodbyes that I held her tight, then whispered, 'Do you think there's a world where you might leave the Army one day?'

'No', she answered, almost defensively. 'It's my life. It's not a job I can just quit. And I want to make Major.'

Just as I'd always been frank and upfront about wanting marriage and children, so had she about being 'Career Army', and there were many times where it felt like we just hadn't heard the other, such had been our joy at finding each other. I reasoned that this was all new and that she would eventually tire of the stolen moments and big breaks in our time together, but I wasn't really certain that that was true. I just knew how good it felt to have a partner you could invite to the cinema randomly on a Tuesday evening and wake up with every day. I really tried to hide my feelings, to enjoy the time that we did have, and I certainly didn't want to pressure her to leave the Army for me. But at the same time, we were falling in love and it cast a shadow over our time together.

Whenever I felt that kind of deep happiness, the butterflies of new love, the sheer pleasure of just being with this woman who brought so much joy and light into my life – I got scared. I hoped that the more solid we became, the more entwined, the more she would open to the possibility of leaving the military. We even talked at length about her requesting a posting in London, but those were much sought after and highly unlikely at that point in her career. She would ask me to move closer to her, to leave London and join her in Wiltshire, but I'm a London boy through and through, despite my stints in Brighton and the States. I couldn't imagine being out in the countryside where Hannah was based. My mum lived here, my friends were here, *everything* was here. There were times when we both felt frustrated and hopeless for our future, but we just couldn't walk away from each other and hoped that, somehow, we would work it out.

Hannah

I was in Starbucks in Cardiff when I told my mum I was dating Jake. I showed her a photo of him and she was silent at first. She took a sip of her latte and said something like, 'Well, OK love. Take care of yourself.'

It was uncomfortable – there are no two ways about it. It wasn't a position we were used to being in together. We were still working out our relationship as mother and daughter. It was all pleasant and nice on the surface, but she was still adjusting to the new me. And we'd never had a conversation like this before. I'd never had a partner so it was all uncharted territory. I told her he was trans too, but I'm not sure that made it any easier for her.

I met Jake's best friends on his birthday, literally a week after we had our first date. At the time he used to have these big parties with karaoke and an open bar with his extended group of friends. He told me that he really wanted me there but wasn't ready to tell everyone that we were dating, which was fair enough as we hadn't even made it seven days by this point. So I went along as a friend. A few tequilas into the evening, however, Jake proudly put his arm around me and announced to everyone 'This is my girl!'

It was a very different vibe to my own social life because Jake's friends are such a diverse bunch. There were several actors and filmmakers, his best mate runs a high-end furniture company, another manages a hotel, it's just a real mix. Also his friends are very international because he went to the Lycée in London, and so there was French and Arabic and Spanish flying around.

Luckily for me, one thing the Army teaches is to be gregarious and outgoing. Not in a show-offy sense, but in the sense that you can socialise easily with a group of people you've never met. Certainly, one of the things I took from the Army is to be able to walk into a function, not know anyone and just go and introduce myself and start a conversation. I had to host loads of senior people in my role, so I had learnt to be a good host to other people and make sure they were well looked after. So being around Jake's mates didn't faze me particularly even though none of them really knew anyone with my sort of experience. They had a lot of questions for me and wanted to hear about my work, which was nice, so I didn't struggle with conversation. After dinner and a few drinks, we had a really lovely, laid-back evening and I even got on the karaoke machine and belted out 'American Pie'. That's my go-to karaoke song. I think I made a decent first impression despite my off-key singing.

Slightly more stressful was meeting his mum and step-father, David, only a week later at his family birthday outing. I drove us to this restaurant in south-west London to have dinner with them, and must admit to feeling pretty nervous in the lead-up. As luck would have it, they just happened to be walking up as I was parking. They noticed us, waved, then waited on the pavement, watching while I struggled to get my big BMW into this tiny spot. I wasn't used to London driving at all. Parallel parking is not something you need to do in the country! It was excruciating. Eventually they gave up and headed into the restaurant as I finally managed to fit my car into the space. A rather mortifying way to meet for the first time, but I had to roll with the punches.

It was a really nice dinner and the restaurant was where Jake and I eventually had our wedding reception, but the evening was fairly fraught with nerves and my desire to make a good impression. It was my first time meeting a guy's parents and, despite my usual confidence helping to keep the conversation flowing, it was quite nerve-wracking. What did make me relax was Jake waxing lyrical about me and my achievements, clearly proud to be there with me. Jake's uncles having served too gave us something in common and his mum was genuinely interested and really warm and welcom-ing, which meant a lot. She could clearly see that her son was happy and given their history that was obviously of paramount importance to her.

At the end of the evening I offered to drive them home and, after some very hasty tidying of my back seat, we dropped them around the corner and Jake popped into the house quickly. As we drove home and debriefed, Jake thanked me for braving the family. It felt like quite the achievement to have met his mother and apparently got the seal of approval. The complete lack of judgement around my trans identity also made the whole experience a lot less hair raising and I know we're very lucky to have been able to avoid all of that.

We talked often about kids and a family right from the start and Jake was always honest about his desire to be a father. His sister had two children and was already planning a third and, while Jake threw himself into being the much loved uncle, I know that he longed for parenthood. It was tough on him, seeing all of his friends and sister with their growing broods and feeling so far behind.

Neither of us wanted kids before marriage and we wanted to be absolutely solid in our relationship before we even considered 'forever'. With the pressures of living so far apart and my Army career, plus the time limits on Jake's embryos, there was a lot to overcome to get to that point. We were most definitely on the same page of wanting to enjoy just being us before committing and beginning a family and there was also a big part of me that felt some trepidation about becoming a mother. It all seemed so completely fantastical and something I had literally never thought possible. It was a challenge to really get my head around at first.

I think that after a year or so my priorities began to shift, as did my outlook and aspirations, although it took a while to fully make my peace with what that meant losing. I suppose that's how it all came to a head and I decided to leave the Army.

We'd been dating for about a year. Although we were spending every weekend together and I had even started driving in at least one night a week, we both knew that we couldn't keep going that way, that we both needed more. I guess we had reached make or break. I had exhausted all avenues for a London posting and things were taking off for Jake, with his filmmaking community mostly London based. To be honest, I'm not sure where else we could see ourselves living anyway. I was leaving later and later every Sunday and driving through the night to spend as much time with him as I could, but that was now becoming exhausting for both of us.

The sticking point though was my long-term aspiration of making Major. That had been my goal when I joined the Army, it being the first rank as an Officer where you are promoted purely on merit. You become a Second Lieutenant by passing Sandhurst and unless you do something wrong, the subsequent ranks of Lieutenant and Captain are based on your time of service. Then, after five years' service as a Captain, you become eligible for promotion to Major. You go to a promotion board where they assess you based on your reports and score you against your peers to decide whether or not you are ranked high enough to be selected to become a Major.

There was a big part of us both that longed for more stability and an end to the endless goodbyes, and I think Jake was starting to doubt that we would ever be more than a weekend romance. He knew how important it was for me to achieve my dream and was very frank that his biggest fear was my starting to resent him if I left without fulfilling that. We rumbled along until January of 2017, during which time I changed role to become the Adjutant of a REME Battalion (a traditional and prestigious role that basically doubles up as both the head of all administration for the unit and assistant to the Commanding Officer). In this role, it was looking very likely that I would deploy to Canada for a period of three months on exercise.

I know the thought terrified Jake but he tried to make the most of it.

'I'll come and visit you, we can ski and see some of the sights. We'll be fine!'

He quickly came back down to earth when I explained that I would be expected to behave as if we were in a conflict over there. No visits, no Skypes, no phone calls. Pretty much radio silence for 12 weeks. I know that Jake struggled with that. We spoke and texted all day, every day. The thought of no contact for three months seemed too tough, too cruel and Jake was very vocal about not wanting me to go.

How did I feel? Honestly, I was torn. I loved being in the Army, being on exercise, but things with Jake were serious now and I hoped that he was my future. I think Jake was terrified of what might happen during that time, and three months is undeniably a long time to go with only limited contact. I knew what Jake was hoping for from me: a clear sign that I was in this for keeps. And for him, that meant finding a way to remain in England.

As a soldier, there is very little that you can do to influence your deployments and I knew there was really only one sure-fire way to make it happen. So it fell upon me to make what was a very tough call, but one that had been a long time coming. The way the promotion system works for the Army is that you go through the assessment process and, a few months later, the results get released and you get told whether or not you've been selected for promotion to Major. I was very fortunate. I scored very highly and was selected in the top bracket of the promotion board, which felt like enough for me to feel that I had done my time, achieved more than I ever dreamt I would and could leave on a high. Despite knowing that it would mean that I never actually got to wear the rank of Major, the very next day I handed in my notice.

I of course felt sadness that we hadn't been able to find a way to have it all, but nevertheless I was excited about the future. A move to London, an imminent change of career and a very firm sign of our commitment to each other as we started to plan a home together. Jake was over the moon and clearly very touched by my decision. He spent weeks and months thanking me endlessly and I could feel a real shift and release in him, as he finally let himself believe that we had a future. The Army had given me a great start and made me the woman I am today and for a long while I firmly believed that it would be my first and last great love, but then Jake came along and I had to make that decision for our long-term future. And ultimately, I chose to be with Jake.

Jake

I've always been quite shy about meeting my friends' or partner's parents. I think that after years of just being generally awkward and introverted, I still have a way to go when it comes to feeling at ease with myself and I think I'll always have the feeling that I'm not good enough. All completely ridiculous for a man of my age, but unfortunately hard to shake! I think I delayed meeting Hannah's parents as long as I could, convinced that they wouldn't like me, until finally I had to bite the bullet. Of course, all of my fears were unfounded and they couldn't have been more welcoming.

Wendy, Brian and Jeff are so warm and easy going but honestly, I'm not sure I'll ever totally relax around them. I mean, they're the girl I like's parents, for goodness' sake! My upbringing was so different to Hannah's, but our family values are very similar. We both come from close, traditional family units, both have a sibling and were both fortunate to have parents who lived together. We also both grew up in homes where we felt slightly out of place, hiding who we really were, the odd one out in that traditional family sphere, and those feelings shaped us from an early age. Those similar experiences have meant that our own views on parenting have so far been fairly closely aligned, which has been important. Despite all of that, I still always feel like I'm on show when I'm around Hannah's parents and struggle hard against that. When your intention is to marry someone it's obviously vital that you get on with their family and I'm so grateful for the love and support that the Winterbournes have shown me over the years – we might have our differences but we have the most important thing in common – our love for Hannah and desire to protect her and make her happy.

Hannah's dad is brilliant. For our wedding he searched tirelessly for a tie in the trans flag colours and was so proud of himself when he found one. It was such a sweet gesture. As I got to know Hannah and we started to think about marriage, I decided to ask for her father's blessing before I proposed. I knew that Hannah would absolutely love it. We are more than aware that there are many people who will think the concept outdated, but for us the tradition of it all felt quite validating in our identities, if a little old fashioned. It also made Brian very happy and proud, although he was very clear that he had no ownership over Hannah and that it was entirely her choice, which I found very sweet.

One August morning in 2017, while Hannah was working her year's notice period from the Army, I made my way over to my mother's house for moral support. I would have liked to do it in person but Hannah's parents lived in Cardiff at the time, so it was quite a journey. After sitting on my mum's sofa, phone in hand, for two hours trying to get up the nerve, she finally exclaimed: 'For God's sake, darling, just get on with it!'

As I waited for Brian to answer, heart pounding, I practised what I would say and then, hearing his warm, friendly voice on the other end: 'Hi, Brian. How are you? I'm just calling because... Well, I was hoping to ask Hannah to marry me, and wondered if that might be OK with you... ?'

Brian laughed kindly. 'Of course you have my blessing. How exciting!' We briefly discussed my plans for when and where, before Brian told me a rather detailed story about his new lawnmower, which certainly took the edge off!

CHAPTER EIGHTEEN

The proposal

Hannah

Something was up. Jake had been acting so oddly. It was September 2017 and we were visiting New York, our happy place and spiritual home. We'd been to the city several times since we started dating, staying for two weeks at a time when we could. We'd rent an Airbnb in the Lower East Side, go out and have espresso in the morning, hit the gym and then just bounce between bars and restaurants, seeing friends late into the night. One of our favourite 'summer in Manhattan' rituals was waking up really early, getting a bagel at the local bodega, and then heading to Central Park so we could be at the boathouse just as they were opening. We would rent one of the boats and Jake would row us around. We'd be out there for hours, in the late summer sunshine, skyscrapers on one side and towering trees on the other, oblivious to the fellow boaters and our time allowance, just floating in our own little world. We'd share a warm bottle of cider and a bagel, take photos of the thousands of terrapins swimming around us and just relax. It was bliss. I was looking forward to our little tradition on this trip but, from the moment we'd arrived in New York two days prior, Jake had been on edge. We'd argued several times and he just didn't seem himself at all. I couldn't explain it. We had planned to go to the lake, and I caught him packing a rucksack in a really panicked way.

I've got to admit, I had an inkling of what was about to happen. You don't watch as many rom-coms as I have and not!

Is he going to do it? I wondered. *It feels like he is but he's being so cranky, maybe he's changed his mind?*

We rowed out onto the pond and an hour went by. Nothing. Two hours went by, nothing. I thought, *Oh OK, maybe not then*, and decided to just enjoy the afternoon, but eventually he rowed us nearer the shore, settling under a tree, dappled sun shining down through the leaves, and took a deep breath. Purely by chance there was a little band playing jazz on a wooden pagoda across the water and, when Jake shakily got down on one knee in the boat and pulled a tiny box out of his pocket, it felt a little bit like that Richard Curtis movie again.

'Hannah, I've got something to ask you. Will you marry me?'

I immediately welled up, swallowing a lump in my throat. I said yes through my tears, and he wrapped me in his arms, with a loud exhale and, apparently, a huge amount of relief. I felt him relax into me with all that pressure dissipating; obviously having built the moment up for weeks before, he was now finally able to smile. Very romantically, he had brought some red, heart-shaped balloons and a mini bottle of champagne and so we had a little toast and sat back in the boat, all anxiety gone, drifting in the breeze.

As we were rowing back, we passed another boat and its occupants spied our balloons and obvious elation. They asked us if we'd just got engaged. It was seemingly quite a popular spot for demonstrations of love and they kindly offered to take a photo of our special moment. The result is a beautiful shot of Jake and me in the middle of Central Park lake, beaming, in our little boat, as I show off the beautiful sparkler on my finger. It now hangs proudly in our hallway, a forever memory of one of Jake's most romantic gestures.

Once ashore and eager to share our news, we went to one of our favourite spots, Tavern on the Green, a short walk through the park. There, we had another toast, on the house, as we called our friends and family to fill them in. Everyone, obviously, was rapturous, especially Jake's mother and my parents.

They knew it was happening of course, as Jake had spoken to my dad. He relayed the phone call to me as we sat in the sun and, I have to confess, that made me tear up again. I know that he did it for my dad and me. He would have found the whole thing pretty mortifying, which made it even more meaningful to me.

The rest of the holiday was wonderful as we were both walking on air. Whenever we told people we'd just got engaged, they would scream and offer to take photos. We also racked up a fair few free drinks in our various regular spots, another bonus! One evening at sunset, we went out to Pier 45 and watched the weekly Sunset Salsa session, many of New York's older folk shimmying away as the sun went down. Jake thought it would make a great photo, down on one knee, the rays bouncing off the water, the sun a red ball behind us, and we re-enacted our special moment as a passer-by took a pic.

273

Suddenly we heard loud applause and as we turned around we saw that the dancers had stopped to watch, and were celebrating with us. It made us both smile and it seemed churlish to tell them that it was just for the camera! Jake was right though, it did make an amazing picture.

CHAPTER NINETEEN

The wedding

Jake

Since going through the rather difficult process of egg harvesting and fertilisation back in 2014, the embryos were pretty much always at the back of my mind. Recently they extended the legal storage time to 55 years, so maybe we didn't quite have the time pressures that we thought, but I was certainly ready to be a father by that point. Hannah had always said that once we were married she'd be as ready as she'd ever be, so we knew that post marriage, that would be our next step. But first, we had a wedding to plan.

We decided to aim for the following March. Hannah didn't want a winter wedding and we needed time to pull everything together, plus it's Hannah's birthday month so we thought that would be a good tie-in! Hannah wanted a big, country wedding, possibly in a stately home or similar. She also wanted a military element, like many of her friends who had gone for full-on military pomp, but we quickly realised that those sorts of weddings were a little pricey for us! I wanted Hannah to have everything that she desired, particularly as she had never thought that she would end up in love or married and it felt important for her to have her dream; we just had a tough choice to make: big, expensive wedding or hopes of surrogacy and children.

At that stage, we knew we couldn't have it all and even Hannah couldn't justify spending thousands on one day when every penny would be needed elsewhere. So, we made our peace with a smaller wedding and began to plan accordingly. One of the trickiest aspects of something less grandiose was trying to whittle our many friends and extended family down to a manageable number, no mean feat. That in itself took months, much bickering and many awkward decisions and conversations. Added to that finding a suitably magical wedding venue and affordable restaurant for the reception and we really had our work cut out. In December 2017, while we were negotiating all of these potential pitfalls, I went over to Paris for my friend Jeremie's 40th birthday weekend.

While I was there I planned to visit my aunt, Berthe, now in her mid-eighties and living on the outskirts of Paris. Having witnessed her parents being forcibly removed by the Nazis in 1939, aged just seven, she had a nervous breakdown and found herself in a mental institute for over a decade, her life shattered by the murder of her parents and the antisemitism that even now continues to permeate our society. We had been in touch sporadically over the years and although my sister had remained in close contact, she had repeatedly declined visits from me after hearing of my transition. Now, frail and struggling, she finally needed as much help as she could get, and I rallied.

I'd been in touch with an older Jewish cousin called Sylvie

who lived in Paris and had arranged to meet her on the Saturday morning, to head over to Neuilly to visit Berthe.

We knocked loudly on the door and waited. No answer. We knocked again and shouted her name. 'She doesn't leave the house, so she's got to be inside,' said Sylvie. It was December and freezing cold in Paris. We started to get desperate, hammering on the door. 'Berthe, Berthe!', and that's when we heard a faint moan coming from behind the door. She'd fallen over and had been trapped semi-conscious for two days, unable to get up or open the door.

I ran to a local locksmith's and had them come and smash the door in. Behind it, crumpled on the floor, was my aunt, confused and dehydrated but still able to smile as she recognised us. I gently lifted her and she felt as frail as a bird in my arms. If we hadn't gone that day she would probably have died alone on her floor, a truly horrific thought after the life she'd led.

We called the ambulance and rode with her to hospital in nearby Courbevoie, as she clutched my hand. At the hospital she was whisked off through swing doors, and I quickly realised the limits of my French, which was fluent as long as it was the heavily slang-influenced dialect of my Lycée days. I knew none of the medical jargon nor much of her medical history, so felt very fortunate that Sylvie was there to jump in. We waited several hours, Sylvie eventually heading home, but when I was finally allowed to go through and see her I will always remember her giving me the sweetest, most grateful smile, pulling me to her and not letting go. When the doctor came in, she proudly said: 'This is my nephew. He rescued me,' which broke my heart a little.

No one likes hospitals, but there was something particularly clinical and businesslike about the French system that truly made our wonderful NHS shine in comparison. Add to that my crash course in medical terminology and the whole experience was a little overwhelming, but I never for a second entertained the notion of leaving her.

I've always had a real soft spot for old people, possibly due to my absolute devotion to my grandmother. If I see someone elderly struggling in the street, I'll always stop and help and will go out of my way to strike up conversation with lonelier-looking older folk in the supermarket or on the bus, most of whom gladly engage. One of my favourite things pre-kids was volunteering on Christmas Day with the elderly community of Wandsworth for the Rotary Club Christmas Day bash, doing a big festive lunch for 400 residents. As soon as the girls are old enough, that will become an annual family outing, and I hope to instil in them the same respect for our elderly folk that I had growing up. I can't, however, claim to have much stoicism or stiff upper lip when I see older people ill or in pain, and I really struggled at first when my aunt was put on a ward populated almost entirely by women, many lost to dementia, battling cancer, diabetes or simply abandoned by family. It was absolutely heartbreaking and I spent many moments fighting back tears, but there was no way I could just leave and forget about her there and so determined to be as present as I possibly could. Between my sister and me, we were there every single week as the days quickly became weeks.

I began to plan my diary around the visits to Paris, the wedding and my day job filling the rest of my time. I would lie awake worrying about Berthe being on that ward on her own. Certainly there was an element of my own baggage and guilt tied up in my commitment to being there for her, but this was my family, lying in a bed alone on that bleak ward of death.

Over Christmas and the holidays, Chloe and I were there for days on end. Hannah was on gardening leave from the Army by then and was an incredible support. She never once questioned why it was so important for me to be there and even joined me several times. It was very difficult to witness my aunt suffering, too weak to stand and with no desire to eat.

'I just want to go home,' she would cry.

'Don't worry. You will, you just need to get your strength back up,' I'd reassure her.

She was already severely underweight and stood no chance of leaving unless that changed. I'd bring baskets of pastries and chocolates and cakes for the whole ward when I visited, handing them out with wild abandon until one of the nurses pointed out that many of the patients were diabetic and sugar could kill them. After that I made a point of double checking who I was giving them to, and hoped I hadn't done too much damage! Berthe would eat chocolate eclairs and little else, but it was better than nothing. Between my sister's visits, mine and my cousin, Sylvie's, Berthe survived for three months on French pastries and water.

I remember the first time Hannah came with me to visit. I was really nervous that this fairly grumpy, closed-minded old woman would realise that Hannah was trans and possibly comment on her deep voice and make Hannah feel awkward, but she greeted her like a lost friend. I left the room for a minute and when I came back they were sitting holding hands, Berthe speaking to her in broken English, telling her about her favourite music. It was all rather touching. Afterwards, when Hannah had to return to London, Berthe said to me: 'La belle blonde, when is she coming back?'

Hannah visited with me quite regularly after that and, although it was always hard going at the hospital, it meant a lot to us all to be there together. We'd dig out old French songs from the 1940s and 1950s to play Berthe on Spotify. We'd read to her or just chat about her past, though she rarely mentioned her parents. One day a priest happened through the ward, offering to bless her. She smiled and politely declined but as he left, she said: 'I thought you were going to tell them I was Jewish. Don't tell anyone.' Her fear of the Nazis still haunted her, 80 years later.

When we were there she was cheerful, chatty and really came alive, but we knew that she was allowing herself to fade when she was alone. Hannah and I would get Berthe vitamin drinks and protein shakes, but getting her to drink them was a battle. She could barely see, with cataracts in both eyes. I watched as the strength began to drain from her body, desperate to get her better, to get her home.

All of that aside, Paris and our errands of mercy really brought Hannah and me together. Paris in winter was beautiful, sparkling lights everywhere, crowds of elegant people sitting out on the 'terraces' under heaters watching the world go by, and even some heavy snow that made the city look like a postcard. I headed back to Paris on Boxing Day and Hannah came out to join me a few days later. Despite the worry hanging over us, I think back very fondly to that time as it was just us, in a foreign city, the long hospital visits bookended by intimate breakfasts and romantic dinners. Knowing that Hannah was by my side throughout gave me an anchor like I'd never had before. With her, wherever we were in the world, it felt like home, and we were closer than we'd ever been.

The wedding planning was stressful, but a welcome distraction. We would spend evenings in our various little rented Airbnbs in Paris, or on the Eurostar home, dreaming up ways to make it as special as possible on our shoe string budget. An old actor friend who used to drive buses sorted out a double-decker to ferry our guests from wedding to reception. Another friend did the flowers at cost price. My suit was kindly loaned, as was Hannah's dress. We cut corners anywhere we could. My stepfather generously offered to pay for the reception, a massive load off our mind, and Hannah's parents covered the wedding venue.

We had a cap of 40 guests including us, so that made for some very tough choices, many of which we weren't happy about but we had to be ruthless. We both had to leave out some of our oldest friends and extended family, the surrogacy and the associated costs always on our minds. Most of our friends and family didn't have to plan for costs close to £25,000 when having their first babies, so they all understood the difficulty of our choices. Still, a few people felt hurt that they weren't there.

We decided on having the wedding at the Chelsea Old Town Hall, a non-denominational venue in the heart of Chelsea. My mother got married there, as did my best friend, and Hannah and I drove past it several times a week and always saw the happiest brides on the steps, confetti thick in the air. It felt very 'us'. Plus there was a long list of celebrities who had tied the knot there, not that Hannah had heard of most of them. I read that Patsy Kensit was one, and as she was one of my very first crushes when, aged five, I had seen her on stage in a production of *Cinderella*, that seemed particularly exciting to me. Hannah, of course, couldn't have cared less, and I loved her for that. She was like, 'Who the hell is Patsy Kensit?'

The back and forths to Paris were a bi-weekly thing now, my sister doing one in two, and I had become very familiar with the city that had been my father's childhood home, my French flooding back as I learnt my way around the Metro and buses. By February, Berthe's condition had deteriorated further, and the doctors had found cancer on her lung.

'Please don't tell her. Just let her get stronger first,' I pleaded with the doctors. I knew that Berthe was tired, more than fed up of her hospital bed and looking for a reason to let go. Of course, the doctors told her and three days later she slipped away. I was devastated not to be by her bedside as she left us, but for the first time I knew that I had done all I could. My sister, Hannah and I had been with her throughout, and shown her that she was loved right until the end. All that was left was to bury her.

In the Jewish faith, just as in Islam, you have a funeral within 24 hours. My sister and her husband joined Hannah and me at a small Jewish burial ground on the outskirts of Paris on a grey day in early March. The rabbi paid his respects; the whole thing was over in an hour. Finally, Berthe

Graf, who saw her parents taken away when she was seven years old and had waited her entire life to see them again, was at peace.

The next week or so was difficult and I struggled between crushing grief and sadness and joy at our impending marriage. I pulled myself together for Hannah, who had been my rock those past months, and resolved to try to enjoy every moment as we readied ourselves for the big day.

Hannah and I had slept apart the night before but met on the morning of the wedding to pick up our cake and drop it off at the restaurant where we were having the reception. In another money-saving manoeuvre, we had worked out that if we bought two normal cakes and placed them on top of each other, rather than buying an official 'wedding cake', we'd save over £300. Hummingbird Bakery duly produced one rainbow and one salted caramel delight, which our friend Amalia helped us mount and decorate with fresh flowers, and we were wedding ready. It being so close to Easter, I also bought a little Easter Bunny cupcake and plonked it on top, which drove Hannah mad. Now we had three tiers!

I got ready with the boys at my mum's house in Parson's Green, where she had moved with my stepfather a few years after they married. I had gone for the full traditional wedding ensemble, cravat, tails, waistcoat, all the things that I had dreamt of wearing as a young trans boy, now a firm reality. As I did up the shirt buttons and Pavlo straightened my tie, I still felt utterly disbelieving that I was about to be a married man, and Hannah was about to become Mrs Graf. For a fleeting moment, I allowed myself to feel proud of everything that I had achieved and, cautiously, very excited for our future together.

*   *   *

Hannah walked down the aisle to the Christina Perri song 'A Thousand Years'. It was planned that she would enter as the chorus hit, but we hadn't really prepared for the length of the intro, so I was standing there, looking nervously at the door at the back of the room, hoping she would appear. My sister helpfully mouthed, 'Do you think she's done a runner?' That obviously helped calm my already jangling nerves!

Hannah finally entered to the lyrics

> *I have died everyday waiting for you*
> *Darling, don't be afraid, I have loved you for a thousand*
>   *years*
> *I'll love you for a thousand more...*

As I took her in, hair up and accentuating her long, slim neck, in the most stunning dress imaginable, shyly smiling at me, I was surprised when my eyes filled with tears. Hannah also welled up as she walked towards me and I felt like the luckiest man alive. Her bouquet of flowers, pink, white and blue, mirrored the colours of the trans flag; her dress was pure white.

As she came to stand next to me, we beamed at each other, turning to the registrar as we were married in front of a room full of our family and friends. It seemed so completely far-fetched, unexpected and fantastical for these two trans people who grew up fearing that they would never even be tolerated to be so visibly celebrated in this way. It was perfect, and Hannah and I barely heard the words as we grinned incredulously at each other, completing our vows.

Just before we were pronounced husband and wife, my best man, Guy, one of the boys I'd looked after for so long, produced the glass that we had carefully selected to break after the ceremony, a throwback to my Jewish roots, and, as we said, '*I do*', we stamped on the glass, breaking it underfoot as the room erupted in cheers.

We were married!

*   *   *

Some weeks prior, we had agreed to let the *Sun* newspaper cover our wedding and worked with them on a short interview. Sharing our story seemed like an amazing opportunity to spread some trans joy and show the world that love and happiness was possible for people like us. The *Sun* has an incredible reach and we saw it as a chance to show its readers that we are just like everyone else and deserve to be treated with the same respect. A photographer from the paper took some pictures as we left the town hall and we thought no more of it, expecting a small feature in the lifestyle pages at the weekend. Once they were gone, we took hundreds of family photos, everyone beaming proudly, the passing cars beeping and shouting their congratulations, a fairly standard occurrence on wedding days. The big red double-decker bus arrived with free-flowing Prosecco on board and, as our guests departed, Hannah and I stayed behind with our amazing photographer, Paul Grace. He took some stunning shots before Hannah finally gave in to the cold and the dark and we hopped in a cab to our reception venue.

The reception was in a lovely, local Italian restaurant in Fulham. It was pretty surreal walking into a room filled with many of our closest family and friends, to be announced as *Mr and Mrs Graf*! Everyone stood and cheered for us, the bride and groom: an unforgettable feeling.

Dinner was lovely, intimate and laid back, no airs and graces. All of the speeches were incredibly moving, my mother's and Hannah's father's in particular, but Guy's speech stole the show. He was 11 years old at the time and just the most brilliant orator. It was hilarious and pitch perfect. He knew me so well and had everyone in hysterics. Then his younger brother, Raf, got out his viola and gave us a rendition of 'Under the Sea' from *The Little Mermaid*, and brought the house down. Our first dance was Guns and Roses' 'Sweet Child of Mine', followed by Metallica's 'Nothing Else Matters', a nod to our rock roots, then everyone joined us as we danced into the night, bouncing around on cloud nine.

A couple of days after the wedding we were sent the article from the *Sun* for copy approval, and were pleased to see that it was a lovely piece, sensitively handled. We were rather predictably still buzzing from our nuptials. It had been such a special day and having our families there celebrating us and our love for each other had been amazing. We had a honeymoon in Tel Aviv to look forward to and beyond that the much anticipated beginning of our surrogacy journey.

Then our agent called. She had received news that our interview would be out tomorrow, and that, rather than nestling in the lifestyle pages, it was to be featured on the front page.

Yikes. Front page.

Obviously, we had decided to share our story but we knew that being on front page of the nation's most read newspaper was going to make some waves. Our main concern was the headline that would accompany our supportive, sensitive and well-written interview. They are crafted to grab attention and sell newspapers, so, understandably, we felt some trepidation.

We waited up for the online version to come out just before midnight, but even we were unprepared for what we saw.

Just under a beautiful photo of Hannah and me leaving the Town Hall, beaming with utter joy, in our finest, was the headline:

TRAN AND WIFE.

CHAPTER TWENTY

A change is gonna come

Hannah

The headline was a great shame. It very much marred all of the great work put in by the writer. Everybody we spoke to said we had to distance ourselves from it, and we knew they were right. We had hoped to put out a story of hope, love, acceptance and joy, but once more our community was the butt of the joke, the very last thing we wanted. We put out a statement on Twitter, detailing the great interview and subsequent respectful interactions, but clarifying that we were very disappointed by the headline. We also apologised to the community for it belittling our broader experience.

And then, for whatever reason, maybe just a slow news day, the tweet went viral. We had politicians pick it up, the UK LGBT press and then the US LGBT press. It went as far as the Australian and Russian press and gained so much traction that we were getting media requests from across the world. It quickly stopped being about the 'Tran and Wife' headline, and started focusing on the story of a trans couple getting married, surrounded by their family and friends.

The next day it was on the front page of the *Telegraph* and the *Express*, with articles about us in *The Times* and the *Daily*

Mail. It was quite ridiculous. It made it seem like we were the first trans couple to ever get married, which, of course, wasn't the case, it was just an easy narrative for the media to perpetuate. Even today, we're frequently referred to as the UK's first trans parents, no matter how many times we tell journalists how inaccurate that is.

Of course, that kind of exposure was hard to shy away from and we lost a lot of our anonymity after that. If our neighbours, local barista or postman hadn't realised we were trans before, they certainly did now. Rather encouragingly, several of those people made a point of telling us that they'd seen the story and that they were happy for us, which meant a lot.

*   *   *

After the wedding and nearly a decade living in single quarters, I was afforded the privilege of military married quarters, which meant a four-bedroom house in Camberley, just outside of London. It was in a very rural area near Sandhurst and to Jake at least, felt like the countryside proper. It certainly wasn't anything fancy but it gave us space that we'd only dreamt of before, and a welcome break from Jake's tiny flat in Barnes. It had a big garden and behind it you could even see wild deer prancing through the woods. It was definitely unlike anywhere he had lived before and was an exciting addition, despite knowing we would only have it for six months, as I worked out my remaining time in the Army.

It was certainly fun playing at being Mr and Mrs Graf at what Jake called 'The Country Pile'. We knew it would be short-lived, so enjoyed it while we could. We'd invite friends and their kids over for weekends and run around the massive garden playing with Nerf Guns. It was fun, but we never fully settled. Those last few months felt a little like living in limbo and I was eager to begin our 'real life' as a married couple in London, ready to expand my world in a whole new way.

As the end of my contract approached and I began to wind things down at work, I realised that adjusting to civilian life wouldn't be easy either. As I handed in my military ID for the last time, I felt a slight panic, but I've always loved a challenge and tried to think of it as such. A new start, a new home, a new life as a married woman and 10-year Army veteran. I knew I was leaving behind so many things that I would miss, not least of all the people who were like family to me, but equally there were benefits to civilian life, particularly the sense of freedom.

By its nature, the military lifestyle dictates everything from what fitness sessions you have to do, to where you live or whether you have to spend your summer on a deployment abroad. Now, I could ground myself, with Jake, and focus on building our home and our family. I certainly relished having a lot more control over my life than I ever had before.

*   *   *

My last few days were strange. I had changed postings twice in my last year and found myself floating without a regular team and so no fuss was made as I left after a decade of service. No last drinks or dinner nor really any sort of fanfare. One day I just went in for the last time, said my goodbyes, and there it was. The end of my military career. More of a whimper than a bang, but I barely had time to mourn it as I leapt straight into meetings and interviews to kickstart the next phase of my life. As I pushed my uniforms to the back of my wardrobe, I wondered if I would ever get the chance to wear them again.

Then, on 30 December 2018, three years to the day Jake and I had our first date, we were driving to see my parents in Cardiff, the phone rang and I answered on hands free.

'Is this Hannah Graf?' a voice asked. *'I am calling from the Army's press team and we were hoping you could give a comment as there are a few media outlets reporting on your MBE, following the release of the New Year Honours List. Could we get a few words?'*

I remember Jake and me looking at each other, shocked, before Jake, wide-eyed, slapped my leg and mouthed:

'OH MY GOD. You're getting an MBE!'

As this was the first I'd heard of it, I responded awkwardly that I wasn't aware that I had been given an MBE (with all my different postings and changes of office, the news had somehow slipped through the gaps and I hadn't been officially notified), but managed to give a short statement expressing my shock and gratitude, acknowledging all the trans people who came before me, before hanging up and turning to Jake.

He Googled the list as I drove, confirming that I was indeed receiving an MBE for my services towards the military's LGBTQIA+ community. Despite it feeling completely surreal, I knew that somehow, someone had nominated me and it wasn't just a joke. I was overwhelmed, thrilled, disbelieving. And couldn't wait to get home to tell my parents.

After the official announcement of my award and despite

the ceremony not taking place until June, things really took off. We were getting lots of offers to do press, public speaking and influencer work, but I wanted the stability of a job with a regular salary, something I'd always had and come to count on. I was slightly concerned that all the front page news coverage we were getting would hinder my chances of being hired by a financial institution, which was where I saw my future career outside of the military, but it appeared that our story hadn't filtered through to the banking sector! I was networking anywhere I could, trying to find a connection who could help me get a foot in the door. I knew several fellow veterans who had found work in finance and hoped that I might be afforded one of those same opportunities. Soon enough, through a series of meetings I was interviewing for HSBC, a bank that has a great track record of diversity and inclusion and looked like a good fit. I must admit to feeling quite the sense of relief when I was offered my very first position outside of the Army, and looked forward to my first day in January 2019.

The next step was making our first home together and, despite finding ourselves very attached to our Barnes stomping ground, we knew that Jake's little flat wasn't big enough for us to really make a home. One of Jake's old school friends, Calandra, stepped in to help and mentioned that her mother had a lovely flat to let in Streatham in south London. It came with a shared garden and great travel connections to my new job. We were sold.

Moving Jake out of his home of 10 years was quite the undertaking. He's not great with change and that flat had been where we'd spent our first night together, got to know each other and eventually fallen in love, and it was filled with happy memories of our first years. Still, even he knew it was time to move on. My life had only ever been nomadic, it was all I had ever really known since the age of 16, so packing up our Camberley house was pretty much a non-event for me, just another stepping stone to our life together.

We were both aware that this would be the first time we had properly lived together, in a place that was ours, as opposed to his or mine, and that adjustments would need to be made. As Jake often said during those first few months, 'There's a reason people try living together before they get married!'

It was a real baptism of fire after both living as singletons for so many years, but once we found our groove we came to love our little garden flat, our first shared home. I soon found my feet in my new job and learnt quickly that I loved the challenges and pressures of the world of finance. I suppose I was very fortunate that I had adapted so quickly, because the next step in our lives as a couple would present hurdles and struggles that we could never have imagined. Starting a family.

CHAPTER TWENTY-ONE

Surrogacy

Jake & Hannah

Jake

As we tentatively set forth into the world of surrogacy, we'd both admit to having had absolutely no clue what we were doing. On our honeymoon in Tel Aviv we had met a gay couple who had just had their first child via surrogacy and highly recommended a US agency that had been great for them. When we returned to England, Hannah and I excitedly got on a Skype call with them and quickly had the wind knocked out of our sails when they quoted costs of up to $110K, well outside of our capabilities. We then looked at some of the British agencies. Fees were considerably less, but still running to the £50K mark. The main problem there was a lot of empty promises and false hope.

Unfortunately, in the UK there are relatively few women who want to act as surrogates, mostly due to how the law is laid out: when the child is born, regardless of whose egg, sperm or embryo it was, the surrogate is the legal parent. She isn't even able to legally transfer those rights until six weeks after the birth, a 'cooling off' period if you will. That means that surrogates are often fearful that the intended parents (IPs) might decide at the last minute that they no longer want the child, leaving the surrogate quite literally 'holding the baby', and, of course, the intended parents worry that their surrogate might decide, upon birth, to keep the child. It's a very tricky situation with long-promised updates to these laws yet to materialise.

We then tried going online, onto the various Facebook surrogacy groups where admittedly many matches are made, but it does feel like an unregulated 'Wild West' with some real horror stories alongside the myriad tales of successful births and arrangements. The other problem here was that the sheer despair of so many of the IPs, coupled with the tiny numbers of surrogates, meant that 'competition' was beyond fierce, with some IPs spending hours a day online courting potential surrogates, time that Hannah and I just didn't have. After many months and dead ends, Hannah and I popped onto the *Lorraine* sofa on ITV one morning and spoke of life as a newly married couple, as well as of our quest to find a surrogate. After the show, we were amazed to receive about 20 messages on our social media from women who wanted to help us to become parents. Another 10 contacted the show directly. While most of these came to nothing, through an old Facebook contact we were told of a paediatric nurse from Belfast who had seen our story and wanted to help. By then, we were somewhat jaded and knew that there was much talk and little action when it came to finding someone to commit to carrying your baby, but we duly scheduled a Skype call with Laura, trying not to get our hopes up again.

A week later on a Tuesday evening in late winter, we met

Laura, a recently separated mother of two from Northern Ireland. I remember one of our first questions was 'Why? Why would you want to give us this absolute ultimate gift?' Hannah and I were incredulous that anyone would be kind enough to help a transgender couple start a family and wanted to understand Laura's motivation. She told us that she had wanted to be a surrogate since having nearly carried a child for a family member 12 years prior and that it had since been her dream. Laura was so open, so frank about it all, that it didn't feel awkward to be discussing something so personal and intimate. We talked for an hour, and even on that first call we really clicked. She told us about her family, her work, and it all came very naturally to be discussing making a baby together. Although on that first meeting we didn't want to put any pressure on Laura, she made it very clear from day one that this was something that she was serious about and very keen to do, which was exactly where we were at. We all understood that this wasn't just talk, and the excitement soon began to build.

The second call a few days later was a little more in depth. We discussed timings, had some very candid chats about how involved in our lives Laura would want to be if we were successful and even talked about what would happen if the embryo developed abnormally or Hannah and I died as Laura was still carrying the baby. Quite the rollercoaster, but all absolutely necessary. Laura also found it hilarious when she would openly discuss her periods and cycle and I'd squirm having to talk about something so very personal to her. Nothing fazed her at all, which made everything a bit easier and made us warm to each other even more. I think it was on that second call, having tried to hold back and keep things casual, that Laura asked if we really wanted to do this, and we both beamed, incredulous that this amazing woman was offering to go on this journey with us. 'Absolutely!', we replied.

The next step was to meet Laura in the flesh and introduce her to the team at The London Women's Clinic. I remember picking her up at Gatwick Airport and sharing a big hug, blown away at what we were about to do. We named ourselves Team Unicorn, and hoped that the magic of this mythical animal would seep into our first attempt at becoming parents. More importantly, spending two days together in London really cemented our relationship and made us all the more determined to give this a proper try.

In July of that same year Laura had a single embryo transferred at the clinic. The lead-up was fraught as nerves built, and when the day came Hannah and I were both pretty tense. Laura, of course, was totally laid back as ever, and smiled her way through.

'Just think positive thoughts,' she told me.

I think she found my nervous energy quite funny, but the stakes for me did feel particularly high.

Hannah and I wanted to be in the room for the transfer and stood behind Laura, preserving her modesty. As they pulled out the syringe there was a spray of liquid across the room. I panicked, of course, convinced that it had been the embryo flying through the air. The nurses reassured me that it was just the solution they use during the procedure and pointed at the screen. The embryo was safely implanted in Laura's uterus. The doctors were brilliant throughout, calming and professional while also trying to manage our

expectations. We knew the statistics and the one-in-two likelihood of a pregnancy didn't fill me with confidence, but those
were our odds. Despite my nerves, I'm sure they had seen
worse than me, and I'll always be glad that Hannah was by
my side, holding my hand. To be honest, it had always worried
me that we only had five embryos. I would rather have had 10
or more, because once they were gone that was it – our chance
to have my biological children would be gone too. I know
now, however, that five is a great number and that many other
people aren't so lucky, and I will always be grateful for that.

Once the transfer was done, there was nothing to do but
settle in for the 12-day wait until Laura could do a pregnancy
test. It was pretty tough, and as someone who struggles with
patience, I was worried, tetchy and anxious, while Hannah
became quiet and withdrawn. I would catch her Googling
things about early signs of pregnancy and then messaging
Laura for updates. At night we clung to each other, whispering reassuring nonsense, daring to imagine what it might feel
like to lie with our baby between us, neither of us really
believing that it was possible. Work went out the window
and the days felt like weeks.

Finally the morning came to take the test and see if Laura
was pregnant. At 9 a.m., we joined our scheduled Skype call,
Laura relaxed as ever, Hannah cautiously hopeful, while I
steeled myself for the worst. Laura had already done the test
and replaced the stick into its little wrapper, so, when we
were all ready, she slowly pulled it out before holding it up
to the camera. Peering at the screen, we were able to make
out two red lines. Two red lines! Laura was pregnant with
our baby. We had done it. The first step of our miraculous

journey to parenthood. Hannah and I burst into tears and Laura just smiled knowingly at us, as though there had never been doubt in her mind.

And then, in true Jake fashion, I asked her to go and do the test again.

*　　*　　*

From the beginning, the pregnancy went smoothly. Hannah had an app on her phone that kept track of how big the baby was compared to different fruits. A grape, a plum, a mango. I think it was nice for her to feel involved, and, while she spoke of 'the odds' and the science of it all, I just tried not to worry, mostly failing. We flew to Northern Ireland for the 12- and 20-week scans to be by Laura's side and see how our baby was growing and developing. Honestly, it was difficult being so far away, not being able to feel or rub the bump and have that physical connection. We tried our best not to plague Laura with calls and texts but she was always very patient and understanding when we were a bit full-on. Ahead of each scan Hannah and I were bouncing off the walls, convinced something would be wrong. Laura, as ever, was calm personified. She'd done this twice before smoothly and without issue.

I squeezed Hannah's hand as the nurse put the gel on Laura's tummy and began the ultrasound that would confirm whether our baby had a heartbeat, that everything was progressing as it should. At first, there was nothing, just lots of indistinct rumblings and shapes. We all held our breath. Then, suddenly, life. The tiny little heartbeat of our daughter filled the air with its rhythmical pounding and we all welled up, beaming through our tears, and breathed a collective sigh of relief. Thus far, all was well.

The 20-week scan, equally nerve-wracking, went just as smoothly. As the nurse ran the scanner over Laura's bump, we saw our baby's head, eyes, heart, brain, organs, once again saying silent 'Thank Yous' to anyone who was listening.

Back in London, we began to prepare in earnest for the birth of our child. Prior to the scan, my own superstitions had prevented me from truly allowing myself to believe that this was real, but now it felt imminent and I could no longer hold back from throwing myself all in. As we began tentatively buying baby clothes and a cot, winter slowly melting into spring, something turned our world, the whole world, upside down. Covid-19. The pandemic.

*   *   *

Lockdown.

That word feels so familiar now, etched into our brains and leaving decades of trauma in its wake, but at the time we just didn't know what was happening. We had been so entirely and utterly caught up in our baby dream that we hadn't really noticed the proliferation of masks on the streets of London, nor the rapidly climbing global death toll, but suddenly it was unavoidable. And terrifying. Hannah and I carried on with our everyday lives, work and baby prep and planning for the birth, but now the government was talking about travel bans and curfews and we were hundreds of miles away from our child.

Hannah switched into Army mode, well-placed to do so as she was receiving updates from her old military family, who advised that we head straight to Belfast, and quickly. The prime minister's announcement on the evening of 23 March 2020, our second wedding anniversary, filled us with terror that we would miss our baby's birth. We leapt into action, packing into the night, trying to remember everything we would need to welcome a baby into an Airbnb in Belfast where we would be staying indefinitely. I got online just as many accommodations were pulling themselves off the site, and luckily found a little house just on the outskirts of the city, near the hospital.

The next morning, just after dawn, we left our house in Streatham, stopping only to drop spare keys with my mum on the way, and tore off up to Holyhead, to catch the ferry across the water. Five hundred miles and twelve hours later, we arrived in Belfast at 2 a.m. on Hannah's birthday and hunkered down, scared and worried and lost, just like the rest of the world.

The best-laid plans of mice and men...

For eight months we had planned our time in Belfast: day trips with Laura and her kids, lunches and dinners and 'getting to know you' time. Laura had kindly offered to have us in the room as she gave birth, something that felt particularly important to Hannah, as the baby's mother, and we had even determined who would hold her first, give her her first bottle, do the first skin to skin. Lockdown derailed all of that.

Our Airbnb was lovely, cosy and comfortable with a little garden, and minutes from a beautiful glen, but because of all the Covid rules we couldn't see Laura, who was isolating at home. Hannah and I were also terrified of catching the virus because it would mean that we wouldn't be able to be there or take care of our baby after the birth. We only left the house to shop, carefully wiping down every item when we returned home, unsure of what to do or how to stay safe, as hundreds of thousands of people died across the world. Hannah and I became closer than ever, away from our families and friends at one of the most nerve-wracking times in our lives, counting down the days until our baby was born, terrified that we wouldn't be there for her birth or aftercare.

Hannah

I had a lot of time to reflect on things while we were in lockdown in Belfast. I worried about whether I would have a mother's instinct. Would I be able to bond with this child? Would it matter that I couldn't breastfeed?

The root of my anxiety was mainly that I'm a transgender woman. So much weight is put on the hormones, the pregnancy, the bonding – the innate motherhood. I just assumed that I would be lacking all those things and thought often about what it meant to be a *natural* mother.

Will I be able to do all the things that other women do with their children? I wondered.

We were making a documentary with Channel 4 about surrogacy at the time, and you can see in that film how much I wanted to be involved with what Laura was going through at every step of the way. I vividly remember hearing that we wouldn't be able to be in the room with Laura as our baby was being born and my worry only growing. I think Jake was less concerned with that aspect, only really caring that our baby came into the world healthy and safely, but then these were his embryos, his genetic tie. Plus, I'm sure that there are many dads who don't necessarily want to be in the room if it's their own wife giving birth, let alone a woman who isn't!

Looking back now, I realise my anxiety was hugely exacerbated by being in lockdown and fear of the pandemic and that had all become commingled with normal first-time parent worries. Regardless, I understood the reasons why only one person would be allowed in with Laura at the birth, and it made total sense that it would be her best friend, Gillian. After all, Laura's comfort and safety was paramount. Realising quickly that plans were out of the window, we allowed ourselves to relax a bit, and played the waiting game.

Jake

On Easter Sunday, 12 April 2020, Laura was induced. We were very much ready for action by then, bags packed and route to the hospital programmed into Google maps. Induction usually gets things moving pretty quickly. Not so in our case. For the next 40 hours we paced up and down our Airbnb, Hannah going out for runs in the glen, as I hiked up a nearby hill and watched as morning turned to afternoon, no change in Laura's condition. With no direct line to Laura, her lovely birthing partner, Gillian, kept us updated by WhatsApp.

Laura's waters broke the following day, 13 April, but still no baby, nor sign of contractions. Gillian told us not to worry, that the doctors weren't concerned, but it was hard not to sit and fret at what might be happening some 20 miles away.

Finally, at 5.30 a.m. on 14 April as we lay sleepless in bed, our phones pinged simultaneously with the message:

'She's here and she's healthy.'

Gillian had also sent a collection of photos from the delivery room of our little girl, covered in blood and screaming blue murder, healthy and fighting. We paused briefly in wonder, shedding a few tears, then threw on our clothes, ran out to the car and drove through the deserted streets of Belfast to meet our daughter for the first time. Pulling into Ulster Hospital at 6 a.m., it was like a ghost town. Large blocks closed and in total darkness, yellow emergency tape across many of the doorways, not a soul in sight. It felt reminiscent of the opening scene of the movie *28 Days Later*, utterly deserted. As we tried to find a way into maternity, I called up to the ward, asking how we might find our baby. The nurse on the phone correctly but frustratingly told us that as we weren't our baby's legal parents yet, she couldn't tell us where she was. We simply had to wait. By this point we were exhausted, not having slept properly in days, and then had to sit in the dark reception for three hours to be let in, desperate to find Laura and our baby and unable to even ascertain which ward she was in. Hannah broke down, and I could only sit and hold her, alone in the hospital lobby. Suddenly, we heard a warm Irish lilt from above as one of the nurses, now filled in on our situation, came down to get us. Relief flooded our bodies as we excitedly climbed the stairs.

As we waited in our own little room off the labour ward, anticipation now through the roof, Laura was wheeled in looking exhausted but happy, with this little bundle in her arms. She handed it to me, and there she was – our daughter.

We all cried, Hannah and I repeating our endless thanks to Laura, who, after a long labour that ended in a caesarean, just wanted to sleep. After many hugs and more tears, she was wheeled out to her own private room. I fed Millie her first bottle, then as she lay on my chest, gently hiccupping, I lay back and marvelled that I was a father to this perfect baby girl.

Hannah

Three days after our daughter's birth, something in me changed. We were back in the Airbnb, and Jake was catching some well-needed sleep, the house utterly still, the birds starting to sing outside our window. Our beautiful newborn baby lay on my lap, her eyes still unable to see, gentle hiccups escaping from her perfect little rose bud lips, her tiny hand resting in mine. Finally, now, I knew that my worries and fears and anxiety had been misplaced. As I sat feeding her, the soft glow from the little night light by our side illuminating her beautiful face as she drank her milk, I realised then that I was everything to her. Without me, in that moment, she wouldn't survive. I also knew then that I would do anything for her, always. It clicked.

This is what being a mother is. And I am enough. I didn't need blood ties or a womb to be a mother to my child. I just was. And I just am.

I smiled in the dawn light, and made her a silent promise, to be the best mother that I could ever be.

Jake

Those first few days were magical, despite the world burning around us. We took our little one on long, sunny walks in the glen, did endless FaceTime chats with family and friends and planned our return to London. We tentatively visited Laura, chatting over her garden fence, leaving presents for her to pick up once we had gone. She was feeling elated and made it clear that despite the long birth it had been an entirely positive experience for her, which had been so important to us. She even hinted that she would consider doing it all again if we wanted. One thing at a time!

The travel ban was still very much in effect, so we wrote to our wonderful local Labour MP, explaining our plight and need to get home with our baby, and were issued permission to fly. We rushed to get her registered, as without her birth certificate we couldn't leave Northern Ireland, but struggled as births weren't being registered at that time, only deaths. After many calls to registry offices we finally found one that would help us and managed to get our daughter a birth certificate.

Millie Winter Graf.

Our firstborn child.

And so we packed up all of our belongings and got back on the road, this time London bound. The flight was almost completely empty and Millie slept right through, barely registering her first time in the air.

Being back in London was unnerving, the city's streets deserted, restaurants, bars and shops closed. Our family and friends met Millie for the first time through a window.

Although we missed many of the milestones of having a first child, we never for a second lost sight of how incredibly fortunate we were to have returned, unscathed, to set up home as a family of three. Hannah had four months of maternity leave that stretched over what felt like an almost endless summer, the enforced lockdown adding to that feeling. Sitting in our little garden, entirely entranced by our perfect little baby, life felt very special indeed.

Hannah

I honestly don't have the words to describe what Laura means to us, nor to sum up our gratitude for what she has done for us. Laura is very no-nonsense and was always very clear as to why she wanted to do this for us: she loved being pregnant, the feeling of life growing inside her, but wanted no more children of her own. She also wanted to give this most precious of gifts to a couple who couldn't do it on their own. No mystery, no coercion, just respectful, mutually beneficial and truly magical. When horrible people online say that we have 'stolen' a woman's baby or pressured Laura into any of this, it makes us all laugh. I doubt there is anyone strong enough on this earth to force Laura into doing anything she doesn't want to, and, as she is all too quick to confirm, the baby was never hers, nor would she have wanted it to be. Considering what an intelligent, self possessed woman Laura is, it feels rather insulting that anyone should even suggest that this wasn't entirely her decision. Certainly not very feminist at all.

About three weeks after Millie was born, Jake and I were

in bed with her one morning when Laura called for a catch-up. As we wrapped up, she casually dropped in: 'No pressure, but I really want to do this again. It's been one of the best experiences in my life and I miss being pregnant. If you're not ready yet that's fine, but once I've healed and definitely in the next year, I'd like to try again, if you're up for it?'

Jake beamed at me, as we had always hoped for a sibling for Millie but didn't feel that it was appropriate to ask Laura so soon after her C-section. We were overjoyed that she was once again on the same page and all happily agreed to try again once Laura was ready. Although that next attempt didn't work and ended in an ectopic pregnancy, heartbreaking all round, we gave it one more shot and our second child, Teddie, was born in June 2022. We all agreed then that, for the moment at least, two was enough.

It's funny, I'd never really considered what kind of mother I'd be as I was so fixated on whether I would be one at all. As Millie's started growing up, I've thought more and more about my own parents and the way I was brought up. My mum and dad were amazing and both very present throughout my childhood.

When I went through my rugby phase, they would be on the icy playing fields early on those cold Sunday mornings, and, when I got into rock climbing, I'd be driven back and forth to the indoor climbing centre every weekend. If I wanted to make cakes or play Lego or do gymnastics – whatever it was, they were enthusiastic and by my side for it. And that's what I really carried forward in how I want to be with Millie and Teddie, which is to just be there and let them be themselves. I can't wait to see their true characters emerge and flourish, and, whatever those are, we just want to be there by their side, their biggest and most vocal champions. So if one of the girls decides that she wants to be a gymnast, I'll be there at gymnastics every weekend, or if they want to play football or rugby, we'll be there in the cold and rain after school every day. Or if they're creative, like their father, then all of that will be encouraged and supported. We will be there for them, whatever choices they make.

Jake

That's how Hannah and I have committed to raising our girls: we want them to know that whoever they are, whoever they love, whatever they want to be, we will support them, unquestioningly and unwaveringly. We don't want them to go through any of the self-doubt or worry of hiding their true selves that we both experienced. If your child feels brave enough, emboldened enough, safe enough to come to you and tell you they're not exactly what you thought them to be, then surely as a loving parent you embrace that, reassure them that everything is OK and let them know that their mummy and daddy accept them utterly and unconditionally.

Anything less just doesn't feel like love.

Hannah

Laura will always be in our lives and the lives of our girls, and we continue to be in frequent contact with her. There will also come a time when we'll explain to our daughters not only the circumstances of their birth, but also that both of their parents are transgender. I'm not daunted by that though. Children understand things in a very pure, simple way that many adults can't grasp. Like any family where a child has come into the world in a slightly unusual way – be it through adoption, IVF, surrogacy – there will always be that conversation when the right time comes, and our children are far from alone. Across the world, we are seeing more and more beautiful and diverse LGBTQIA+ families, more people and parents who identify differently from what society's norms dictate, more children born out of the sheer tenacity of parents who just want to love a child. Millie and Teddie will both know that they were born out of pure love, and nothing matters beyond that.

Jake

As we sit here in our cosy little flat, watching Millie dancing around in the garden, ecstatic that spring is finally here, Teddie clapping her sister's every move, Hannah and I are fully aware of how lucky we are. The girls are growing fast and interacting more now. There is nothing more beautiful than Teddie's face lighting up as Millie comes crashing into the kitchen every morning, foisting her favourite toys on her bemused little sister. One of our biggest hopes is that they will forever remain the best of friends, helping each other weather every storm along the way.

And outside of our little bubble, the storm rages on. Hannah and I walk through the world every day knowing that our mere existence disgusts those factions who believe that we shouldn't have basic rights or protections and certainly shouldn't be parenting children. I'm sorry to admit that, despite now being used to feeling that hate, it still chips away at us and hurts us. Sadder still is the knowledge that there are people who will revel in the pain that their pointless and mindless vendetta causes us. To my wife and me there is something truly heartbreaking in knowing that, in Great Britain in 2023, there are still people who want to erase us simply for being ourselves.

Despite all of that noise, life is good. It's March as we write this, and the days are stretching out a little longer, crocuses are peeking their heads above ground in the local park, and buds are erupting on all sides of our little garden. Life goes on. After darkness, the sun will shine, flowers will bloom and, one day, this storm will fade out too. Hannah and I hold onto that hope, and do our best to spread it as widely as we possibly can, for all of those who so badly need it right now.

For us, it will never stop feeling like some kind of miracle that we found ourselves and then we found each other, against all the odds. And together, despite everything and everyone who has tried to drag us down with their hatred and transphobia, we have built a world for ourselves as a family, filled with happiness and with love.

Our story is only beginning.

And, finally, we are becoming us.

Acknowledgements

In writing this book, we are more than aware that we are not the trailblazers, we are not the first trans couple, parents, military Officer or actor, merely some of the first who have seen the love, understanding and support that we have been so privileged and fortunate to receive. Before us came the heroes, the pioneers, the real trailblazers who carved this path for us to follow in their footsteps. We stand on the shoulders of giants and would like to take this opportunity to name but a few and to thank them for their kindness and grace.

To our dear friends Bernard Reed and his late wife Terry, founders of the GIRES charity, who have done more for our beautiful trans community than most will ever know, in the name of their trans daughter, Niki.

To Ayla Holdom and Nicco Beretta, who very much saved us, guided us, and made us proud to be ourselves.

To our daughters' godparents, Amalia, Linda, Pavlo, Rana and Sophie, ever-present figures of love and guidance in their lives.

Big thanks to our amazing agent Max Parker and our brilliant Buffy, always working in the background.

Thanks to our publisher Hannah Black, who has worked so patiently alongside us on this book and extended deadlines more than a handful of times. With thanks to Lotte Jeffs for the support you have given us.

Our endless gratitude to Laura Warke, who made us parents and gave us the family we had always dreamed of.

Infinite love goes to our girls, Millie and Teddie. You make us smile every single day and we will walk through fire to protect you. Mummy and Daddy love you so much.

Another huge thanks to our friend and unwavering ally, Lorraine Kelly, who has allowed a happy transgender couple to grace her morning sofa over many years, and opened hearts and minds across the nation.

Special mentions, in no particular order: to the Silver/Kaye clan who have shown us so much love through the years. To Sam Rouche, who despite the distance is always in our hearts. To Philip and Charlotte, the best neighbours and friends anyone could ask for. To Katie, Amy, Wash and the rest of our American family. You are all loved and missed.

A special thanks to all of the lovely people, parents and allies who are always there to jump in with love and support when the evil trolls are out in force.

Another huge thank you to the rest of our beautiful LGBTQIA+ community who leap in to help fight our battles, when they are more than aware that doing so will draw the hate in their direction. Sometimes we just need to take a step back, and we hugely appreciate you stepping in.

A final special mention to all of the trans children and

young folk who feel so invisible. We see you. You are beautiful. You have a bright future ahead, and we look forward to seeing you all shine.

Jake's personal acknowledgements:

A little word for my wonderful wife. Hannah, you stand by me through thick and thin, the rough and the smooth. You make me feel safe. I'm never happier than when we're off on one of our adventures together and I can't wait for many, many more. You are our rock and we love you to the moon and back.

To my sister Chloe, who continues to work with me on a relationship that (mostly!) goes from strength to strength.

To my boy Yanal Bilbeisi, my old pal Jo Gell, and all of those friends and family that we have lost along the way.

Hannah's personal acknowledgements:

To the wonderful father of my children, thank you for correcting my terrible spelling, making me food when I am hungry and hugging me when it all gets too much. You taught me that I was worthy of being loved and that I deserved a family and happiness, and for that I will be eternally grateful. I am also sorry that I am messy and can never find things.

To all the soldiers and Officers I had the privilege to serve with, thank you for all the support you showed me and for teaching me how to laugh at myself.

To Ali, Andy, Chris, Glynn, Steve and Woody. I love you all and your beautiful families, thank you for being my best friends and for keeping me grounded when I started to get ahead of myself.

To Alexandra, you have been so influential in my life, possibly more than you know. You are the most kind-hearted woman I know and I wish I saw you more.

To Buffy, Ellen, Emily, Hayley, Megan and my other childhood friends. I am sorry that I wasn't better at staying in touch, but you were integral in me becoming who I am, so thank you and I hope we get the opportunity to reconnect soon.

Resources:

AKT (Albert Kennedy Trust): https://www.akt.org.uk/
GIRES (Gender Identity Research & Education Society):
   https://www.gires.org.uk/
LGBT Switchboard: https://switchboard.lgbt/
Mermaids: https://mermaidsuk.org.uk/
Not A Phase: https://notaphase.org/
Stonewall: https://www.stonewall.org.uk/
TransActual: https://www.transactual.org.uk/